The
Challenge and Spirituality
of
Catholic Social Teaching

The
Challenge and Spirituality
of
Catholic Social Teaching

REVISED EDITION

Marvin L. Krier Mich

ORBIS BOOKS
Maryknoll, New York 10545

Founded in 1970, Orbis Books endeavors to publish works that enlighten the mind, nourish the spirit, and challenge the conscience. The publishing arm of the Maryknoll Fathers and Brothers, Orbis seeks to explore the global dimensions of the Christian faith and mission, to invite dialogue with diverse cultures and religious traditions, and to serve the cause of reconciliation and peace. The books published reflect the views of their authors and do not represent the official position of the Maryknoll Society. To learn more about Maryknoll and Orbis Books, please visit our website at www.maryknollsociety.org.

Library of Congress Cataloging-in-Publication Data

Mich, Marvin L. Krier.
    The challenge and spirituality of Catholic social teaching / Marvin L. Krier Mich.
— Rev. ed.
        p.   cm.
    Includes bibliographical references (p.   ) and index.
    ISBN 978-1-57075-945-1 (pbk.)
    1. Christian sociology—Catholic Church.   2. Spirituality—Catholic Church.
3. Catholic Church—Doctrines.   I. Title.
    BX1753.M5 2011
    261.8'309--dc22

                                                                                    2011014800

Contents

Acknowledgments

This book is primarily a story of transformation. More accurately, it is the stories of transformation in the Spirit. While it unpacks the core themes of Catholic social teaching, it also tells the stories of our saints, contemporary and ancient, who, under the power of the Spirit, live out the meaning of the "glad tidings to the poor," the gospel of Jesus Christ. Each chapter brings forth insights from the biblical tradition, which is the narrative of God's Spirit at work in the world. Working on this revision has renewed my appreciation of our Catholic tradition of protecting the life and dignity of each person. I hope that this book will assist you in your journey as a follower of Jesus and his gospel of life.

I want to thank Jack Jezreel, the director of JustFaith, for the invitation to work on this text and for his suggestion to revise and update the first edition. The first edition, published in 2005 by Sowers Books (part of the JustFaith ministries), was used in the JustFaith curriculum for five years. During that time both the JustFaith staff and participants in the JustFaith program surfaced a number of suggestions for improving the text. I want to thank Sharon Bidwell on the JustFaith staff for gathering feedback from people who had used the text and for her own very helpful insights and suggestions.

With very short notice, Susan Perry, senior editor at Orbis Books, took on the editing of the revised edition. Her careful attention in checking my sources and overall guidance of the project was a marvelous gift to this writer. Thank you, Sue!

I also want to thank my co-worker at Catholic Family Center, Brigit Hurley, who willingly took care of the fort while I hid away to meet the tight production deadline. Rev. Denise Yarbrough and Sue Howard, leaders in the Greater Rochester Community of Churches—Faith in Action Network, also came to my rescue by picking up some of my work with GRCC. I am grateful to my wife Kristine for supporting my laser beam focus on the project during the three month revision schedule.

It is a joy to share the principles of our Catholic social tradition, biblical insights, and the stories of holy men and women who make that tradition a lived reality by the witness of their lives. I pray that we are effective and holy witnesses to that rich tradition in our lives.

Introduction

The joys and the hopes, the grief and anguish of the people of our time, especially of those who are poor or afflicted, are the joys and hopes, the grief and anguish of the followers of Christ as well.[1]

The Catholic bishops, gathered in the Second Vatican Council (1962–1965), expressed this conviction about the responsibilities of the followers of Christ. We are to "take on" the joys and hopes and the grief and anguish of our times. Our mission is to bring the good news of the gospel to those who are suffering, neglected, hungry, and in poverty and to those who are threatened by abortion, war, and other forms of violence.

In other words, we are to face the harsh realities of our time, including:

- a child poverty rate of 20.7 percent in the United States (in Rochester, New York it is 47.1 percent);[2]
- 43.6 million people were living in poverty in the United States in 2009;[3]
- 925 million in the world are hungry;[4]
- 1.21 million abortions were performed in 2008 in the United States;[5]
- destruction of the rain forest in Brazil proceeded at a rate of more than 100,000 square kilometers a year, which is roughly equivalent to the State of Virginia;[6] and
- 75 to 90 percent of the victims in conflicts in Bosnia, Rwanda, Sudan, Afghanistan, and Iraq have been civilians.[7]

What does it mean to "take on" these issues of the poor and vulnerable? How do the followers of Christ respond to these very complex problems? The Catholic community has been wrestling with these questions from its very first days. Today we "get our bearings" by consulting the church's social teachings and its living tradition. They are founded on a number of important sources including:

- the life and words of Jesus who came "to bring glad tidings to the poor . . . liberty to captives . . . and recovery of sight to the blind" (Lk 4:18–19);
- the passion for justice of the Hebrew prophets calling for "justice to surge like water" (Am 5:24);
- the early martyrs, fathers, and mothers of the church;
- the bishops, popes, and councils who articulated the church's concern for justice peace, and the poor and vulnerable; and
- the lived experience of the people of God.[8]

We will be listening to those voices—popes, bishops, and holy men and women through the ages—in the pages of this text. The wisdom of this tradition challenges our minds and our hearts to expand our compassion to care for the "least of these." Also included are the stories of the saints and those who live out these teachings in order to inspire and touch our hearts and to show us what following Christ looks like in reality.

The Catholic Church does not have an official "mission statement." If it did, these words from Pope Benedict XVI's encyclical *Deus Caritas Est* (God Is Love) would be a good starting point: "The Church's deepest nature is expressed in her three-fold responsibility: of proclaiming the word of God (*kerygma-martyria*), celebrating the sacraments (*leitourgia*), and exercising the ministry of charity (*diakonia*). These duties presuppose each other and are inseparable" (25).

In other words, the mission of the church is to proclaim the good news, to celebrate the sacraments, and to care for the needy. As Christians we can't pick and choose among these commands; as we live out our lives, we must include all three. We could not imagine a Catholic community that does not celebrate the Eucharist because the Eucharist is central to our identity as Catholics. In the same way, the church would not be the church if it did not serve the needs of the poor and vulnerable. These three are inseparable. The Holy Father continues: "For the Church, charity is not a kind of welfare activity which could equally well be left to others, but is a part of her nature, an indispensable expression of her very being" (25).

The work of charity and justice that the church undertakes in the name of the gospel is at times controversial, as was discovered by a small band of Catholics from Rochester when they visited their legislator in Albany, New York. The legislator met the delegation in his office in Albany as part of the New York State Catholic Conference's "2011 Albany Forum." He was very attentive and respectful as members of the group addressed a number of life issues and issues of social justice, including support for Catholic schools, funding for the working poor in the New York State budget, and their objections to a bill, the Reproductive Health Act, that would strengthen abortion rights in New York.

The legislator responded to these concerns by stating that "as a Catholic" he did not think that it was the job of the church to be involved in the political process. The church should be involved in the work of "redemption." He said that he believes that the "peace and justice" focus is ruining the church. A colleague, Brigit Hurley, who was leading the delegation, was shocked by his response. She tried to explain why the Catholic Church was involved in the "political" work of advocating funding for "Wheels for Work" (a program to help low income workers get used cars so they have reliable transportation to get to work) and subsidized child-care for workers and against the Reproductive Health Act. The delegation left on a note of "let's keep talking" about the advocacy work of the church.

As a delegation, we were grateful that the legislator listened attentively to our concerns and was honest about his position as a Catholic. We plan to continue this conversation when we visit the legislators over the summer months when they are back in the Rochester area. We have established relationships with other legislators and feel that, over time, they have come to better understand the various levels of our outreach to the poor and our advocacy work through Catholic Charities.

However, this visit to Albany gave us pause to think: How *do* we communicate our advocacy work to the Catholic community? What is the role of the church in tackling the difficult issues of our time in Albany, New York, or Lincoln, Nebraska, or in our nation's capital in Washington?

Popes, bishops, theologians, religious men and women, and lay people have reflected on those questions throughout the centuries. This book will highlight the work of some of those leaders, including people like Bartolomé de Las Casas, who advocated for the rights of the indigenous people in the New World before the court of the Spanish King in the sixteenth century, and Dorothy Day, who advocated against war in the twentieth century. And the members of our small delegation visiting Mr. Hanna in Albany are part of that long tradition of holy people who take on the grief and anguish of their neighbors.

The popes and bishops have articulated the church's response to social issues in a body of thought known as Catholic social teaching. The foundation of that teaching is the great commandment of the Bible: to love God and to love our neighbor. The church sees this work as part of God's work of salvation and the coming of God's reign "on earth as it is in heaven." The Bible demonstrates that God did intervene in politics as, for example, when God sent Moses to confront the pharaoh in Egypt. Then Jesus continued that liberating work of God when he announced his ministry in Nazareth with the words of the prophet Isaiah, "The Spirit of the Lord is upon me, because he has anointed me to bring good news to the poor. He has sent me to proclaim release to the captives and recovery of sight to the blind, to let the oppressed go free" (Lk 4:18). The church continues that ministry of Jesus, the work of God, led by the Spirit. This is the tradition that the Catholic Church continues in our day when it proclaims the gospel, celebrates the sacraments, and cares for the needy.

In 1971, the Synod of Bishops stated the church's mission for the "redemption of the human race" in these terms: "Action on behalf of justice and participation in the transformation of the world fully appear to us as a constitutive dimension of the preaching of the Gospel, or in other words, of the Church's mission for the redemption of the human race and its liberation from every oppressive situation."[9]

Almost four decades later, in his encyclical *Caritas in Veritate*, Pope Benedict XVI clarified the role of the church as neither trying to "replace the State" nor staying on the "sidelines in the fight for justice": "The Church cannot and must not take upon herself the political battle to bring about the most just society possible. She cannot and must not replace the State. *Yet at the same time she cannot and must not remain on the sidelines in the fight for justice.*"[10]

In *Deus Caritas Est* Pope Benedict explains that the church brings a spiritual energy to the struggle for justice in addition to stressing the gift of reason—the church "has to play her part through rational argument and she has to *reawaken the spiritual energy* without which justice, which always demands sacrifice, cannot prevail and prosper" (28). Benedict describes this spiritual energy that flows from God who is the source of all that is and who calls humanity to unity.

> The Spirit is also the energy that transforms the heart of the ecclesial community into a witness before the world to the love of the Father, who wishes to make humanity a single family in his Son. . . .

Love is therefore the service that the Church carries out in order
to attend constantly to man's sufferings and his needs, including
material needs (19).

The *Compendium of the Social Doctrine of the Church* links the "conversion of
hearts" to work for the "healing" of human institutions and structures.

*It is from the conversion of hearts that there arises concern for others, loved as
brothers or sisters.* This concern helps us to understand the obligation
and commitment to heal institutions, structures and conditions of life
that are contrary to human dignity. The laity must therefore *work at
the same time for the conversion of hearts and the improvement of structures,*
taking historical situations into account and using legitimate means
so that the dignity of every man and woman will be truly respected
and promoted within institutions.[11]

The Catholic Church lives out its social mission in many settings and
through diverse institutions, including Catholic Charities, Catholic Relief
Services, the St. Vincent de Paul Society, Catholic schools, Catholic health
care, and through the local parishes. For most Catholics the parish is the
primary experience of how the church lives out its threefold ministry of
preaching, celebrating the sacraments, and loving one's neighbor. The U.S.
bishops have called parishes to become "Communities of Salt and Light."
In a document by that same name, they provide a framework for how the
church is to live out its service to the neighbor. They see seven components for the social mission of the parish:

- anchoring social ministry in prayer and worship;
- sharing the message through preaching and education;
- supporting family, work, and citizenship;
- serving the "least of these" through outreach and charity;
- advocating for justice through legislative action;
- creating community by organizing for justice; and
- building solidarity, even beyond parish boundaries.[12]

The works of charity include serving the needs of the local community
as well as going beyond the parish boundaries, as in the case of helping
the victims of Hurricane Katrina and victims of disasters in other countries such as those caused by earthquakes in Japan and Haiti. The bishops

also identify works of justice such as legislative advocacy, which may involve visiting legislators and signing petitions, and community organizing, another work of justice, that empowers grassroots leaders to address the concerns of the community.

The local parish is also called to support parishioners as they carry out their vocation as parents, citizens, and workers. The bishops note that "The most challenging work for justice is not done in church committees, but in the secular world of work, family life, and citizenship."[13] The church offers guidance for the faithful as parents, citizens, and workers through parish and diocesan programs and the documents of the United States Conference of Catholic Bishops, such as *Faithful Citizenship, Economic Justice for All,* and *Everyday Christianity.* Connecting the wisdom of the Bible and the Catholic tradition to the busy world of parenting, working, and civic engagement is an ongoing challenge for parish leaders and all who seek to live out their faith in their everyday life.

Understanding the Terminology

It is important to understand the language we are using. That became very clear to me a few years ago when I offered a course entitled "The Theology of Social Ministry." A woman in her forties enrolled and after a few sessions she realized that we might not be talking about the "social" ministry she expected, that is, how to organize "social gatherings" at church, such as an ice cream "social." She was surprised to discover that the class would be reading papal encyclicals and episcopal statements on economic justice and life issues!

My use of the word *social* refers primarily to the *social institutions* of society—including the economy, government, health care, and civil society. Because social institutions are created and maintained by the community, these institutions and their policies can be changed. The decision of the Supreme Court, *Roe v Wade,* is an example of a policy established by an institution, the Supreme Court. Such a policy or law can be changed, it is not written in stone. The Catholic Church is working to overturn this policy because, according to church teaching, it does not protect unborn humans. Other "social" policies that the church is addressing range from eliminating the death penalty, to implementing a living wage, and reforming immigration laws.

The *social ministry* of the church includes the works of charity and the works of social justice. The works of charity address the immediate needs of our neighbor, both next door and around the world. The Catholic Church is known for its excellent ministries of charity including the St. Vincent DePaul Society, Catholic Charities, and Catholic Relief Services. Some of these programs and agencies that serve the immediate needs of the poor are also involved in works of justice, addressing social policies that impede the flourishing of individuals. For example, both Catholic Charities and Catholic Relief Services are involved in two-fold advocacy efforts to educate parishioners on the issues and to pressure legislators to make the appropriate changes in funding and policy. As noted above, the U. S. bishops encourage parishes to be engaged in legislative advocacy.

Social encyclicals and *social teachings* include the letters of the popes and bishops that address issues of the economy, war, globalization, human and economic development, the environment, and protecting the dignity of life of unborn children. For instance, in July 2009 Pope Benedict issued his first *social* encyclical, *Caritas in Veritate*, which presented his ideas about reforming economic structures, civil society, and the role of government. He had issued two previous encyclicals that were *not* labeled social encyclicals because their main focus was not on social institutions and structures. The first encyclical, *Deus Caritas Est*, was an in-depth reflection on the theological meaning of love, and the second encyclical, *Spe Salvi*, focused on hope.

The social teachings of the church address current social issues in light of the message of the Bible and the insights of reason and the Catholic tradition. The social issues are examined in light of the responsibility of Christians as individuals and also the responsibilities of the church as an institution. These documents examine the policies and practices of society as well as the underlying cultural attitudes. For example, the taking of human life through abortion is discussed in terms of the understanding of the value of human life in the Bible, in the Catholic tradition, and as part of a universal human ethic. However, the popes and bishops tend to probe further by examining the "culture of death" or the cultural acceptance of violence that leads to using abortion to solve the problem of an unwanted pregnancy. They urge Christians and all people to build a culture of life (as discussed in chapter 3). A similar analysis is made in the discussion of racism in chapter 7. Fr. Bryan Massingale pushes the church to be more attentive to the cultural roots of racism and the unspoken acceptance of "white privilege." Throughout this text, then, Catholic social teaching examines issues, the cultural undercurrents of the issues and the theological resources available for responding, and makes general policy recommendations for the church and society.

In Caritas in Veritate Pope Benedict divided society into three large areas: (1) the role of *government* at all levels—local, state, national, and international; (2) the area of the economy including *marketplace, businesses, and finance*—where most of us work and do our shopping; and (3) *civil society*, which includes all the rest—non-profit agencies, civic organizations, churches, synagogues, temples, mosques, and other religious bodies, community organizations, neighborhood groups, families, and social groupings. The challenge is how to energize all of these areas of society to serve the common good and to protect the dignity of each life.

In the church's concern about abortion, for example, Catholic social teaching will address *government* attempts to pass legislation to protect life, it will address *economic factors* that may increase abortion among the poor, and it will invite the *civil society* through faith communities, schools, non-profit organizations, and families to teach a culture of life. In all of these areas the church is addressing the individuals involved but also trying to shape *social policies* and attitudes.

While Catholic social teaching has been part of the church from the very beginning as recorded in the Acts of the Apostles, its modern expression began with Pope Leo XIII's encyclical, *Rerum Novarum*, in 1891. In this encyclical Pope Leo addressed the question of justice for workers during the time of the Industrial Revolution. Since that time, popes and bishops have continued to address an ever-broadening range of issues.[14]

Seven Themes—A Starting Point

The breadth of Catholic social teaching is both immense and complex. In an effort to make this tradition a little more "user-friendly," three committees of the National Conference of Catholic Bishops came together in 1995 to produce a summary of Catholic social teaching. This summary, entitled *Sharing Catholic Social Teaching: Challenges and Directions*, was for use in parishes and Catholic schools.[15] The joint committee noted that it was not easy to summarize the sophisticated body of teaching that has developed over the last one hundred years so it distilled the main points of Catholic social teaching into seven themes that "are at the heart of our Catholic social tradition" to be seen "as a starting point for those interested in exploring the Catholic social tradition more fully."[16]

The seven themes identified by the U.S. bishops are:

1. the life and dignity of the human person;
2. a call to family, community, and participation;

3. rights and responsibilities;
4. an option for the poor and vulnerable;
5. the dignity of work and the rights of workers;
6. solidarity; and
7. care for God's creation.

At the heart of all Catholic social teaching is the *dignity of human life*. As the bishops point out: "This central Catholic principle requires that we measure every policy, every institution, and every action by whether it protects human life and enhances human dignity, especially for the poor and vulnerable." This one sentence summarizes all the encyclicals and pastoral letters of the past hundred years and it "offers consistent moral guidance for the future."[17]

The U.S. bishops stated that while all of the social issues deserve our attention, all issues do not carry the same urgency. They believe that "abortion and euthanasia have become preeminent threats to human dignity because they directly attack life itself, the most fundamental human good and the condition for all others. They are committed against those who are weakest and most defenseless, those who are genuinely 'the poorest of the poor.'"[18]

Pope Benedict concurs that "Only if human life from conception until death is respected is the ethic of peace possible and credible; only then may non-violence be expressed in every direction, only then can we truly accept creation and only then can we achieve true justice."[19]

These seven "starting points" provide a framework for the last seven chapters of this book. The first chapter addresses the overarching theme of "following Christ in a consumer society," however the following chapters do not follow the order listed above. Rather, we begin with "Care for God's Creation," the starting point of all life. Throughout much of the text, these central principles are linked with specific issues. For example, chapter 2 links creation with environmental issues; chapter 3 pairs human dignity with abortion and the death penalty; chapter 6 links rights and responsibilities with poverty and racism; and chapter 8 matches solidarity with the ethics of war.

While the bishops term these seven themes of Catholic social teaching "starting points," this text recommends that we *start with our own experience*. Instead of beginning with the church's teaching, we begin with our experience of "the grief and anguish" of the poor and vulnerable and with our experience of social issues. Vatican II called this approach "reading the signs of the time." This methodology reverses the order of theory and practice. Earlier understandings emphasized *theory as knowledge* and *practice as the application* of the knowledge. Following this older approach, social ministry was considered merely a matter of applying church teaching to the situation at hand.

Reading the Signs of the Times

The new understanding of the theory-practice relationship gives a new status and higher priority to our lived experience. In other words, "Practice is no longer merely the aftermath of theory so that practice reflexively flows from theory."[20] Instead, practice is a source of insight that affects theory and influences how we interpret the world and our tradition. Practice, in this approach, is not simply the ability to *apply knowledge* to a concrete situation, rather practice is a *source of knowledge*.

To convey this richer understanding of "practice," the Greek word "praxis" is often used instead of "practice." In this view, the experience or praxis of Christians is a source of knowledge and insight. The lived experience of Christians engaged in social ministry is another source of knowledge and *authority*, along with scripture, tradition, and human reason. This richer understanding of praxis has led to a new appreciation of the importance of reflecting on the Christian's lived experience.

This new understanding of the importance of lived experience and practice demands that we examine our experience more thoughtfully. A useful approach for analyzing a social setting is a method known as the "pastoral circle." The pastoral circle starts with an examination of experience and then moves to social analysis, theological reflection on a particular issue, and pastoral planning and action.[21]

This method developed many years ago in Latin America as some of the early liberation theologians struggled with the basic issues of oppression, poverty, hunger, and illiteracy. As Peruvian theologian Gustavo Gutiérrez explains, theology comes after a day filled with service and working for justice, it is "what you do when the sun goes down." The experience of *commitment to service*, which must come first, is then followed by the work of reflecting on that activity in light of the Bible and Catholic teaching. Father Gutiérrez writes,

[F]irst is the commitment of charity, of service. Theology comes afterwards, it is the second act. . . . The pastoral activity of the Church does not flow as a conclusion from theological premises. Theology does not produce pastoral activity; rather, it reflects upon it. Theology must be able to find in pastoral activity the presence of the Spirit inspiring the action of the Christian community.[22]

This newer methodology can complement the older methodology that moves from theological insights to action. In reality, the faithful are often moved to act because of the teachings of the church and the words of Jesus and the prophets; at other times we reflect on the Bible and Catholic social teaching in light of our experience of service to others.

Social Analysis and the Pastoral Circle

The pastoral circle and social analysis require us to dig more deeply into the issues and to ask "why": Why are so many people coming to our soup kitchen and homeless shelters? What are the root causes of poverty and how can we address those causes? Why are so many women having abortions?

The four phases of the pastoral circle are:

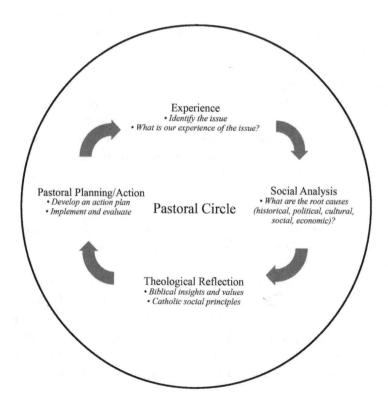

Experience
• *Identify the issue*
• *What is our experience of the issue?*

Pastoral Planning/Action
• *Develop an action plan*
• *Implement and evaluate*

Pastoral Circle

Social Analysis
• *What are the root causes*
(historical, political, cultural,
social, economic)?

Theological Reflection
• *Biblical insights and values*
• *Catholic social principles*

The first phase, "insertion," is the experience of getting in touch with the issue. As pragmatic Americans, we often want to move quickly from the problem we see before us to forging solutions and taking action. However, moving to the second step, the approach of the pastoral circle tells us to slow down and analyze *why* this particular problem exists. What has caused it? In the third and fourth phases, we reflect as a faith community on our biblical and social teachings in order to craft a response and to come up with an effective plan of action.

To gain some understanding of this process, let's return to the second step, that of social analysis. Social analysis is used to look at various institutional and structural factors—they may be economic, political, social, and/or cultural forces—that are at work. Here's an example of how social analysis might tackle a particular issue.

St. Theodore is a downtown church with a small park across the street. Homeless people congregate in the park during the day and sometimes ask the parishioners for handouts. The social ministry committee has been serving a meal for the poor for the last five years, but some of the committee wants to dig a little deeper into what is happening.

They began their long process of social analysis with the economy, trying to determine how the *resources* of their community are organized. They discovered that the factory jobs that once employed workers with a minimal education are no longer available in the area. The garment industry, for example, has left town—and often, the country—in search of lower labor costs. When the group continued to explore the economic conditions of the area, they realized that the educational resources were not distributed equally in the community. Some of the inner-city schools had very little money, which meant that the students did not have even the basic necessities for school. The committee saw how this lack of education forced the poor who live in the inner city to accept service-sector jobs with low pay and little hope for career advancement. They came to understand how the lure of the drug culture that promises quick wealth could appeal to so many young people in those neighborhoods.

The committee then undertook a political analysis to determine how the community can organize to wield *power*; it discovered that the homeless were just one of many groups of people—mentally ill, the poor, minority groups—without political power. Finally, in analyzing the community's social structures, they attempted to determine how the society organizes relationships, in the family and in the neighborhood. This phase of their study brought the committee face to face with the clear stratification in the society: poor, working class, middle class, upper class. They discovered just how segregated their city was by class.

Finally, they turned to a cultural analysis to look at how society organizes *meaning* through the lenses of the media, the arts, and religion. They saw a culture interwoven with both implicit and explicit racism that made it particularly difficult for young black males to find employment. These young men were also subjected to racial profiling by police and security staffs at area stores and malls. The committee saw that this situation often led to a loss of meaning and hope in the black community. The despair in the community led some to escape by abusing drugs and alcohol.

When the social ministry committee at St. Theodore's brought its reflections together at the end of the year, its members realized that individuals must take personal responsibility for their decisions, but they also realized how limited the choices were for many of their fellow citizens who have not had the advantages of faithful parents, good schools, and adequate resources. The committee decided to continue offering the meals, but decided in addition to add a few projects that would tackle the root causes of hunger, such as supporting the living wage legislation in the county and working with two inner-city schools to improve the educational opportunities for the students there.

The following anecdote illustrates the usefulness of social analysis. Once upon a time, the social ministry committee of a local parish went on a picnic, along with their families, to enjoy the beauty of creation and to celebrate all they had accomplished that year. They held the picnic at a park on the banks of a beautiful river. When they were ready to light the charcoal to cook the hot dogs and hamburgers, a few of the children cried out that something was floating down the river. Running to the river, the adults were horrified to see that a body was floating there. They pulled out the body and, detecting a faint heart beat, someone began to administer CPR while someone else called an ambulance.

As they covered the body in a car blanket, the children cried out that another body was coming down the river, and another. One of the leaders who had taken a course in social analysis left the group and headed upstream. Her fellow parishioners asked why she was abandoning them when there was so much to do. She responded, "I'm going upstream to find out why these people are ending up in the river."[23]

Types of Authority in the Church

As the Second Vatican Council reminds us, the mission of preaching the gospel and transforming society has been given to the whole church; as members of the church each of us is to live out our baptismal commitment.[24] The entire Christian community participates in shaping and being shaped by this tradition. As active Catholics, we not only receive the teaching of the tradition, but we have a role to play in shaping that tradition with our expertise and our lived experience. Aware of the importance of experience as a source of theological wisdom and insight, we realize that the wisdom of the entire people of God—the *sensus fidelium*—is needed for the authentic development and reception of Catholic social teaching. Bishops, theologians, religious educators, and the laity each have distinctive roles, but each role is important.

Bishop Richard Sklba, a scripture scholar and a retired bishop of Milwaukee, has clarified the way the various kinds of authority in the church complement each other. He has identified three types of authority: the authority that comes from the *lived experience* of Christians who struggle between grace and sin; the authority that comes from competence, skill, or learning, that is, the *authority of expertise*; and the authority that comes from *delegation*. For example, an expert might know all the reasons that a person should stop smoking. Someone else with experiential authority that goes beyond the intellectual insights of the expert may have struggled with trying to stop smoking. A third may have the authority to make sure that no smoking takes place in a particular building or may approve legislation on behalf of the community that outlaws smoking within restaurants or other public buildings. Bishop Sklba believes that "the same kinds of diversification of authority exist in the Church." He explains the necessity of all three authorities:

> One of the roles of the bishop is not merely to represent the delegated responsibility for tradition but rather to make sure that the Church community experiences a healthy balance between those three kinds of teaching authorities. The bishop ensures that knowledge, experience, and delegation are speaking to one another.[25]

Maintaining a "healthy balance between these three kinds of teaching authorities" is not an easy task. Many of the controversial moral and social issues within the church reveal the tensions between these diverse authorities. We often think of the troubling issues such as birth control, the role of women, and the rights of gays and lesbians. But the social and economic teachings of the church are equally controversial: for example, the limited right to private property, the role of the government in economic affairs, and the morality of the death penalty. These complex questions need the insights and wisdom from all the authoritative sources within the people of God. Bishop Sklba's point is that the bishops' role is to keep these authoritative voices speaking to one another.

The Second Vatican Council articulated the responsibility of the entire people of God: "With the help of the Holy Spirit, it is the task of the entire People of God, especially pastors and theologians, to hear, distinguish, and interpret the many voices of our age, and to judge them in the light of the divine Word."[26] In naming theologians, pastors, and the people of God, this passage is consistent with Bishop Sklba's three types of authority that must work together to discern the meaning of the gospel in today's world. The bishops of the Council also suggested that the laity should take initiative in living out the gospel in their arenas of influence:

> For guidance and spiritual strength let them [the laity] turn to the clergy; but let them realize that their pastors will not always be so expert as to have a ready answer to every problem, even every grave problem, that arises; this is not the role clergy: it is rather the task of lay people to shoulder their responsibilities under the guidance of Christian wisdom and with careful attention to the teaching authority of the church.[27]

In 1971 Pope Paul VI reinforced the message that the task of the whole Christian community is to wrestle with the meaning of the Gospel in our diverse and complex world:

> In the face of such widely varying situations it is difficult for us to utter a unified message and to put forward a solution which has universal validity. Such is not our ambition, nor is it our mission. It is up to the Christian communities to analyze with objectivity the situation which is proper to their own country, to shed on it the light of the Gospel's unalterable words and to draw principles of reflection, norms of judgment and directives for action from the social teaching of the Church.[28]

This book gives voice to the three authoritative voices in the church: the official teaching of popes and bishops, the insights of theologians and spiritual leaders, and the experience of the people of God struggling to be faithful Christians. It draws upon Catholic social teachings, biblical insights, and the stories of holy men and women throughout history, including a number of stories that come from people in the Catholic Worker movement. There are over 185 Catholic Worker communities around the world: 168 in the United States (in thirty-seven different states), six in three Canadian provinces, and fifteen in ten other countries.[29] These communities are a great way to connect with the ongoing prophetic social ministry of Dorothy Day.

Catholic social teaching, then, is the dynamic, living tradition of the whole Catholic community. The entire church receives the teaching and the entire church is part of shaping and passing that teaching on to the next generation. It is a living tradition and you and I are part of it. By our authentic Christian living may we become authoritative witnesses. May we also be heirs to its "prophetic vision and courageous action." In the words of John Coleman:

> Ultimately, the future of this tradition will depend less on our ability to parrot its significant terms such as subsidiarity, a just wage, etc., and more on our ability to read the signs of the times in fidelity to the Gospel of human dignity as Leo, Pius XI and XII, John—with all their historical limitations, biases, and failures—tried to do in their times. History will surely unveil all too well our shortcomings. May it also—as it does for this legacy of the popes—show our prophetic vision and courageous action.[30]

1

The Challenge of Being Prophetic: Gospel and Culture

Jesus invites us into a new way of living, a new way of being in the world. In baptism we were plunged into the waters of death and we died to the old way of living. To symbolize our new identity we were given a white garment, a new set of clothes that represents the light of Christ who will enlighten our path in a world of darkness. We were anointed with the oil of catechumens to strengthen us for the battle with evil, self-doubt, and lethargy. As my pastor, Father Bill Donnelly, puts it, we have been rubbed with the oil of baptism so we could slip out of the grasp of the devil. We were welcomed into a new family, a new community, committed to living the values of Jesus.

At baptism the second anointing was with chrism—the oil also used to anoint priests and bishops—to remind us of our high calling. The priest or deacon prays as he anoints "as Jesus was anointed Priest, Prophet, and King, so may you live as a child of God." We too are expected to be priestly, prophetic, and kingly, three images that highlight three distinct aspects of ministry and discipleship.

What a marvelous gift it is to be welcomed into the community of the beloved disciples, to be claimed for Christ, to be reborn into a life of grace, rejecting the clamor of evil. What a high calling and what an honor! What has happened since our welcome into the church? What has happened to the church itself since its baptism by the Spirit on that first Pentecost? How exactly has the church been an agent of the Spirit "renewing the face of the earth"?

Each of us could tell our own story of Christian discipleship, a story of faithfulness and grace, and of infidelity and sin. The Catholic Church could also tell the saga of fidelity and infidelity, the story of wrestling with the meaning of God's word in new circumstances and, at times, missing the mark. The church, like individual Christians, has had its moments of grace and sin, yet throughout the journey we are confident that the love

17

of God calls us back and continues to sustain us. When the church or individual Christians have missed the mark we know that God is waiting for our return.

The Nature of Discipleship

The story of Christian discipleship is complex and multileveled, not only through history, but in our own day as well. History reveals many paths to being a faithful servant of God's work in the world for individuals and for denominations. In Christianity, as in life, one size does not fit all. Each Christian follows God's calling, revealed in the circumstances of her life, discovered in her unique gifts and talents, and in the longing of her heart. Many paths wend through the forest and many tributaries flow into the river of discipleship.

Such diversity within Christianity should not be surprising to us, because from the very beginning there have been diverse interpretations of how Christians are to live out the good news. Twenty-seven books in the Christian scriptures (the New Testament), including four different gospels, tell the story of the same person, Jesus. There is not simply one way of telling the story, nor is there just one way of being a disciple of Jesus. No single approach exhausts the meaning of the Christian faith. Even within specific denominations there are diverse, and at times, competing interpretations of discipleship.

One ancient way of describing the diversity of discipleship and ministry is found in the baptismal rite that names three distinct images of leadership, those of priest, prophet, and king, that highlight three distinctive ways of being a leader in the community.

The *priestly ministry* focuses on calling the community together for worship and connecting the sacrifices of our lives with the sacrifice of Christ. The priestly ministry celebrates God's love, forgiveness, and peace in our everyday lives through the sacred rituals of the liturgy and the sacraments.

The *prophetic ministry* awakens the faith community when it is not living according to God's covenant, when its members are not living fully the command to love God and to love our neighbor. The prophet is single-focused and often sees the world in black and white with few shades of gray. A prophetic community is also willing to take hard stands, such as defending the dignity of every life when confronting the controversial issues of abortion, euthanasia, the death penalty, and speaking out against war, racism, and poverty. The prophetic voice names the violence of abortion and the injustice of poverty; it stands with the poor, the unborn, and all victims of oppression. While the prophet criticizes violence and injustice, he or she also energizes the community with the clarity of God's word, giving hope to those who are overwhelmed by the forces of evil and pointing to a better world of *shalom* and well being.

Kingly leadership focuses on order and justice in the faith community and the secular society. Kingly service is concerned with worldly realities, the governance of the secular community, the common good, and public order. The church's kingly ministry seeks to shape social policy and advise presidents, mayors, and legislators. Rooted in the faith language of the Christian community, the kingly approach seeks to articulate its moral and social positions in reasonable ways in order to be understood by the wider community. Making known the tradition of the just war ethic fits into this kingly style of teaching, presenting arguments in ethical language rather than using specifically religious terms.

While the prophetic ministry calls the church to reach for the ideal, the kingly function cautions that idealism with the realism of what is possible and responsible. According to Fr. David O'Brien and ethicist Thomas Shannon, "Yet it is precisely the effort to be *both* prophetic and responsible that distinguishes Catholic social teaching and makes it so significant in the modern world." O'Brien and Shannon believe that "the church as a whole is trying to be both idealistic and realistic because that is what it is called to be."[1]

As individual Christians, we are called to be prophetic, responsible, and sacramental. While these three ministries give full expression to Christian discipleship, no one person can perfectly balance all three ministries; each of us tends to emphasize one ministry, giving less attention to the others. The various Christian denominations also tend to highlight one of these types of ministry. In general, Christianity was more prophetic in the first three centuries and then in succeeding centuries it began to shift to more kingly and priestly emphases.

The Catholic Church includes all three types of ministry. Throughout history, however, religious movements within Catholicism often attempted to reclaim and give prominence to the prophetic dimension. St. Francis of Assisi, for example, is one among many leaders who called the church to the prophetic message of radical love and evangelical poverty. Similarly our leaders may be prophetic on one occasion and priestly or kingly on the next occasion. For instance, Pope John Paul II was prophetic when he visited Poland and supported Solidarity, the workers' movement; he was kingly when he met with world leaders, and priestly when he presided at liturgy and celebrated the sacraments.

The social teachings of the Catholic Church also reflect the different hues of these three ministries. The social documents serve a kingly role when they urge leaders and laity to work for a just social order. At other times, the voice of the church is very prophetic. For instance, the 1971 Synod document, *Justice in the World*, addressed economic injustice in the developing countries in stark terms. Pope John Paul II's encyclical, *Gospel of Life*, named the "culture of death" in prophetic language. At times, the priestly ministry is also evident in the social documents when the bishops and pope urge the community to be rooted in prayer and fasting as essential components of building a more just world. The pastoral letter of the U.S. bishops, *The Challenge of Peace*, asked Catholics to pray and fast as a way to open hearts to the way of peace.

All three types of leadership and vision will be evident in these pages; however, I have tried to highlight the prophetic voice of Catholic social teaching and witness. It awakens us to a new way of hearing the gospel, and it challenges our uncritical accommodation of Catholic faith to American culture.

Living the Gospel in U.S. Culture

The gospel is always expressed and lived out in a specific time, place, and culture. As Catholics in the United States it is important for us to take a careful look at our culture and how it shapes our thinking and decisions. Our U.S. culture has many positive values, but it also has some negative aspects.

Positive dimensions include the values of democracy, freedom, and individual initiative, the emphasis on equality and rights of all, accountability, and transparency. It seems that our church could learn from the U.S. culture how to better implement these values in its structures and policies. On the negative side, three aspects of U. S. culture are contrary to the message of the gospel and the Catholic social tradition, namely, excessive individualism, violence, and materialism. Therefore a large part of this chapter is focused on the challenge of materialism, although it will also briefly treat individualism and touch on violence. Chapters 3 and 8 will explore violence in more detail.

One of the blessings of living in the United States is the cultural attitude that frees individuals to take personal initiative in every area of life. It is often the freedom to follow one's individual dream that attracts people to our shores. But, as with every good thing, it can be taken too far and individual freedom and initiative can become so excessive as to harm the social fabric, what we call "the common good."

Sociologist John Coleman, S.J., notes: "Many ethicists or political philosophers in the United States favor a view of the unencumbered individual as an autonomous chooser, cut off from essential relationality." This could easily be expanded to say that many Americans, not just the ethicists and philosophers, favor a view of the "unencumbered individual." Coleman adds, "This is, of course, diametrically opposed to the Catholic understanding of the human person as profoundly, and *essentially*, relational." In other words, "strong notions of solidarity and communitarianism do not resonate as well in the United States as they do in papal social teaching."[2]

It will become obvious that this exploration of Catholic social teaching is going to challenge the excessive individualism of our culture. We will see, for example, that the church does not always defend the right of private property. Individual ownership is not the highest priority or value in our Catholic tradition. Nor does the church teach that the right of individual privacy as determined in the debate around abortion is the highest value. Catholic teaching may challenge our assumptions about the relationship of the individual to the community in a number of areas. This is the prophetic edge of the Catholic tradition.

Our popes and bishops would concur with the recommendation of Father Charles Curran when he states,

> In my judgment, the major problem in contemporary U.S. culture today is the danger of individualism. In this context, the Catholic is called both in his or her own actions and especially in concert with like-minded people to inject a more communitarian approach into public life in the United States. The most significant way in which Catholics can transform existing culture and mediating institutions is by changing this predominate individualism into a more communitarian reality.[3]

This emphasis on community and interdependence is a persistent leitmotif of Catholic social teaching and spirituality, as is a concern about violence in its many forms.

In 1994 the U.S. bishops reflected on violence in American culture with these words: "The Kerner Commission called violence 'as American as apple pie.' Sadly, this provocative statement has proved prophetic. No nation on earth, except those in the midst of war, has as much violent behavior as we do—in our homes, on our televisions, and in our streets."[4]

The bishops identified some of the details of violence in America (using 1994 statistics):

- we face far higher rates of murder, assault, rape and other violent crimes than other societies;
- the most violent place in America is not in our streets, but in our homes—more that 50 percent of the women murdered in the U.S. are killed by their partner or ex-partner;
- 13 American children die every day from guns;
- our entertainment media too often exaggerate and even celebrate violence—children see 8,000 murders and 100,000 other acts of violence on television before they leave elementary school;
- the violence of abortion has destroyed more than 30 million unborn children since 1972.[5]

These are startling realities and numbing statistics, yet the gospel of Jesus and the teaching of the church compel us to address the root causes of violence in our communities and in our nation. These questions will be explored in later chapters.

Following Christ in a Consumer Culture

A few years ago our family was having a yard sale to unload some of our unwanted possessions. It was amazing how much "stuff" we had accumulated! About that same time our nineteen-year-old daughter returned from Europe after completing a four-week course in drawing in Florence and three weeks of backpacking in Europe. After living out of a backpack for almost two months, her first comment on opening her bedroom door was, "Boy, I have a lot of stuff!" She didn't realize how many possessions she had until she had lived without most of it for a few weeks.

That is probably true for most of us. We go along with the expectations of our society. We want to "fit in." Our children want what their friends have, and we adults want what our friends have. We try to create a higher standard for living for our children, who in turn learn from us and from our culture that life is about moving ahead, making progress, keeping the economy moving. How do we bring the values of the gospel to our consumer society? This is not an easy task, and one size does not fit all. Some are called by gospel values to a more radical life-style of voluntary poverty while others, the majority of us, are called by gospel values to a stewardship of our resources—striving to live simply and care for the needs of others. So we must wrestle with that central project of our culture: being a consumer, but being a consumer who is attentive to the values of the gospel and the Catholic tradition.

It is very hard to separate our religion from our culture because Christianity is always part of the culture. Jesus spoke and acted within his Jewish culture and St. Paul and others took Christianity to the Greek and Rome worlds, altering the message so it would be understood within those cultures. Just as in our day, at that time some of the cultural realities assisted in spreading Christianity and other cultural attitudes and practices were antithetical to the gospel. Because Jesus had reached out to the lepers, the sinners, and the other outcasts of his time, Christianity attracted many poor and marginal people and the early church continued the ministry of reaching out to all people, including those with little status in the society.

Throughout the centuries, Christianity in the West took on more and more of the cultural and political assumptions of Rome. As an institution the church assumed the cultural trappings of the Roman approach to law and order. Roman concepts of diocese, curia, and a hierarchy of ordination with three levels of ordination for deacons, priests, and bishops found their way into the Roman Catholic Church. The Eastern Catholic Church, in turn, utilized Greek notions and concepts. After the "fall of Rome" in 476 C.E. the church took on more responsibility for maintaining public order and addressing the needs of the poor.

The blending of religion and culture often makes it difficult to gain a perspective on our own culture. Some thoughtful Christians may wonder if Christianity has lost its soul by having been absorbed by the culture. Others may confuse loyalty to the gospel with loyalty to our country. Father Richard Rohr believes that "too many . . . Catholics do not understand that to be Catholic means to be Christian first and American second. They do not put the invitation of the gospel ahead of the demands of nationalism." When this happens, Rohr claims we "fall into the idolatry condemned by the prophets and rejected by Jesus."[6]

John Kavanaugh, a Jesuit priest, has focused on the challenge of "following Christ in a consumer society" in his writing and ministry. He notes that Americans on both ends of the political spectrum challenge his work:

> I have found the greatest resistance and challenge to my ideas from people who might be located at either far end of the spectrum. Some of them seem to have so strongly identified faith with Americanism that they reject any critique of the United States as being

communistic or even anti-Catholic. Others, it seems to me, have become so identified with American secular liberalism that they see any appeal to a radical Catholic of Christian faith as mere pietism.[7]

It is not easy to follow Christ in a consumer society because we are constantly bombarded with the cultural mantra of work and spend, work and spend. Harvard economist Juliet Schor documents how American households find themselves locked into this insidious cycle. Households go into debt to buy products they do not need and then they must work longer than they want in order to keep up on the payments. Schor makes the astute observation that "shopping is the chief cultural activity in the United States."[8]

Authoritative voices from our Catholic tradition can help our reflections on the challenges of following Christ in a consumer society. These voices include a British economist, Popes John Paul II and Benedict XVI, the Christian scriptures, early teachers of the church, and St. Francis of Assisi.

E. F. Schumacher (1911–1977)

Robert Ellsberg aptly captured the life and message of Ernest Fritz Schumacher as "a prophet in the guise of an economist."[9] Like other prophets, E. F. Schumacher called Western societies to repent from their sins of greed and exploitation in the patterns of production and consumption that were devastating the resources of the earth and leading to violence among the nations. He called for a fundamental reorientation: "We need a gentle spirit, a nonviolent approach" that would recognize the wisdom that "small is beautiful."[10]

Not religious as a youth, Schumacher was an unlikely prophet: "I was raised in Germany in the atmosphere of scientific materialism," he explained, "though with a veneer of Christianity—Lutheranism." During his years at the University of Bonn, he recalled, "I reacted very strongly, like many young people, against veneers of religion and culture, and that was the beginning of my own version of the anti-Christian trauma." He noted that it wasn't just a case of youthful rebellion: "There's much truth to that reaction too, of course, because the churches have become associated with so much that's wrong about our culture."[11]

While Christianity wasn't attractive to him, neither was his scientific materialism that "left the taste of ashes in my mouth" so he continued searching for a more satisfying worldview. Schumacher won a Rhodes scholarship to study at Oxford in England and also spent two years in New York City pursuing a diploma in economics at Columbia University. He returned to Germany in 1934 just as Hitler was coming into power. He was critical of the Nazis so he and his wife moved back to London. When World War II broke out in 1939 and he was unable to return to Germany, England became his adopted country for the rest of his life.

In 1950 while working as the head economist for the British National Coal Board, one of the largest industrial enterprises in Europe, he came across a book about Buddhism. "My eyes had been firmly closed to truth," he said, "but Buddhism opened them. As I read the book I kept saying, 'This is what I've been looking for!' And I wanted to learn all I could about it."[12] At age forty-four he was invited to Burma to work as an economic advisor to the Burmese government. In addition to his service in the Burmese government, he was eager to learn more about Buddhism. During his three-month assignment, he spent his weekends at a Buddhist monastery learning to mediate and eventually finding an inner peace: "He realized he had found the gold he was seeking. With words paraphrased from the scripture he described the experience: 'I came to Burma as a thirsty wanderer and there I found living water.'"[13]

Paradoxically, by studying Gandhi and Buddhism Schumacher found his way back to Christianity. From the late 1950s on, he was drawn to the liturgy and the social teachings of the Catholic Church and eventually converted to Catholicism. The Catholic tradition provided not only a spiritual haven for his soul, it also provided the moral foundation for his economic theories of human scale and appropriate technology. As a convert to Catholicism, Schumacher utilized the Catholic moral framework of the four cardinal virtues of prudence, justice, fortitude, and temperance. He believed that "There is perhaps no body of teaching which is more relevant and appropriate to the modern predicament than the marvelously subtle and realistic doctrines of the 'Four Cardinal Virtues' and in particular, temperance that means knowing when 'enough is enough.'"[14]

John Coleman placed E. F. Schumacher as

> a contemporary voice of what I call social Catholicism. . . . By this I mean the stream of Catholic thought that built on Thomistic principles, as particularly reapplied in the work of Jacques Maritain. Its adherents stressed that human institutions ought to be manageable in size, respectful of the human scale, and sanely run so that they did not damage the people involved in them.[15]

Schumacher's thinking, like other voices of social Catholicism, is caught in the tension between socialism and capitalism resulting in "an almost paradoxical character: they're 'conservative revolutionaries' or 'reactionary radicals,' mixing the old and the new with all the risks that involves."[16]

In an essay entitled "Buddhist Economics" he drew upon the wisdom of that ancient tradition in linking simplicity of lifestyle and nonviolence:

> Simplicity and non-violence are obviously closely related. The optimal pattern of consumption, producing a high degree of human satisfaction by means of a relatively low rate of consumption, allows people to live without great pressure and strain and to fulfill the primary injunction of Buddhist teaching: "Cease to do evil; try to do good."

He continued:

> As physical resources are everywhere limited, people satisfying their needs by means of a modest use of resources are obviously less likely to be at each other's throats than people depending upon a high rate of use.
>
> Equally, people who live in highly self-sufficient local communities are less likely to get involved in large-scale violence than people whose existence depends on world-wide systems of trade.[17]

Schumacher held that "production from local resources for local needs is the most rational way of economic life."[18] He challenged the assumption that bigger is better: "We are inclined to admire bigness, to marvel at super technology, supermedicine, supersonic speeds and superorganizations; the bigger the better. Wisdom teaches that 'small is beautiful,' for 'small' can always find a place, can always be absorbed or counterbalanced in harmony."[19] These insights led him to pioneer what is now called "appropriate technology," that is, earth- and user-friendly technology matched to the scale of community life.[20]

In 1973 he published *Small Is Beautiful: Economics as if People Mattered*; it sold over a million copies and was picked up by the fledgling environmental movement. The essay on Buddhist economics gathered a good deal of attention. When asked whether that essay was more informed by Catholic writings and thinkers, including papal encyclicals, Newman, Gilson, and Thomas Aquinas, he responded, "of course. But if I had called the chapter 'Christian Economics,' nobody would have paid any attention!"[21]

In his second book, *A Guide for the Perplexed*, Schumacher went deeper into spiritual concerns and focused on the loss of a "vertical dimension," which he described as the paradox between having technical solutions and not knowing how to answer the question, "What am I to do with my life?"[22] (Professor Schumacher appears to have shared a lot in common with his fellow German, Joseph Ratzinger—Pope Benedict XVI—who has emphasized the "vertical dimension," that is, the transcendent vocation of humanity in his writings, especially *Caritas in Veritate*.)

This "prophet in the guise of an economist" offered another way of thinking and acting, rooted in the wisdom of Eastern religion and Catholicism, that would resist materialism and protect the environment. He contrasted "the consumerist way of life, which multiples human wants, with the simple life whose aim is to achieve maximum well-being with the minimal use of the earth resources."[23] His writing showed that while "economics as if people mattered" was truly rooted in Catholic social teaching, it was also a universal ethic.

The strain of traveling around the world to support the growing interest in the "Small Is Beautiful" movement took a toll on his health. His daughter wrote: "The more he preached nonviolence, the more he seemed to do violence to his own person by pushing himself to the limits. His crusade had taken on its own momentum. Fritz was carried along in its momentum."[24] He died on September 4, 1977, only four years after the publication of his famous book.

Pope John Paul II

Like Schumacher, Pope John Paul II consistently warned the West about the danger of materialism and consumerism. Even though he grew up under a Communist state, Pope John Paul II believed that consumerism is a more insidious enemy of Christianity than the communism of the Soviet system. Communism is explicitly antireligious whereas materialism and consumerism are more subtle enemies of gospel values.

Pope John Paul II offered a clear moral directive: "It is not wrong to want to live better; what is wrong is a style of life which is presumed to be better when it is directed towards 'having' rather than 'being,' and which wants to have more, not in order to be more but in order to spend life in enjoyment as an end in itself."[25] Having is the goal of a consumer culture, and it presumes that we will *be* more if we *have* more.

The cultural attitude of consumerism is, in the pope's thinking, definitely connected to the ecological crisis: "Equally worrying is the ecological question which accompanies the problem of consumerism and which is closely connected to it. In his desire to have and to enjoy rather than to be and to grow, man consumes the resources of the earth and his own life in an excessive and disordered way."[26]

Pope John Paul II consistently spoke out on the need for simplicity in the Christian's life, especially for those of us living in the more developed nations. In 1979 when he came to the United States, Pope John Paul II addressed an enthusiastic audience in Yankee Stadium:

> Christians will want to be in the vanguard in favoring ways of life that decisively break with the frenzy of consumerism, exhausting and joyless. It is not a question of slowing down progress, for there is not human progress when everything conspires to give full reign to the instincts of self-interest, sex, and power.
>
> We must find a simple way of living. For it is not right that the standard of living of the rich countries would seek to maintain itself by draining off a great part of the reserves of energy and raw materials that are meant to serve the whole of humanity. . . . It is in the joyful simplicity of a life inspired by the Gospel and the Gospel's spirit of fraternal sharing that you will find the best remedy for sour criticism, paralyzing doubt, and the temptation to make money the principal means and indeed the very measure of human advancement.[27]

The U.S. bishops picked up Pope John II's message noting that "Our religious tradition has always urged restraint and moderation in the use of material goods." They went on to talk about the benefits of living simply.

> Changes in lifestyle based on traditional moral virtues can ease the way to a sustainable and equitable world economy in which sacrifice will no longer be an unpopular concept. For many of us, a life less focused on material gain may remind us that we are more than what we have. Rejecting the false promises of excessive or conspicuous consumption can even allow more time for family, friends, and civic responsibilities. A renewed sense of sacrifice and restraint could make an essential contribution to addressing global climate change.[28]

Getting our bearings about consumerism and possessions is not easy in the American culture. The messages of the marketplace are almost overwhelming. It is essential that the pope and bishops address this concern, but our parishes must also work to find ways to combat the mantra of consumption. During the Sundays of the Easter season members of our parish in Rochester, New York renew our baptismal promises using a contemporary version that asks whether we "reject the spirit of consumerism and materialism which is so prevalent in our age." Similarly, each Advent our parish invites us to prepare for Christmas in a way that does more good for creation and those who have less, rather than buying gifts for those who already have more than they can use. Our parish has also tackled the Cinderella syndrome around Christian marriages that costs thousands of dollars, exploring simpler ways for two Christians to celebrate the marriage vows.

Pope John Paul II, E. F. Schumacher, and the staff of St. Mary's Church are trying to remind us of the timeless teaching of Jesus about the lure of possessions.

Christian Scriptures

While a dominant cultural message in the United States is "buy baby, buy," the biblical tradition offers a radically different approach to accumulating possessions. Jesus warned his followers of the dangers of an attachment to wealth and the heedless acquisition of material possessions: "And he said to them, 'Take care! Be on your guard against all kinds of greed; for one's life does not consist in the abundance of possessions'" (Lk 12:15). Jesus taught that at the end of time we will be judged on how we have used the resources entrusted to us for the good of those in need (Mt 25:14ff). "In these ways Jesus opened up to us a new living based not upon consumption, but upon prudent use of the goods of this world with a special concern for the poor."[29]

In commenting on the wisdom of the Bible, scripture scholar Luke Timothy Johnson suggests that we view the Hebrew and Christian Scriptures as "a body of witnesses to what it means to live a human life before a creating, sustaining, and saving God."[30] He goes on to explain that when we look at the Bible in this way, we find "a great deal being said about the way people use possessions." The focus is not so much on the things themselves as "what they mean for those who claimed them."

Professor Johnson believes that *our attitude toward possessions is either one of idolatry or true faith*—a stark choice indeed! In using the word "idolatry" he focuses on the fact that our response to possessions tells us what we perceive as of *ultimate value* in our lives. Possessions become an idol if they enslave worshipers of "the true God who calls humans out of such fearful, compulsive self-grasping into a new life of freedom that enables them to use things without being owned by them." He goes on to say that "The first and most fundamental meaning of possessions, then, is their expression of the human response of idolatry or faith before the mystery of existence."[31]

Before we assume that we have chosen faith rather than "idolatry" because we do not worship idols, Johnson unpacks the meaning of idolatry in contemporary terms: "Idolatry, in simple terms, is the choice of treating as ultimate and absolute that which is neither absolute nor ultimate. We treat something as ultimate by the worship we pay it."[32] Worship in this context is not the worship of our lips or standing at the altar with incense, but the worship of service. Hence, my god is that which I serve. "Whatever I may claim as ultimate, the truth is that my god is that which rivets my attention, centers my activity, preoccupies my mind, and motivates my action." That for which I give up anything else is my god.[33]

The Bible focuses on riches as the classic object of idolatry, but other realities can become idols for us—beauty, power, pleasure, succeeding, stamp collecting, or a million other things. The Gospel of Luke gives a couple of examples of idolatry. One is the parable of the rich man with the barns.

> [Jesus] said to them, "Take heed, and beware of all covetousness; for a man's life does not consist in the abundance of his possessions." And he told them a parable, saying, "The land of a rich man brought forth plentifully; and he thought to himself, 'What shall I do, for I have nowhere to store my crops?' And he said, 'I will do this: I will pull down my barns, and build larger ones; and there I will store all my grain and my goods. And I will say to my soul [life], "Soul, you have ample goods laid up for many years; take your ease, eat, drink, and be merry." 'But God said to him, "Fool! This night your soul [life] is required of you; and the things you have prepared, whose will they be?" So is he who lays up treasure for himself, and is not rich toward God'" (Lk 12:15–21).

Johnson comments that Jesus explicitly and emphatically rejects the identification of "life" with "abundance of possessions." The man in the parable is not a fool because he is rich. "He is a fool because he identifies his very existence with the security he thinks comes from having grain stored in barns." He has made the mistake of equating his life, his being, with what he has. Rather than realizing his life is in God's hands, he trusts in his possessions. This man identified his life with his possessions. He identified his being with his having, which is a fatal mistake. We continue to be tempted to trust in our possessions or some other god, although the Bible teaches us to trust only in God.

Also in the Gospel of Luke we find a reference to possessions in the story of Lot and his wife and the burning of Sodom and Gomorrah. When Lot's wife turned back to look at Sodom she became a pillar of salt. Luke believed that she turned back in longing for the possessions she had left behind. So he says, "Remember Lot's wife. Whoever seeks to gain his life will lose it, but whoever loses his life will preserve it" (Lk 17:33). Luke believed that Lot's wife was tragically confused. She identified her *being* with her *having*, her life with her possessions. Because she could not respond to God's call, she lost the life that she had tried to build up through what she possessed. Johnson maintains that "there is no doubt about the sharpness of Jesus' teaching here." Because the Greek word that Luke used really means "to possess," "Whoever seeks to gain his life will lose it" could also be translated as "Whoever seeks to possess his life will lose it." Luke's point is simply that one who would try to hold onto life as a possession will lose it.[34]

Johnson adds, "The mandate of faith in God is clear: we must, in some fashion, share that which has been given to us by God as a gift. To refuse to share what we have is to act idolatrously." Johnson gives us the image of a clenched hand to expresses our attitude toward God and our possessions:

> The significance of the sharing of possessions, whether by once-for-all donation or by steady almsgiving or by a community of goods . . . expresses our self-disposition toward God and the world. The clenched hand, the stance of holding and hoarding our possessions . . . manifests and makes real our closure against God and the world. The open hand, the sharing of possessions, . . . reveals and makes actual our availability to God and the world.[35]

The Christian scriptures describe the many ways we can share our possessions:

- The disciples dropped their fishing nets and ran after a preacher they had just met.
- Martha and Mary made space for Jesus in their home and likewise made room for his teaching in their hearts.
- The first believers in Jerusalem who were "one of heart and mind" shared all without discrimination.[36]

The church of the apostles continued the biblical teaching that rich and poor alike should share in the bounty of creation. In two places in the Acts of the Apostles, St. Luke sketches a summary of how the followers of Jesus "shared all things in common."

> They devoted themselves to the apostles' instruction and the communal life, to the breaking of bread and the prayers. A reverent fear overtook them all, for many wonders and signs were performed by the apostles. Those who believed shared all things in common; they would sell their property and goods, dividing everything on the basis of each one's need. They went to the temple area together every day, while in their homes they broke bread. With exultant and sincere hearts they took their meals in common, praising God and winning the approval of all the people (Acts 2:42–47).

> Now the whole group of those who believed were of one heart and one soul, and no one claimed private ownership of any possession, but everything they owned was held in common. With great power the apostles gave their testimony to the resurrection of the Lord Jesus, and great grace was upon them all. There was not a needy person among them, for as many as owned lands or houses sold them and brought the proceeds of what was sold. They laid it at the apostles' feet, and it was distributed to each as any had need (Acts 4:32–35).

This picture of a community that shares all so that the needs of all will be met is an ideal picture, an image of sharing by which later communities could judge themselves.[37] The phrase "there was none needy among them" refers to Deuteronomy 15:4, which promised that when the laws of almsgiving were perfectly kept there would be no more needy persons. Luke is suggesting that the first Christian community fulfilled the Jewish desire for a community without poverty. As the history of Christianity unfolded, the monastic tradition emerged as an attempt to keep alive in the church this tradition of sharing possessions.

In his encyclical, *Deus Caritas Est*, Pope Benedict XVI offered his own commentary on the passage from Acts 2:44–45 and its meaning for the church today.

> As a community, the Church must practice love. Love thus needs to be organized if it is to be an ordered service to the community. The awareness of this responsibility has had a constitutive relevance in the Church from the beginning: "All who believed were together

and had all things in common; and they sold their possessions and goods and distributed them to all, as any had need" (*Acts* 2:44–5). In these words, Saint Luke provides a kind of definition of the Church, whose constitutive elements include fidelity to the "teaching of the Apostles," "communion" (*koinonia*), "the breaking of the bread" and "prayer" (cf. *Acts* 2:42). The element of "communion" (*koinonia*) is not initially defined, but appears concretely in the verses quoted above: it consists in the fact that believers hold all things in common and that among them, there is no longer any distinction between rich and poor (cf. also *Acts* 4:32–37). As the Church grew, this radical form of material communion could not in fact be preserved. But its essential core remained: within the community of believers there can never be room for a poverty that denies anyone what is needed for a dignified life (20).

The Letter of James clearly teaches that a living faith is to be expressed by responding to the needs of others in love—a message that Pope Benedict reiterates as well. Scripture scholar Luke Timothy Johnson explains that avoiding injustice is not enough: "Faith in God demands fidelity to the needy."[38] "If a brother or sister is ill clad and in lack of daily food, and one of you says to them, 'Go in peace, be warmed and filled,' without giving them the things needed for the body, what does it profit? So, faith by itself, if it has no works is dead" (Jas 2:15–17).

James restates the traditional Jewish belief for the followers of Jesus: "Religion that is pure and undefiled before God and the Father is this: to visit orphans and widows in their affliction, and to keep oneself unstained from the world" (1:27). According to James, care for the needy is not some optional program of social reform; care for the needy is an expression of faith in God.

Early Church Tradition

The teaching of Jesus on the dangers of possessions and the importance of sharing God's gifts with the needy permeated the early church. The writings of the early church after the biblical era are compelling and eloquent on this point, as a few selections demonstrate.

At the end of the first century the author of the *Didache*, which is Greek for "teachings," instructs the Christians:

Give to anyone that asks, without looking for any repayment, for it is the Father's pleasure that we should share his gracious bounty with all people. . . . Never turn away from the needy; share all your possessions with your brother, and do not claim that anything is your own. If you and he are joint participators in things immortal, how much more so in things that are mortal?[39]

In the second century the writer of *The Shepherd of Hermas* was concerned about the welfare of the rich as well as the poor. Hermas, a liberated Christian slave, taught that the rich must become detached from their wealth before they can be genuine Christians. A Christian proves that he or she is detached by a willingness to help all who are in trouble financially, emotionally, and spiritually. "Instead of fields, then, buy souls that are in trouble. . . . Look after widows and orphans and do not neglect them. Spend your riches and all your establishment you have received from God on this kind of field and houses."[40]

In a similar vein, the early church wrestled with the question of whether a rich person could be saved. After considerable conversation and prayer, the church concluded that "they were allowed a chance of salvation if they lived modestly and distributed their possessions generously to the poor."[41]

Clement of Alexandria, writing in the early third century, reaffirmed the scriptural position that the source of all humanity's troubles is the desire for wealth. Clement, who saw no value in poverty, was trying to appeal to the cultured and the rich of Alexandria. He offered a moderate principle that we use the resources of the earth to meet our needs and what is not needed for our basic needs must be shared with the needy. Clement mocked rich people's need for extravagant bathroom facilities: "It is farcical and downright ridiculous for men to bring out urinals of silver and chamber pots of transparent alabaster, as if grandly ushering in their advisers, and for rich women in their silliness to have privies made of gold. It is as if the wealthy were not able to relieve nature except in a grandiose style!"[42]

John Chrysostom, the greatest preacher of the early church (354–407), focused on the danger of serving greed rather than the goal of serving God—effectively turning greed into an idol. The avaricious man is a slave of money, a double agent who masks his real allegiance, a Christian who worships mammon, not Christ. In response to the charge of idolatry, Chrysostom sharply replied:

But I've never made an idol . . . nor set up an altar nor sacrificed sheep nor poured libations of wine; no, I come to church, I lift up my hands in prayer to the only-begotten Son of God; I partake of the mysteries, I communicate in prayer and in all other duties of a Christian. How then . . . can I be a worshiper of idols? . . . You pretend to be serving God, but in reality you have submitted yourself to the hard and galling yoke of ruthless greed.[43]

Chrysostom preached that the rich injure themselves as well as the poor by their neglect of the poor: "Don't you realize that, as the poor man withdraws silently, sighing and in tears, you actually thrust a sword into yourself, that it is you who received the more serious wound?"[44] With blunt language, Chrysostom turns the tables on the rich: "The rich are in possession of the goods of the poor, even if they have acquired them honestly or inherited them legally." If they do not share, "the wealthy are a species of bandit." He goes on to explain the patristic principle of the universal purpose of creation: "Do not say 'I am using what belongs to me.' You are using what belongs to others. All the wealth of the world belongs to you and to others in common, as the sun, air, earth, and all the rest."[45]

The right of all people to benefit from the resources of the earth is a persistent teaching of the early church. St. Ambrose, the archbishop of Milan, explained this principle to his fourth-century audience: "God has ordered all things to be produced so that there should be food in common for all, and that the earth should be the common possession of all. Nature, therefore, has produced a common right for all, but greed has made it a right for a few."

The early church leaders were not attacking the rich; rather, they attacked greed and avariciousness. Ambrose "deplores the ruthless greed of the avaricious, their heartless exploitation of the poor, and the ostentation of their luxury."[46] The archbishop of Milan believed that giving to the poor was actually restitution for stolen goods. "You are not making a gift of your possessions to the poor person. You are handing over to him what is his."[47]

In continuity with the biblical tradition, the early church taught of care for the earth and the universal purpose of the goods of the earth. This teaching echoed through the centuries and rang with exceptional clarity in the life of Francesco Bernardone, Francis of Assisi.

Francis of Assisi

Born in 1182, Francis was the son of Pietro Bernardone, a wealthy cloth merchant in Assisi, a modest-sized town nestled in the Umbrian hills between Rome and Florence. Francis was one of the "privileged young men of Assisi, attracted to adventure and frivolity as well as tales of romance."[48] But sickness and a battle wound gave him time to think about the direction of his privileged life. As he recovered from his illness he became much more aware of his own vulnerability and dependence on God. The turning point of his conversion came during an encounter with a leper when God's grace allowed him to overcome his revulsion for all that the leper stood for. He embraced the leper and claimed that the embrace changed "bitterness to sweetness." "From that moment on, Francis would make his home with the lepers and marginalized of the world, and there find Christ, the suffering, crucified Savior."[49]

In a dramatic moment in the public marketplace, Francis stripped off his clothes. Handing his rich clothing to his shocked father, he said, "Hitherto I have called you father on earth; but now I say, 'Our Father, who art in heaven.'"[50] The bishop quickly covered Francis with a peasant's frock, which Francis marked with a cross.

When he was twenty-three years old Francis found direction for his life in the voice of the Crucified One who spoke to him from a cross in the ruined church of San Damiano. He heard the Lord tell him to "rebuild my church." Interpreting the message as an instruction to physically rebuild the dilapidated church in which he was praying, Francis began rebuilding the crumbling walls while continuing to serve the needs of the lepers. "The spectacle which Francis presented—the rich boy who now camped out in the open air, serving the sick, working with his hands, and bearing witness to the gospel—attracted ridicule from the respectable citizens of Assisi."[51] But his radical conversion had "a subversive appeal." Before long, other young men and women followed his example.

Seeking further direction from the gospel, Francis and his companions came across those passages wherein Jesus instructed his disciples to take nothing for the journey as he sent them out to preach conversion and the kingdom of God. This instruction would be their mandate. He now realized that the command of Jesus to rebuild the church did not mean its bricks and mortar but rather it was to call the church to "the radical simplicity of the gospel, to the spirit of poverty, and to the image of Christ in his poor."[52] In his conversion he turned toward the poor and away from the "sacred violence" of his day, the Crusades, as he opted for radical nonviolence.

Francis turned to nature with a radically new appreciation. All things great and small, living and inanimate reflected the Creator's love and were, therefore, deserving of reverence and respect. Theologian Leonardo Boff maintains that what allowed Francis to enter into the fraternity of all creation was the asceticism of poverty. For Francis, poverty "is a way of being by which the individual lets things be what they are; one refuses to dominate them, subjugate them, and make them objects of the will to power."[53]

According to Boff, poverty requires the "renunciation of the instinct to power, the dominion over things," because the desire for possessions is what stands between true communication between persons and with all creation. As Francis became poorer, he became more fraternal; he saw poverty as the way into the experience of universal fraternity with creation. Francis realized that he was a creature, a fellow companion with all the rest of creation. He was "not over things, but together with them, like brothers and sisters of the same family."[54]

Francis came to embrace creation by first embracing his fellow human beings, especially the poor. The poor reminded him of his true nature: a dependent creature unable to be self-made, self-sufficient, or self-fulfilled. Francis entered into a radical companionship with the poor, and through them, with all of creation. His life and his new relationship with all of creation—which included the elements, the stars, animals, the poor and the sick, sultans and crusaders, princes and prelates—represented "the breakthrough of a new model of human and cosmic community."[55]

A New Breed of Men and Women

Our Christian vocation is to be a disciple of Christ in our own political and cultural setting. While we celebrate all that is good in our cultural values, at the same time we must have a discerning eye and ear regarding the messages of our culture. Father Richard Rohr reflects his Franciscan spirituality as he points out the paradox of Christian discipleship and spiritual growth: "Paradoxically, our soul does not grow by being fed. It does not develop by taking more and more into itself, by adding experience, by increasing information or activity. Spiritual development is not a matter of addition but subtraction. It is not an aggressive activity but a passive activity, not by taking in but in letting go."[56]

Our spirits are filled not by acquiring more, but by giving thanks for the relationships and gifts that are already part of our lives: our family, our community, our faith, our home, our work, and creation. We are enriched not by adding more "stuff," but in seeing goodness and beauty in our present situation. While our culture imbues us with the message that possessions bring happiness, our faith tradition teaches us that possessions do not bring us happiness. Rather, the door to everlasting joy is opened by pursuing the lasting values of fidelity, love, community, justice, and peace.

Some of us will be called to the radical witness of *voluntary poverty*. Those living as part of the Catholic Worker movement take on voluntary poverty as do those committed to religious life. As a graduate student in Rome I witnessed the joy of voluntary poverty in the Missionaries of Charity. One evening the sisters asked if I could drive them to the train station in the middle of the night. Mother Teresa had just reassigned four of them to open a house in Sicily, so they were catching the night train from Rome. They packed a few belongings in a cardboard box, and within a few hours they had said their good-byes and were off to a new place. They were laughing as we lifted their "fancy luggage" onto the train in stark contrast to the dower faces of the other passengers on the platform. How could women who had so little be so joyful? How could these women who had let go of so much be so full of life? Their commitment to poverty and gospel-living had filled them with a different kind of richness.

Others in the Christian community are called to *stewardship* and to the tempering of our desire for more. Although most Christians are not called to voluntary poverty, the gospel does invite us to be joyful stewards of what we have. Personally I feel very blessed to have a modest home in the city of Rochester. We have a small city lot, but the yard is filled with flowers, bushes, a birdfeeder, squirrels, birds, and occasionally a woodchuck, skunk, or opossum. Giving thanks for what we have, even if it is less than others have, is an important part of being a faithful steward.

Even though we live in a consumer society, many holy people are living out gospel values in our churches and our workplaces. They use their resources to strengthen the community and care for the needy. Brigit, my coworker, and her husband Jeff are raising their three children on a modest income. Jeff is a social worker and Brigit works part-time so she can home-school their children. While their car may be rusty and dented, they decided to adopt a baby girl from China. They put their resources, their money, and their energy into creating a home for one of God's unfortunate children. That is what Christian stewardship looks like. This is the nature of Christian compassion and holiness.

As John Kavanaugh notes, "holiness will never occur where there is no passion or zeal for justice." Holiness "will never be found where there is no sense of one's own personal poverty nor a correlative love of the poor." He explains what he means by sanctity:

Sanctity is the acceptance of one's humanity, the acknowledgment that one is a loved sinner, and the overflowing of that experience of being unconditionally loved into compassion and honest labor. . . . The saint does the only utterly new and sacred thing on the face of the earth. The saint has learned to give all—even his or her very self—freely away in a true revolution of life and love.[57]

Brigit and Jeff and the Missionaries of Charity are among the saints of our time. They remind us that the sanctity and compassion of Jesus can be part of our time and our place. They keep alive the passion and vision of the followers of Christ in the early church.

This vision of holiness is expressed in the words of the *Epistle to Diognetus* written at the end of the second century to the tutor of the Emperor Marcus Aurelius. The author explained that in gratitude for God's gifts, as Christians we should imitate God by loving our neighbors: "Happiness is not found in dominating one's fellows, or in wanting to have more than his weaker brethren, or in possessing riches and riding roughshod over his inferiors." The author explains, "No one can become an imitator of God like that, for such things are wholly alien to his greatness." To imitate God the following is required: "But if a man will shoulder his neighbor's burden; if he be ready to supply another's need from his own abundance; if, by sharing the blessings he has received from God with those who are in want, he himself becomes a god to those who receive his bounty—such a man is indeed an imitator of God."[58]

The early Christians lived a "reversal of values" in the pagan culture of their time. In the year 180 Athenagoras of Athens, a Greek Christian, noted that Christians did not place great importance on their property, their reputations, and their freedom. These were not the focus of their highest values. Athenagoras pointed out that Christians' belief in an all-bountiful God resulted in an astonishing reversal of current pagan values and brought into existence "a new breed of men and women who refuse to abandon the poor and the helpless to fate, but who rush to their assistance in times of crisis."[59] Jeff, Brigit, the Missionaries of Charity, and you and I are all called to be this new breed of men and women in our day.

A Prayer for Social Justice (Pope Pius XII)

Almighty and eternal God, may your grace enkindle
in all persons a love of the many unfortunate people

whom poverty and misery reduce to a
condition of life unworthy of human beings.
Arouse in the hearts of those who call you God a
hunger and thirst for social justice and for fraternal charity
in deeds and in truth.
Grant, O Lord, peace in our days, peace to our souls, peace to
our community and peace among nations.
Amen.[60]

Discussion Questions

1. Professor Johnson believes that our attitude toward possessions is one of idolatry or true faith. What is he trying to say by this stark contrast?

2. Discuss the quotes from the Acts of the Apostles on personal possessions. How does the church today try to "share all things in common?" Why is this hard to do in our American culture?

3. St. Francis entered into a radical companionship with the poor and through them with all of creation. How is "care for the earth" connected with "care for the poor?"

4. In 180 C.E. Athenagoras of Athens noted that Christians did not place great importance on their property, their reputation, and their freedom. Christians were "a new breed of men and women." Do you know any people who reflect the values that Athenagoras described? Tell about them.

2

God's Gift of Creation

Pope Benedict XVI challenges Catholics:

Can we remain indifferent before the problems associated with such realities as climate change, desertification, the deterioration and loss of productivity in vast agricultural areas, the pollution of rivers and aquifers, the loss of biodiversity, the increase of natural catastrophes and the deforestation of equatorial and tropical regions?[1]

The pope expresses a sense of urgency "in the face of signs of a growing crisis," but this crisis is also an "opportunity for discernment and new strategic planning" (par. 5). However, the process of discernment can be enriched by listening to the values and wisdom of the words of Jesus, the prophets of the Hebrew Scriptures, the Fathers and Mothers of the church, the teachings of our bishops and popes, and the lived experience of the People of God. Their voices have given shape to our Catholic social tradition.[2]

As caretakers of creation we should be under no illusion about the challenges that we face—the personal challenges of conversions and lifestyle decisions, our systemic challenges of addiction to fossil fuels, and the resistance of individuals and institutions that benefit from the status quo and the exploitation of our natural resources. The life and death of Dorothy Stang, a defender of the poor and the Earth, demonstrate the challenges that caretakers of creation face as they work to protect the gift of creation so that all may benefit from the its goods.

Sister Dorothy Stang

In 1966 when she was thirty-four years old, Sister Dorothy Stang from Dayton, Ohio went with four other sisters to rural Brazil. Her religious community, the Sisters of Notre Dame de Namur, was responding to the request from Pope John XXIII that American religious communities send ten percent of their members to serve in Latin America. The five sisters studied Portuguese and Brazilian culture at the Center for Intercultural Formation in Petrópolis. During this time they also studied liberation theology with Gustavo Gutiérrez and Jon Sobrino. Liberation theology urged the church to identify with the poor by sharing in their poverty and empowering the poor to claim their rights. The sisters lived with the poor and formed small Christian communities to reflect on the Bible and its meaning in their lives. Through this ministry, the poor began to recognize their rights as human beings and they began to challenge the unjust economic system of rural Brazil. Not surprisingly, the wealthy landowners became suspicious of the sisters and the work they were doing.

Sister Dorothy moved to the state of Para where peasant farmers were migrating. The Trans-Amazon Highway was opening up the rain forest to loggers, cattlemen, and settlers, and the government offered free land (250 acres) to settlers to develop the area. Conflict arose as wealthy ranchers and loggers coveted the land of the settlers. Government officials, police, and judges were beholden to the wealthy landowners, and the conflict over the land turned violent. Hired thugs would sow weeds among the crops, burn the farms of the settlers, or kill the settlers, union leaders, priests, and religious. In addition to defending the rights of the poor, Dorothy became a leader in the environmental movement, which was trying to prevent the destruction of the rain forest.

By the 1990s the environmental movement in Brazil and around the world was keenly aware of the importance of the rain forest as a source of oxygen for the planet and for its irreplaceable species of fauna and flora. The rain forest in Brazil was being destroyed at a rate of more than 100,000 square kilometers a year, roughly equivalent to the State of Virginia! The forest was "clear cut" for the valuable cedar and mahogany or the ranchers burned the forest to create fields for farming and cattle grazing. The clear-cutting destroys the soil, which quickly becomes a desert due to the loss of the decaying vegetation and the bleaching effect of the hot sun. Burning the forest adds to the air pollution and accelerates global warming as it releases large amounts of carbon into the atmosphere. At the same time, whole species of animals, insects, and plants are destroyed, eliminating valuable parts of God's creation. It is worth noting that approximately 25 percent of all pharmaceutical products used in the world come from plant species in the Amazon.

Dorothy Stang saw the link between the rights of the poor and the necessity of protecting the environment. With other environmentalists she confirmed the "intrinsic connection between the abuse of women, exploitation of the poor, and the desecration of the earth."[3] She worked with the government to establish preserves incorporating sustainable development that would keep 80 percent of the land as forest. Sustainable development meant persuading farmers to plow under vegetation rather than burning it, thereby preserving the nutrients for the soil and lessening air pollution. Sustainable development also meant establishing businesses to bring the natural produce of the forests to markets rather than bringing in cattle and non-indigenous crops that destroy the environment. And Dorothy convinced the farmers to plant tens of thousands of trees in an effort to reforest the land.

All of this activity by Dorothy and the poor settlers did not go unnoticed by the large landowners. In 2004 she was detained and questioned by the authorities, and death threats against her increased. Two ranchers put up $25,000 to have her murdered. On the day before her death she called her brother David in Colorado with serious concerns. She told him that ten villages had been burned in an attempt to scare off the farmers. Even though she had reported these events to the police and other officials, nothing had been done.

> On the morning of February 12, 2005, in a gentle rain, Dorothy set off for an important meeting with the farmers. Dorothy knew the two men [Rayfran das Neves Sales and Clodoaldo Carlos Batista] who blocked her way, and she engaged them in conversation, pulling a map from her ever-present plastic bag to show that the area was a reserve for sustainable development and the logging would be illegal. When one of them asked if she had a weapon, she produced a well-worn Bible from her bag, and proceeded to read to them from the Beatitudes. She invited them to the community meeting, blessed them, and turned to leave. They called her name and when she turned back they shot her in the abdomen. After she fell face down, she was shot five more times and killed. The voice of this seventy-three-year-old nun was silenced.[4]

Bringing her killers to justice was not easy in a region controlled by the loggers and cattlemen and known for political corruption. After five years of court battles a jury found Vitalmiro Bastos de Moura guilty on April 12, 2010, of ordering Sister Dorothy's death because she had blocked him from taking land the government had given to farmers. Mr. Moura, a rancher who had previously been acquitted of orchestrating her murder, was sentenced to thirty years. On May 1, 2010, a jury convicted fellow rancher Regivaldo

Galvao of the same charge. Mr. Galvao, the last of four defendants to stand trial in the case, was sentenced to thirty years in prison.[5]

Today the struggle continues in the rain forest in the state of Para where Sister Dorothy was killed. A grassroots organization, "Dorothy Committe" is working to stop illegal logging. On January 10, 2011, its members blocked the road at the entrance of the "Sustainable Development Project Hope." The Dorothy Committe reports that once again the scene is one of "tension and threat."[6] According to *The Denver Post*, a French priest, Henri des Roziers, who is working with the settlers in this region, has a $38,000 price on his head. The forces of greed are relentless.

When Dorothy's brother, David, learned of his sister's death he said "I just broke down. I cried all day. I'd totally underestimated the power of that dark side."[7] David Stang worked for five years to bring his sister's killers to justice and to make sure that "the dark side" was not victorious. His sister's murder thrust David from his existence as a blissfully retired person tending his coin and stamp collection into an international drama of land wars and death lists. His perseverance eventually paid off when the murderers were exposed and held accountable for their crime.

David commented on Dorothy's tenacity: "She was not by any means a sweetly pious nun who retreated to a life of prayer and contemplation. She was tough, smart and intensely political, and it was precisely her fervent earthly work on behalf of the poor that got her killed" he said. "None of this ooey-gooey little nun bit. She was like a Mack truck."[8]

This tenacity runs in her brother's blood as well; he vows to keep her legacy alive. For example, when Father des Roziers invited him to attend the opening of a new school named for Dorothy during the heart of the violent conflict, David did not hesitate. After a journey that included two airplane flights and a four-hour drive in a pickup truck on a rutted jungle road deep into the frontier, he was greeted by hundreds of people: "The workers wore hard hats and were standing at attention. The kids came out in their uniforms. Everyone sang songs. There were hugs and tears. If I'm a symbol of pride to them, then, yes, I'll be there." Devastated by Dorothy's murder, David Stang is determined keep her message alive: "When are we going to realize that the Earth belongs to every human being?"[9]

Our Lived Experience

"When are we going to realize that the Earth belongs to every human being?" This is a truth that Dorothy and David Stang learned through struggle and suffering. The witness of this woman, her brother, the Sisters of Notre Dame de Namur, and the poor settlers in Para is a powerful lesson, and their lived experience forms part of the Catholic social tradition, a living tradition in which each of us plays a part. Our lives and our actions either contribute to or take away from the witness of that tradition as each person's life and actions send out ripples in the pond. Although some people's experience is dramatic, many of our lives are seemingly mundane, yet each of us can be a witness of our love for the poor and our care for creation.

Howard Hunter's life as an apple farmer in Michigan sends out ripples to his children and grandchildren and to all who come to his orchard for apples. Howard Hunter, a 98-year-old apple farmer in Michigan, reflects on what he has learned from tending an apple orchard for many years: "The orchard taught us how to raise apples and to cooperate with nature, not control it." His philosophy is rooted in a belief that things will turn out fine even if the outcome is not what we expect. Hunter remembers an unseasonably cold, clear evening years ago. His son Stan came to his father and said, "It's a beautiful night, but I think the apples are frozen." Hunter looked at the apples himself and saw that they were frozen but said to his son, "It's still a beautiful night."

Tending his apple trees has taught Hunter and his family about the vicissitudes of farming as a challenge toward strength, knowledge, and humility. These lessons have been absorbed by Hunter's granddaughter, Cindy, who visits with her three-year old son. "Every time I step into this house or walk through the orchard, I feel a sense of well-being. . . . It is not unlike what one might feel walking into a church. . . . A great many people have felt this same sacredness when they've come for apples at Hunter's Orchard."[10]

The sacredness of creation is a message that Cindy has learned from her grandfather's farm and forms part of her lived experience. Each of us can tap into similar lived experiences in order to better understand the sacredness of creation. Day-to-day experiences can be sources that shape our values and our commitment to protect creation. Similarly, as Christians we can also turn to the Bible to shape our values and commitments, fully aware that past misunderstandings of the biblical teaching may have actually been part of the problem.

Biblical Perspectives

Then God said, "Let us make man in our image, after our likeness. Let them have dominion over the fish of the sea, the birds of the air, and the cattle, and over all the wild animals and all the creatures that crawl on the ground. . . ." God blessed them, saying: "Be fertile and multiply; fill the earth and subdue it. Have dominion over the fish of the sea, the birds of the air, and all the living things that move on the earth." (Gen 1:26, 28)

The lesson of Genesis is that humanity has responsibility over nature and some level of power over it, as a steward has some level of authority over the resources of the owner.

Some commentators believe that *misinterpretation* of this text has actually led to the exploitation and domination of nature. Historian Lynn White, Jr., in particular, suggested that by vigorously embracing the Genesis mandate to hold "dominion" over the Earth and to "fill and subdue it," the Judeo-Christian tradition broke the hold of animistic belief in the intrinsic sacredness of nature. White's thesis is that the Judeo-Christian tradition taught that exploiting people is wrong, but that exploiting nature is right and proper. With these attitudes Christianity set the stage for the emergence of modern science and technology in the West, but accordingly bears a heavy burden of responsibility for ecological degradation.

While the Judeo-Christian tradition may have been part of the problem, White also believes that it can be part of the solution:

> Both our present science and our present technology are so tinctured with orthodox arrogance toward nature that no solutions for our ecological crisis can be expected from them alone. Since the roots of our trouble are so largely religious, the remedy must also be essentially religious, whether we call it that or not. We must rethink and refeel our nature and our destiny.[11]

Biblical scholar Dianne Bergant believes that White's criticism has some truth to it. She summarizes a common misunderstanding of the Genesis text. "After all, are we not superior to all of creation? Have we not been told to subdue the earth and have dominion over the fish and the birds and every living thing (cf. Gen 1:26, 28)?" She points to Catholic catechetical materials that used a pyramid to explain humanity's place in creation: rocks and minerals on the first level, vegetative life on the second level, animate life on the next level, and finally, humanity at the top of the pyramid. "In this way, we learned that God created the lower levels of the natural world to serve the ends of the higher level. How well this was illustrated; how well we learned it, and how wrong we have been!"

According to Bergant, such a human-centered worldview is "certainly not biblical." The Bible has a God-centered worldview. "It is false to think that humankind is itself the measure of everything. God is! The value of creation does not lie in its usefulness for us. It lies in the fact of its existence from God. The Bible is very clear on this point. The world is not ours; it is God's. . . . We are stewards. We are accountable to God."[12]

Rabbi David Saperstein explains the Jewish understanding of "dominion." The rabbinic tradition taught that "it is important for us to exercise dominion in the context of replenishing the earth." Jews "acknowledge that we have no rights of ownership or authority over the world. We enjoy only a borrowed authority; God remains the master of God's creation."[13]

Chapter 2 of the Book of Genesis includes a second account of creation, in which God asked Adam to name his fellow creatures:

> The LORD God said: "It is not good for the man to be alone. I will make a suitable partner for him." So the LORD God formed out of the ground various wild animals and various birds of the air, and he brought them to the man to see what he would call them; whatever the man called each of them would be its name. The man gave names to all the cattle, all the birds of the air, and all the wild animals; but none proved to be the suitable partner for the man (Gen 2:18–20).

The text continues with the story of God taking a rib from the man and creating woman to be man's suitable partner and companion. In naming the animals, the man establishes a relationship with each creature. The message of this story is that God created human beings to be in relationship with all of creation and to find a suitable partner and companion in another human being. Fathers Michael Himes and Kenneth Himes explain that "humanity is sexed in order that human beings may be driven into relationship with one with another."[14] And this relationship is one of being a partner, a companion. The Himes brothers believe it is time to recover the theme of companionship as way of understanding our relationship with each other and with all of creation. "Companionship implies mutuality. It excludes the reduction of either side of the relationship to a tool of the other's purposes."[15] The natural world is not intended for domination and subjugation by humans, but for companionship.

The Himes brothers argue that "companionship" is a better image for our relationship with creation than the image of "stewardship." The stewardship theme can be interpreted as God having created all that is and then handing creation over to humanity. However, when the image of steward-ship dominates our imagination, God can be removed from the scene as human beings are given oversight of the Earth. In a subtle way, human be-ings move to center stage in the drama of caring for creation. Stewards are not anxious for the master to return; we enjoy being in charge and may forget that we do not own creation, that we are only caretakers. In many ways, then, it is better to speak of our *companionship with* all of creation, rather than our stewardship over creation.[16]

The Book of Genesis shows that the sin of Adam and Eve caused a rupture in the harmony of the Garden of Eden. As a result, they were driven from the garden, the place of harmony and well-being. Humanity's sin continues to affect creation, as the prophet Hosea cries out:

> There is no fidelity, no mercy, no knowledge of God in the land. False swearing, lying, murder, stealing and adultery. In their lawless-ness, bloodshed follows bloodshed. Therefore, the land mourns, and everything that dwells in it languishes: the beasts of the field, the birds of the air, and even the fish of the sea perish" (Hos 4:1b–3).

Sin, exploitation, and greed distorted the "right relationships" between people and with nature. Therefore, the Jewish religion established the in-stitutions of Sabbath and the Jubilee to restore the proper balance between human relationships, with creation, and with God. "The Sabbath rest gave relief from unremitting toil to workers and beasts alike. It invited the whole community to taste the goodness of God in creation."[17] The Jewish tradition also developed the Sabbath year. Every seventh year, the land and the people were to rest, and human restraint would restore nature. Finally, after seven sets of seven years, a special "year of favor from the LORD" would take place. In that year, the Jubilee Year, not only would the land lie fallow, but debts would be forgiven so that human relationships would be restored and the poor would have a new beginning.

The Hebrew Scriptures are also filled with prayers in which creation it-self praises God. For example, when Shadrach, Meshach, and Abednego were thrown in the fiery furnace they broke into praise with all of creation:

> Let the earth bless the Lord;
> > praise and exalt him above forever.
> Mountains and hills, bless the Lord;
> > praise and exalt him above all forever.

Everything growing from the earth, bless the Lord;
    praise and exalt him above forever.
You springs, bless the Lord;
    praise and exalt him above forever.
Seas and rivers, bless the Lord;
    praise and exalt him above forever.
You dolphins and all water creatures, bless the Lord;
    praise and exalt him above forever.
All you birds of the air, bless the Lord;
    praise and exalt him above forever.
All you beasts, wild and tame, bless the Lord;
    praise and exalt him above forever. (Dan 3: 74–81)

The Book of Psalms, used in the Liturgy of the Word and the Liturgy of the Hours, echoes the praise that creation gives to God along with humanity. "The heavens declare the glory of God, and the firmament proclaims his handiwork" (Ps 19:2).

Jesus maintained the Jewish tradition of proclaiming the Jubilee Year in which humanity and creation are liberated: "The spirit of the Lord is upon me," he announced in the synagogue in Nazareth, "to announce a year of favor from the Lord" (Lk 4:18–19). The writings of Paul also teach that creation, too, is waiting for liberation: "Yes, we know that all creation groans and is in agony even until now . . . while we await the redemption of our bodies" (Rom 8:22–23).

Jesus repeatedly used the beauty of creation to illustrate his message of salvation. The birds of the air and the lilies of the field were a reminder of God's care. Wisdom about the spiritual life was to be gained by observing the fig tree: "Notice the fig tree, or any other tree. You observe them when they are budding, and know for yourselves that summer is near. Likewise when you see all the things happening of which I speak, know that the reign of God is near" (Lk 21:29). Jesus saw in the seed cast on the ground a lesson of the Word of God trying to take root in our lives (Lk 8:11).

Jesus also used the earthy realities of bread, wine, oil, and water to symbolize the new covenant he established with humanity and all creation. This new covenant overcomes all hostility and restores the order of love that God intended from the creation of the Earth. Christ is the firstborn of a new creation that participates in God's grace and God's salvation.

From Boniface to Francis of Assisi

As the Christian faith spread throughout Europe it carried with it both an appreciation of creation but also a fear of pagan religions that worshipped nature. Christianity's praise of creation was thus tempered by its fear of idolatry. In the eighth century St. Boniface stands out as a symbol of this confrontation with nature worship. An Anglo-Saxon by birth, Boniface left England when he was forty to preach the gospel to the people of Saxony (now part of Germany). Boniface was willing to adapt Christianity as far as possible to the local culture, but he was unwilling to accept the worship of trees, a common feature of Germanic folk religion. So in 723 Boniface took an ax to a tree dedicated to the god Thor. A crowd of onlookers expected that lightning bolts would rain down upon Boniface for his sacrilege. When he remained unscathed, his challenge to the idol Thor demonstrated to the people the truth of Christianity, and his act of defiance inspired a wave of conversions.[18] However, an unintended consequence of his action was a diminished awe for the sacredness of nature.

For a thousand years Christianity in Europe confronted the worship of nature in pagan religions. This confrontation with pagan nature worship meant that Christian theology and practice overreacted to the fear of idolatry and downplayed respect for nature. Five hundred years after Boniface, Francis of Assisi opened a new chapter of Christian theology and spirituality regarding creation. With the threat of the worship of nature resolved, Francis turned to nature with a radically new appreciation. All things great and small, living and inanimate reflected the Creator's love and were, therefore, deserving of reverence and respect.

As noted in the first chapter, Francis entered into the fraternity of all creation. His humility and poverty were keys to this new appreciation of nature. For Francis, poverty "is a way of being by which the individual lets things be what they are; one refuses to dominate them, subjugate them, and make them objects of the will to power."[19] Consequently, as Francis became poorer, he became more fraternal; he saw poverty as the way into the experience of universal fraternity with creation. Francis realized that he was a creature, a fellow companion with all the rest of creation. He was "not over things, but together with them, like brothers and sisters of the same family."[20] Francis entered into a radical companionship with the poor and, through them, with all of creation. His new relationship with all of creation represented "the breakthrough of a new model of human and cosmic community."[21]

Creation as the Sacrament of God

The Catholic liturgical tradition recognizes the goodness of creation and uses the "earthy" components of creation—water, ashes, oil, fire, wine —and bread in sacred worship. Bishop Anthony Pilla of Cleveland stated, "Catholic sacramental practice embraces the gifts of creation and uses them for praise and thanksgiving. Fundamental to that practice is the conviction that creation is itself holy and appropriately used for worship."[22]

Sacraments reveal God's love for us and they also reveal God's grace. "By being thoroughly itself, a sacrament bodies forth the absolute self-donative love of God that undergirds both it and the entirety of creation." We think of the seven sacraments of the Catholic Church as revealing God's grace, "[b]ut every creature, human and nonhuman, animate and inanimate, can be a sacrament."[23] This discovery that every part of creation is a sacrament of God's love is the beginning of a great reverence for creation. It is important to remember that the sacraments of creation are to be appreciated and respected for what they are, and not seen as a tool to achieve human goals.

Water is one example of a sacrament of God's love, a gift that is honored by many religions. In this way it is a "sacramental common ground" or a "sacramental commons." This broad honoring of the gift of water is highlighted by the National Catholic Rural Life Conference in its advocacy and spirituality:

> Water, a creative force, is essential for all life. It is the common heritage of all creation, a sacred gift. Water cleanses: it washes away impurities, purifying objects for ritual use as well as making a person clean, physically and spiritually. No other substance on Earth carries so profound a spiritual meaning.
>
> For Judaism and Christianity, water is prominent in initiation rituals. The pouring of fresh, living water, symbolizing the spirit of God, makes manifest a new spiritual life. The cleansing character and power of water is essential in Islam as well, as Muslims become ritually pure before approaching God in prayer. Water also has a special place in Hinduism because of its spiritually cleansing powers as Hindu believers strive to attain physical and spiritual purity. For Indigenous Peoples, water connects everything in a vast unity, celebrated through rituals of cleansing and gratitude.
>
> Water is a sacramental commons because water sustains all life. The contamination of water or the act of withholding it from

anyone is an affront to the sacredness of water. It is our collective responsibility to preserve fresh water, and to make fresh water available to all people. Water management and resource distribution must be guided by considerations for the common good of the people of the world and the natural systems of the planet itself.

Water is a gift, inspiring in all of us a response of gratitude. A spirituality of gratitude takes us beyond the consideration of water as only a physical, economic, social, or cultural good to its status as a gift of the Creator, having a unique life-giving role in creation.[24]

The Catholic sacramental understanding of creation is a powerful resource for appreciating water and all the other gifts of creation. This understanding is evident in this poem by the Trappist monk Thomas Merton. He calls the creatures and elements of nature "saints":

The forms and individual character of living and growing things, of inanimate beings, of animal and flowers and all nature, constitute their holiness in the sight of God. . . .

The special clumsy beauty of this particular colt on this April day in this field under these clouds is a holiness consecrated to God by His own creative wisdom and it declares the glory of God.

The pale flowers of the dogwood outside this window are saints.

The little yellow flowers that nobody notices on the edge of that road are saints looking up into the face of God. . . .

The lakes hidden among the hills are saints, and the sea too is a saint who praises God without interruption in her majestic dance.

The great, gashed, half-naked mountain is another of God's saints.

There is no other like him. He is alone in his own character; nothing else in the world ever did or ever will imitate God in quite the same way. That is his sanctity.[25]

Merton reminds us to notice the flowers by the side of the road, to appreciate the mountains and all creatures as God's saints; all are expressions of God's love. The Catholic sacramental tradition shapes our appreciation of creation, and we in turn celebrate it in our liturgies and in the way we live our lives with gratitude and respect for this great gift of God.

The Voices of the Popes and Bishops

Our bishops and popes add their voices to the lived experience of the saints and holy people and the witness of the Bible. In 1990 Pope John Paul II used his World Day of Peace Message to remind us that peace is threatened by the plundering of natural resources: "In our day there is a growing awareness that world peace is threatened not only by the arms race, regional conflicts and continued injustice among peoples and nations, but also by a lack of due respect for nature, by the plundering of natural resources and by a progressive decline in the quality of life" (1).[26] He reminded Christians that their "duty toward nature and Creator are an essential part of their faith" (15).

This World Day of Peace Message highlighted, really for the first time, official Roman Catholic teaching on the environment. With its lively style, its comprehensive coverage, and its incisive analysis, it communicated a note of urgency. The text addresses specific problems and does not remain an abstract philosophical statement. Specific problems touched on include the "greenhouse" effect, acid rain, soil erosion, the destruction of marine resources, tropical deforestation, and the waste of resources consumed by spending on armaments. The pope warned that consumerism and instant self-gratification are root causes of our environmental predicament.

> Modern society will find no solution to the ecological problem unless it takes a serious look at its life-style. In many parts of the world, society is given to instant gratification and consumerism while remaining indifferent to the damage which they cause. . . . Simplicity, moderation, and discipline, as well as a spirit of sacrifice, must become part of everyday life, lest all suffer the negative consequences of the careless habits of a few (1).

At the end of the statement Pope John Paul II broadens the "pro-life" agenda of the church: "Respect for life and for the dignity of the human person extends also to the rest of creation, which is called to join man in praising God" (16).

Irish theologian Enda McDonagh thought this message was "a landmark in the greening of the Church." He hoped that the pope's voice would be heard and acted upon in parishes, church schools, and dioceses around the world. Amid the praise, Father McDonagh did see room for improvement in that the message did not focus attention on the impact of ecological destruction on poor women, and it did not look at the issue of rapid population growth, which places pressure on the limited resources of the earth.[27]

Following the lead of Pope John Paul II, in 1991 the U.S. bishops crafted a pastoral statement, *Renewing the Earth*, which offered this summary of the themes of Catholic social teaching regarding the environment. They stated that ecological responsibility includes these dimensions:

- a *God-centered and sacramental view of the universe*, which grounds human accountability for the fate of the earth;
- a consistent *respect for human life*, which extends to respect for all creation;
- a world view affirming the ethical significance of *global interdependence and the common good*;
- an *ethics of solidarity* promoting cooperation and a just structure of sharing in the world community;
- an understanding of the *universal purpose of created things*, which requires equitable use of the earth's resources;
- an *option for the poor*, which gives passion to the quest for an equitable and sustainable world;
- a conception of *authentic development*, which offers a direction for progress that respects human dignity and the limits of material growth.[28]

The bishops followed up that statement by organizing the Environmental Justice Program (EJP) to educate and motivate Catholics to a deeper reverence and respect for God's creation, and to engage parishes and dioceses in activities aimed at dealing with environmental problems, particularly as they affect the poor. EJP is active in the public policy arena as it advocates for environmental policies that protect the poor, promote environmental health and safety, ensure that the right to private property is balanced with the claims of the common good, and promote sustainable environmental and economic development.

In the 1990s global climate change and the "greenhouse effect" mentioned by John Paul II became a highly debated issue. The U.S. bishops added their voice to the conversation in 2001 with their statement entitled *Global Climate Change: A Plea for Dialogue, Prudence, and the Common Good*. The bishops addressed the contentious context of the debate and suggested that "Our national debate over solutions to global climate change needs to move beyond the uses and abuses of science, sixty-second ads, and exaggerated claims. Because this issue touches so many people, as well as the planet itself, all parties need to strive for a civil and constructive debate about U.S. decisions and leadership in this area."

The bishops included a call for personal conversion and responsibility:

Each of us should carefully consider our choices and lifestyles. We live in a culture that prizes the consumption of material goods. While the poor often have too little, many of us can be easily caught up in a frenzy of wanting more and more—a bigger home, a larger car, etc. Even though energy resources literally fuel our economy and provide a good quality of life, we need to ask about ways we can conserve energy, prevent pollution, and live more simply.[29]

To organize a coordinated impact within the Catholic community, the United States Conference of Catholic Bishops (USCCB) established the Catholic Coalition on Climate Change in 2006. This coalition brings together twelve national Catholic organizations to offer advice and assistance in implementing its mission. With the help of the National Religious Partnership for the Environment and the full support and cooperation of the U.S. Conference of Catholic Bishops, in 2009 the Coalition launched the Catholic Climate Covenant, called The St. Francis Pledge to Care for Creation and the Poor. The St. Francis Pledge is a promise and a commitment by Catholic individuals, families, parishes, organizations, and institutions to live our faith by protecting God's creation and advocating on behalf of people in poverty who face the harshest impacts of global change.[30]

As noted in the beginning of this chapter, Pope Benedict XVI added his call to protect creation with his *2010 World Day of Peace Message: If You Want to Cultivate Peace, Protect Creation*.[31] "Creation is the beginning and the foundation of all God's works" and its preservation is essential for the peaceful coexistence of humanity. Benedict's message echoes his 2009 encyclical, *Caritas in Veritate*, especially in its emphasis on the notion of gift: "The environment must be seen as God's gift to all people, and the use we make of it entails a shared responsibility for all humanity, especially the poor and future generations." He explains that "seeing creation as God's gift to humanity helps us understand our vocation and worth as human beings" (2).

The pope situates the ecological crisis with the other crises—economic, food-related, and social—that are ultimately also moral crises. These crises "require us to rethink the path which we are traveling together" (5). "Rethinking the path" includes:

- Recalling the ancient teaching of the church that "the goods of creation belong to humanity as a whole" (7)
- Taking on new lifestyles "in which the quest for truth, beauty, goodness, and communication with others for the sake of common growth are factors which determine consumer choices, savings and investment" (11)
- Focusing on a lifestyle marked by sobriety and solidarity (5)
- Taking into account the needs of the poor and future generation (2)

As Pope John Paul II had done before him, Benedict links care for all of life, including the unborn, in his environmental ethic. "The book of nature is one and indivisible" which includes "human ecology," that is "not only the environment but also individual, family and social ethics." He continues, "hence I readily encourage efforts to promote a greater sense of ecological responsibility which . . . would safeguard an authentic 'human ecology' and thus forcefully reaffirm the inviolability of human life at every stage and in every condition, the dignity of the person and the unique mission of the family" (12). Here, Benedict offers a new metaphor to speak of the unity of the Catholic moral vision.

Cardinal Joseph Bernardin used the image of a "seamless garment" as a way of suggesting the linkage of life issues and social justice issues, which led to the impression that all of the issues were of equal importance (more on this in the following chapter). By offering a new image, the "book of nature," Benedict reaffirms the insight of Cardinal Bernardin that the pro-life issues and social justice cannot be separated—"the book of nature is one and indivisible." Benedict's teaching cuts both ways: It challenges environmentalists to recognize that "human ecology" must be part of their concern as well as the natural environment, and it challenges those in the pro-life community to broaden their understanding of life issues to include protecting the environment. The pope believes that the current crisis can be turned into an "opportunity for discernment and new strategic planning" (5), for a renewed and concerted commitment by world leaders and by those at every level of society (14).

Benedict XVI expresses a cautionary note when he speaks of "grave misgivings about notions of the environment inspired by ecocentrism and biocentrism." He explains his concern: "In the name of a supposedly egalitarian vision of the 'dignity' of all living creatures, such notions end up abolishing the distinctiveness and superior role of human beings." This superior role is seen in humanity's position "as a steward and administrator with responsibility over creation, a role which man must certainly not abuse, but also one which he may not abdicate" (13).

While I would agree that it is good to be critical of "biocentrism," emphasizing humanity's "superior role" over creation is somewhat troublesome. In the past it has been a distorted sense of human superiority that has led to the exploitation and domination of creation. I would nudge the Catholic tradition toward a bit of "species humility" as a counterbalance to self-proclaimed superiority.

Species Humility

In 1996 theologian Elizabeth Johnson, in her presidential address to the Catholic Theological Society of America, warned about the danger of arrogance in teaching the concept of human superiority. She asked "What is humanity's place in the great scheme of things?" Previous theologies would have placed human beings with their rational souls as superior to the natural world. Such a ranking easily "gives rise to arrogance, one root of the present ecological crisis." But how is our "superiority" established?

> Consider for a moment, however, green plants. Predating the human race by millennia, green plants take in carbon dioxide and give off oxygen. Through this process of photosynthesis they created the atmosphere which makes life of land animals possible. Human beings could not exist without these plants that neither think nor move. They, on the other hand, get along fine without us. Wherein, then, lies superiority?[32]

Johnson wisely suggests that "with a kind of species humility we need to re-imagine systematically the uniqueness of being human in the context of our profound kinship with the rest of nature." With re-imagining our place in creation, a number of questions emerge, including:

- How to preach salvation as healing and rescue for the whole world rather than as solely an individual relationship with God?
- How to let go of contempt for matter, contempt for the body and sexuality, and how to revalue them as good and blessed?

- How to interpret human beings as primarily "earthlings" rather than as pilgrims or tourists whose real home is elsewhere?
- How to recognize the sacraments as symbols of divine graciousness in a universe that is itself a sacrament?
- What kinds of new spiritualities will emerge as we become creation-centered?[33]

The environmentalists in the Catholic community are beginning to explore these questions as we re-imagine humanity's relationship with creation.

When I read Pope Benedict's message carefully, my eyes lingered on these words in the last paragraph: "The quest for peace by people of good will surely would become easier if all acknowledge the indivisible relationship between God, human beings and the whole of creation" (14). I was caught by the phrase "the indivisible relationship between God, human beings and the whole of creation." I wondered if this could open a whole new way of looking at creation, namely, that our relationship with all of Earth is on a par with our relationship with one another and with God. Then I realized that it was not a totally new way of looking at the relationship of these three. The biblical covenant in the Exodus account established a threefold relationship between God, the chosen people, and the land they would inherit. This covenant was a prototype of the universal covenant that God establishes with all humanity and all of creation. I wonder if we can claim that the "great commandment" to love God with all your strength and to love your neighbor as yourself should be amended by adding the words "and to love creation."

In 1982 Father Thomas Berry wrote that "While we have recognized the inseparable nature of communion of God with the human community, we have not yet realized that this communion, to be perfect, must include communion with Earth."[34] Clearly, Pope Benedict is moving the church to see our relationship with the Earth as part of the "indivisible relationship between God, human beings and the whole creation." Thomas Berry has been a creative force in moving Christianity to understand humanity's relationship with creation in a new way. He suggested that we see humanity "within the community of life systems," and he reinterpreted the "superiority" of humanity within the context of the rich diversity of the creation: "Earth in its integral structure and functioning participates in the divine goodness more perfectly and represents it better than any single creature on Earth."[35]

While this thinking may sound very close to the "biocentrism" that Pope Benedict cautioned against, it is also very Catholic and is found in the teaching of the thirteenth-century theologian Thomas Aquinas. When speaking about the diversity of creation in his *Summa Theologica* he wrote:

> For God brought things into being in order that God's goodness might be communicated to creatures, and be represented by them; and because God's goodness could not be adequately represented by one creature alone, God produced many and diverse creatures, that what was wanting to one in the representation of the divine goodness might be supplied by another. For goodness, which in God is simple and uniform, in creatures is manifold and divided; and hence the whole universe together participates [in] the divine goodness more perfectly, and represents it better than any single creature whatever.[36]

Thus, the "nudge" toward species humility is not a new idea in Catholic theology.

In addition to suggesting that *others* protect the environment, the Vatican City State itself has become a leader in "going green." Solar panels have been installed on the roof of the Paul VI Audience Hall, the energy efficiency of its buildings has been improved, and the Vatican has purchased carbon-offset credits. This small city-state that houses the papal apartment and is the center of the Roman Catholic Church has become the first completely carbon-neutral state in the world.[37]

Impact on the Poor

In his 1990 message Pope John Paul II noted the linkage between addressing structural forms of poverty and protecting the environment.

> It must also be said that the proper ecological balance will not be found without directly addressing the *structural forms of poverty* that exist throughout the world. Rural poverty and unjust land distribution in many countries, for example, have led to subsistence farming and to the exhaustion of soil. Once their land yields no more, many farmers move on to clear new land, thus accelerating uncontrolled deforestation (11).

These words describe the situation that Sister Dorothy Stang faced in Brazil. But the connection between poverty and ecological balance is evident in all countries and regions. The poor suffer doubly, from poverty and from the devastation of the environment.

In the factories along the Mexican–U.S. border, thousands of young people, mostly women, make consumer goods for export in factories known as *maquiladoras* while they live and work in unhealthy squalor in an environment spoiled by toxic waste. In visits to this region, I saw deformed children and workers with cancer resulting from exposure to the chemicals. Even the dirt roads in the barrios were patched with a toxic chemical by-product from producing freon—a chemical outlawed in the United States but tolerated in Mexico. The children walk barefoot on these chemically laden roads, which become even more dangerous when it rains.

Agribusiness farming in developing countries focuses on cash crops, such as strawberries or bananas, to export north, which creates wealth for a few from the backbreaking labor of the many. In the Dominican Republic orange groves produce juice that is exported, while in the same country Coca-Cola markets its orange-flavored soda, *Fanta*, which has no nutritional value.

In the United States, the poor suffer doubly as well. While the well-off can choose to live amid acres of green, the housing for the poor is often near factories, refineries, mining facilities, or in homes and apartments with chipping lead paint. The results are not surprising: birth defects, general ill health, disease, and mental and emotional disabilities resulting from environmental abuses.

Rosemary Radford Ruether challenges us to see the connections between ecological abuse, racism, and class:

> The environmental movement needs to be about more than saving seals and defending public parks from lumber companies, although these are worthy causes. It needs to speak of environmental racism and classism, about the poisoning of the environments where poor black, Latino, and indigenous people live in inner cities and rural areas. An environmental movement that does not make these connections across class and racial lines is an escapism for hikers, and not a serious call for change. . . . [38]

Elizabeth Johnson suggests that we view creation itself as the "new poor." "Solidarity with victims, option for the poor, and action on behalf of justice widens out from human beings to embrace life systems and other species to ensure vibrant communion in life for all."[39] Johnson extends the option for the poor and concern about justice for the oppressed to include the rest of the family of creation.

In addition to the papal statements on the environment, local bishops' conferences, regions, and specific dioceses have produced helpful statements and offered leadership on this issue. In fact, local religious leaders have produced over fifty statements from around the world on environmental problems.[40] One excellent example of Catholics providing leadership on ecological issues comes from the northwestern region of the United States and one diocese in Canada, the location of the Columbia River and its watershed.

The Columbia River Watershed

The bishops, along with the religious and secular leadership of British Columbia, Montana, Idaho, Washington, and Oregon worked together for four years on a pastoral letter on the environment. What brought them together was the Columbia River and tributaries in Montana, Idaho, Washington, and Oregon. From its origin in British Columbia the Columbia flows 1,200 miles into the Pacific Ocean, with a watershed that covers 259,000 square miles.

This international pastoral letter highlights two helpful insights into Catholic social teaching. First, the letter utilizes the wisdom of Native Americans who inhabited the Columbia river watershed long before the Europeans arrived, and, second, the letter views humanity as part of creation and not at the top of the food chain or the pyramid of creation.

The bishops recall the first human communities that lived near the *Che Wana*, the Great River, who fished for salmon, hunted wild game, and gathered roots and berries. They speak of the native religion with respect.

> Native religions taught respect for the ways of nature, personified as a nurturing mother for all creatures. They saw the salmon as food from this mother, and the river as the source of their lives and the life of the fish. They adapted themselves to the river and to the cycles of the seasons. Among the *Wanapum*, the River People, some elders were set apart as dreamers and healers, respected for their visions and healing powers.

A few pages later the bishops expressed their gratitude and apologies:

> The indigenous peoples have a wealth of spirituality, culture and traditions that call forth a need for appropriate respect and preservation. We are brothers and sisters in God's creation and we are

grateful to the First Nations and the Native Americans for the lessons they teach about respect for nature. We apologize for cultural insensitivities and lack of justice, both past and present.

This is a truly catholic stance—to be open and grateful for the wisdom and insight of all people, even those who are not Christian. History reveals that church leaders have not always been appreciative of the culture and religion of indigenous peoples. The bishops then extend a hand of cooperation and collaboration:

> Today, we extend an offer of peace and friendship to native peoples of our region. We pledge to work with them to seek equitable resolutions of conflicts over treaty rights, to work with them to enhance their engagement with other cultures, to foster their economic development and to participate with them to promote care for creation. We call upon the members of our parish communities, government officials, those with economic interests and the general public to join in these efforts.[41]

The second contribution of the letter is a more humble attitude for humanity in the order of creation. The bishops do not speak of human superiority, but instead situate humanity within the ecological community.

> People live in the world of nature, not apart from it. They need to alter that world at times in order to provide for their needs. . . . We can live in greater harmony with our surroundings if we strive to become more aware of our connection to, and responsibility for, the creation that surrounds us.
>
> Such a challenge can be met only if we implore the assistance of the God who creates the universe and who continually sends forth the Spirit for the ongoing renewal of the human race and for the renewal of the face of the earth.[42]

The bishops did not see the publication of the letter as the end of the process, but rather as part of "an ongoing conversation process, to resolve regional conflicts with respect, . . . and to promote sustainable ecological relationships."[43]

The bishops and the steering committee of the Northwest are to be commended for a text written in a nonsexist manner that draws upon the wisdom of many disciplines and traditions. By drawing upon diverse, authoritative voices in articulating Catholic social teaching on the environment, they have made a real contribution to the living Catholic social tradition and to the process of forming church.

These voices of the Catholic social tradition help us learn to live with gratitude and companionship with creation. Finally, these words of wisdom from the first Americans, the people of the Longhouse, capture their reverent attitude toward all of creation:

> We who walk about on the Earth are to express a great respect, an affection, and a gratitude toward all the spirits which create and support life. We give a greeting and thanksgiving to the many supporters of our lives—the corn, beans, squash, the winds, the sun. When people cease to respect and express gratitude for these many things, then all life will be destroyed, and human life on this planet will come to an end.[44]

May we, with all people of the Earth, continue to respect and give thanks for the gift of creation.

Prayer of St. Basil

O God, enlarge within us a sense of fellowship with all
living things,
our brothers and sisters the animals,
To whom you gave the earth as their home in common with us.
We remember with shame that in the past we have exercised
high dominion
with ruthless cruelty,
So that the voice of the earth, which should have gone up to
you in song,
has been a groan of travail.
May we realize that they live not for us alone but for themselves
and for you,
and that they love the sweetness of life.
Amen.[45]

Discussion Questions

1. The ancient wisdom of the church teaches that the resources of the earth are meant for all people. Why is this such a difficult teaching to follow in our society and in Brazil where Sister Dorothy Stang ministered for thirty-nine years?

2. The Bible gives humanity "dominion" over creation. How has this notion from the Bible been used to dominate nature? What is the more accurate understanding of biblical dominion?

3. What does it mean to say that everything in nature is a "sacrament of God's love"?

4. What does it mean to say there is an "indivisible relationship between God, human beings, and the whole of creation"?

3

Human Dignity: Respect for Every Life

Arturo was an ornery, homeless man who slept under the pope's window, protected by the massive Bernini columns, in front of St. Peter's Basilica in Rome. The Missionaries of Charity would visit him a few times a week around 11:00 p.m. as he was pulling his dirty blankets around his bearded face. While doing my doctoral studies in Rome, I helped the sisters once a week, making sandwiches and driving around Rome to visit the homeless. As we visited the street people of Rome in the late evening, I could see how precious each person was, even those who were ornery, like Arturo. Even though he was rather grumpy he always accepted our cheese sandwich and a cup of warm milk, but his disposition never changed. Sister Agnes explained that practically everything had been taken from Arturo; all he had left were his anger and gruff personality. Because his identity was one of his last possessions, he clung to it fiercely. And gracious Sister Agnes was able to appreciate his human dignity, despite the ornery exterior.

Often the poor themselves are the ones who teach about human greatness and dignity. On one especially cold December night in Rome with temperatures in the 30s we were bringing blankets to people sleeping on the streets. Carmen slept in the portico of Sacra Cuore (Sacred Heart) Church near the central train station. She had a pile of plastic garbage bags that served as her bed and covers. When we offered her a woolen blanket to fend off the damp coolness of the night air, she declined, saying that we should "give the blanket to someone who really needs it." She would manage on her bed of cardboard and plastic garbage bags. Even in her desperate state she thought of others who might be worse off than she! If I were in her shoes, I am sure I would have grabbed a couple of blankets.

We can easily see the value and dignity of innocent infants who pull at our heartstrings; sometimes we can glimpse the human dignity of the poor. However, seeing the sacredness of life of those in our prison systems is more difficult. During our annual trip to the state capital, Albany, to meet with our legislators, we invite ex-offenders, residents of Freedom House, to join us for the Albany Forum sponsored by the New York State Catholic Conference. Freedom House is a residential program run by Catholic Charities for men who are addressing chemical addictions.

On one visit three Latino ex-offenders were part of my delegation of six as we visited our state senator, Joseph Robach. My fellow delegates had three strikes against them: they were recovering addicts, Hispanics, and ex-offenders. By society's standards they were losers.

Each of them found the inner strength to face their chemical addiction, to finish their prison terms, and to begin a new life. They were living in a residence for men who wanted to overcome their addictions. Roberto, Carlos, and Luis broke through all of those stereotypes on that March afternoon. Dressed in suits and ties they spoke with honesty, eloquence, and conviction about their experiences. The legislator, a white, conservative, middle-class Catholic, sat with his mouth open in amazement as they shared their experience of addiction, prison, and recovery. Senator Robach was surprised when they said that prison was *not* a deterrent for them when they were in the depths of their addiction. They saw prison as an improvement over their desperate lives on the street. They admitted that, at times, even death seemed an improvement to their suffering and misery as addicts.

We were urging the legislator to help revise the harsh drug-sentencing laws in New York State, known as the Rockefeller Drug Laws. The legislator needed to hear the reality of their experience to help craft new laws that would not only promote public safety, but also truly address the problem of drug addiction. Harsh prison sentences were clearly not the answer. The dignity of these three men shone through in that forty-five minute conversation. With honest eloquence, despite all they had been through, they described how they wanted to start over and to give back to society. Their dignity as human beings was undeniable. The road ahead was not going to be easy, but they were working hard to move beyond their past and to help create a better future for themselves and others still caught in the revolving door of addiction and prison.

Every person—the unborn, the poor, the rich person, the addict, our irritating neighbor or relative—is precious. Every person deserves respect, even those who do not act respectfully to others. As Dorothy Day, the co-founder of the Catholic Worker movement, said: "To serve others, to give what we have is not enough unless we always show the utmost respect for each other and all we meet."[1] The witness of Dorothy Day to the radical respect for the dignity of every person touched many people, including Sister Mary Scullion of Philadelphia.

All Have the Same Human Dignity

Sister Mary Scullion had a conversion after attending the Eucharistic Congress in Philadelphia in 1976. At the Congress she was inspired by the lives and words of Mother Teresa, Dorothy Day, and Brazilian Bishop Dom Helder Camara, who all worked with the poor. She came away with a new vision, beginning to see the hungry and homeless in her midst. "Before this, I would go to Mass and think I was fulfilling my obligation. But now, I began to see that there was hunger in our city and around the world, and I came to realize how much more needs to be done."

In her efforts to serve the poor, she met Joan Dawson-McConnon, at the time a graduate student with a degree in accounting and soon to earn a master's degree in taxation. Joan had the same impulses, having learned from her family that caring for others was the primary expression of faith. Joan understood that "faith was something you acted on." They brought together their unique gifts—Scullion, the out-front partner, and Dawson-McConnon, the behind-the-scenes finance person—to express their faith in protecting the dignity of Philadelphia's poor. They started Project Housing, Opportunities, Medical Care, Education (H.O.M.E.), a multilevel operation of services, residential space, and commerce. They established a new community center in an abandoned rectory, including thirty-nine units of new housing for women with children. These homes were rehabilitated and sold to working poor people, but only after the women were trained in home ownership, financing, and managing money. They also provided permanent housing for men and women off the street with chronic mental illness.

Joan expresses their core conviction: "Whether she's [Mary] talking to extremely powerful and wealthy people or someone sitting on a vent, everyone gets talked about and thought about in the same way. *All have the same human dignity. It is something she really believes.*"[2] That is the Catholic view of human dignity in reality, the foundation of Catholic social teaching and social ministry.

Created in God's Image

The sacredness of human life emerges from the first pages of the Bible:

Then God said, "Let us make humankind in our image, according to our likeness; and let them have dominion over the fish of the sea, and over the birds of the air, and over the cattle, and over all the wild animals of the earth, and over every creeping thing that creeps upon the earth." So God created humankind in his image, in the image of God he created them; male and female he created them (Gen 1:26–27).

The *Catechism of the Catholic Church* echoes that biblical teaching by noting the equal dignity of all people: "Created in the image of the one God and equally endowed with rational souls, all . . . have the same nature and the same origin. Redeemed by the sacrifice of Christ, all are called to participate in the same divine beatitude: all therefore enjoy an equal dignity" (no. 1934).

This teaching on the dignity of each person, which is the starting point and the foundation of all Catholic social teaching, means that every person is precious, that people are more important than things, and that we are to make every effort to respect that dignity and help each person to flourish.

The Book of Genesis teaches that humanity is created in the image of God, which establishes the central dignity and sacredness of each person. "*As such every human being possesses an inalienable dignity that stamps human existence prior to any division into races or nations and prior to human labor and human achievement (Gen 4–11).*"[3]

The biblical vision calls on the community to protect the dignity of each person, especially those who are vulnerable and on the fringe of society: the widow, orphans, the weak, and the stranger (Exod 23:9, Lev 19:34).

The Gospel of Life

Pope John Paul II, who kept the biblical teaching on the dignity of the human person at the center of his papacy, was a tireless protector of the dignity of life as

- a critic of war, especially the two wars in the Persian Gulf
- a critic of the death penalty
- a critic of economic injustice and the violence of poverty
- a defender of worker rights
- a critic of abortion and euthanasia
- a critic of the ecological crisis
- an apostle of the "Gospel of Life"

The centerpiece of his pro-life message is the encyclical *The Gospel of Life*, released on March 25, 1995, in which he defined life as sacred from the "very beginning until its end." Physical life is not an absolute value, but is a "primary good respected to the highest degree. Upon the recognition of this right, every human community and the political community itself are founded." John Paul II viewed "the value of every human life and the right to have each life respected" as the church's "good news," an essential part of the gospel.

Pope John Paul II taught that the incarnation reveals not only God's love for humanity, but also the "incomparable value of every human person.... The Gospel of God's love for man, the Gospel of the dignity of this person and the Gospel of life are a single and indivisible Gospel" (2). The pope linked the good news of salvation with the good news of the value of every person—making an inseparable connection between the church's religious message and its social agenda.

The Gospel of Life makes an urgent appeal to be "A precise and vigorous reaffirmation of the value of human life and its inviolability, and at the same time a pressing appeal in the name of God: Respect, protect, love and serve life, every human life! Only in this direction will you find justice, development, true freedom, peace and happiness" (5).

The encyclical identified diverse sources of violence against life, including:

- threats from nature that are made worse by the indifference and negligence of those who could help,
- hatred that leads to murder, war, and genocide,
- violence against children in the form of poverty, malnutrition, and hunger,
- war and the arms trade,
- the criminal drug culture, and
- attacks against life in its earliest stages and in its final stages.

While the encyclical covers a wide assortment of threats against human life, its primary concerns are abortion and euthanasia, which are defined as "a grave moral disorder" and a "violation of the law of God" (57, 65).

Pope John Paul II also addressed cultural attitudes that may lead to a disdain for the weak, handicapped, or sick. The culture of death "is actively fostered by powerful cultural, economic, and political currents which encourage an ideal of society excessively concerned with efficiency." He continues: "A life which would require greater acceptance, love, and care is considered useless or held to be an intolerable burden, and is therefore rejected in one way or another." He named an attitude in the culture wherein people with greater needs are seen as a threat to others' well-being: "A person who, because of illness, handicap or, simply, just by existing, compromises the well-being or lifestyle of those who are more favored tends to be looked upon as an enemy to be resisted or eliminated. In this way a kind of 'conspiracy against life' is unleashed" (12).

Eighteen years later Pope John Paul II added his concern that life is being perceived as an "object" to be controlled through abortion, euthanasia, and cloning. He urged world leaders and all people to say "yes to life!" He went on to say, "Respect life itself and individual lives: Everything starts here, for the most fundamental of human rights is certainly the right to life. Abortion, euthanasia, human cloning, for example, risk reducing the human person to a mere object: life and death to order, as it were!"[4]

The dignity of the human person is central in every aspect of the church's social teaching and in its critique of dangerous cultural attitudes. For example, the U.S. bishops pointed out that "the basis for all that the Church believes about the moral dimensions of economic life is its vision of the transcendent worth—the sacredness—of human beings. The dignity of the human person, realized in community with others, is the criterion against which all aspects of economic life must be measured."[5] The dignity of the human person, then, is the *raison d'être* for all the social justice and pro-life activity in the church.

Cardinal Bernardin and the Consistent Ethic of Life

Cardinal Joseph Bernardin was the primary leader in the American church who linked the church's teaching on pro-life issues and war and rooted these issues in the dignity of the human person. In 1980, as the archbishop of Cincinnati, Joseph Bernardin was asked to chair the committee that was to draft the U.S. bishops' pastoral letter on war and nuclear weapons, *The Challenge of Peace*. When that work was finished in May 1983, he was asked to chair the bishops' Pro-Life Committee. Bernardin, now archbishop of Chicago, saw connections between the issue of war and the issue of abortion. He committed himself to "shaping a position of linkage among the life issues."[6] He noted that "the central idea in the letter is the sacredness of human life and the responsibility we have, personally and socially, to protect and preserve the sanctity of life."[7] His perceived linkage between Catholic social teaching about nuclear weapons and abortion led him to articulate a consistent ethic of life.

Bernardin named a few of the ways life was threatened:

- nuclear weapons threaten life on a previously unimaginable scale,

- abortion takes lives daily,
- public executions are becoming weekly events in the most advanced technological society in history,
- euthanasia is openly discussed and advocated.

The archbishop recognized that "each of these assaults on life has its own meaning and morality; they cannot be collapsed into one problem." Yet he explained that "they must be confronted as pieces of a larger pattern. . . . I am persuaded by the interrelatedness of these diverse problems. . . ."[8] While others had made this connection before, Bernardin gave the notion a sustained focus and attracted national attention because of his visibility and leadership within the church.[9]

Some pro-life groups argued that this "seamless garment" approach diluted their political impact. Others argued that the principle of protecting innocent life distinguished the unborn child from the life of the convicted murderer. Still others argued that while nuclear war is a *threat* to life, "abortion involves the actual *taking* of life, here and now." Bernardin agreed with those distinctions, but countered that "I also find compelling the need to *relate* the cases while keeping them in distinct categories."[10]

The issues included in the consistent ethic of life (CEL) are not fixed. Usually the CEL includes abortion, euthanasia, capital punishment, poverty, and war. Pope John Paul II and Benedict XVI, as noted in chapter 2, included protection of creation as a pro-life issue. The pro-life umbrella also includes cloning and embryonic stem cell research.

Using the image of the "seamless garment" has its strengths and weaknesses. On the positive side, the consistent ethic of life "rightly emphasizes the inner coherence and objective connectedness of these issues." On the negative side, however, "there have been times when such an approach left the impression that these issues are of equal importance." According to Bishop Thomas Olmstead of Phoenix, "nothing could be farther from the truth."[11] To correct the mistaken impression all the issues are of equal importance Pope John Paul II clarified the priority of rights in the Catholic tradition:

Above all, the common outcry, which is justly made on behalf of human rights—for example, the right to health, to home, to work, to family, to culture—is false and illusory if the right to life, the most basic and fundamental right and the condition for all other personal rights, is not defended with the maximum determination.[12]

A few years later in his encyclical *The Gospel of Life*, the pope repeated and simplified his understanding: "It is impossible to further the common good without acknowledging and defending the right to life, upon which all the other inalienable rights of individuals are founded and from with they develop" (101).

Pope Benedict XVI said that the principle of the "protection of life in all its stages, from the first moment of conception until natural death" is "not negotiable."

> As far as the Catholic Church is concerned, the principal focus of her interventions in the public arena is the protection and promotion of the dignity of the person, and she is thereby consciously drawing particular attention to principles which are not negotiable. Among these the following emerge clearly today:
>
> — protection of life in all its stages, from the first moment of conception until natural death."[13]

The U.S. bishops stated that while respect for life compels the needs of the poor and unemployed, "abortion and euthanasia have become pre-eminent threats to human dignity because they directly attack life itself, the most fundamental human good and the condition for all others. They are committed against those who are weakest and most defenseless, those who are genuinely 'the poorest of the poor'" (5).[14] They explain:

> [T]he basic principle is simple:
>
> *We must begin with a commitment never to intentionally kill, or collude in the killing, of any innocent human life, no matter how broken, unformed, disabled or desperate that life may seem.* In other words, the choice of certain ways of acting is *always and radically incompatible* with the love of God and the dignity of the human person created in His image (21).[15]

every
innocent
human life

The bishops include a number of issues in this principle: abortion, cloning, euthanasia, genocide, torture, racism, and the targeting of noncombatants in acts of terror or war.[16]

While it is clear that all issues do not have the same moral standing, the magisterium is also clear that these issues must be seen as a whole. In 2006 Pope Benedict shared his thoughts with the Swiss bishops: "I see ever more clearly that in our age morality is, as it were, split in two." One morality focuses on "the great topics of peace, non-violence, justice for all, concern for the poor and respect for creation. . . . The other part of morality . . . concerns life. One aspect of it is the commitment to life from conception to death, that is, its defense against abortion, against euthanasia. . . ." He continues,

> I believe we must commit ourselves to reconnecting these two parts of morality and to making it clear that they must be inseparably united. . . . Only if human life from conception until death is respected is the ethic of peace possible and credible; only then may non-violence be expressed in every direction, only then can we truly accept creation and only then can we achieve true justice.[17]

In his first social encyclical, *Caritas in Veritate*, Pope Benedict is quite clear that these two sets of issues are essentially linked (as noted in chapter 1): "The Church forcefully maintains this link between life ethics and social ethics" (15). Later in the encyclical he uses the metaphor of the "book of nature": "The book of nature is one and indivisible; it takes in not only the environment but also life, sexuality, marriage, the family, social relations: in a word, integral human development" (51).

Just before the 2008 presidential election Cardinal Justin Rigali and Bishop William Murphy urged Catholic voters not to ignore the social justice issue of supporting policies that help mothers facing challenging pregnancies or the pro-life issue of overturning Roe v. Wade. This linked social ethics with life ethics: "Our faith requires us to oppose abortion on demand *and* to provide help to mothers facing challenging pregnancies."[18]

The Rev. Jim Wallis, an evangelical leader and advocate of the consistent ethic of life, tells the story of how the issues of poverty and abortion are linked.

> Recently, I met a woman who had an amazing story to tell. She began by saying that her daughter was graduating from Harvard and how proud she was. Because I teach part-time at Harvard, I figured she was making that connection. I smiled and told her that she should indeed be proud of her daughter and that I thought Harvard was a great school. But then she added, "I was a low-income woman at the time. And if I hadn't got food stamps and health care, I would have aborted my daughter. And now she is graduating from Harvard. (A tear now ran down her face, and mine.) I want you to tell people that if they want to prevent abortions, they need to support low-income women like me.[19]

In the 2008 version of *Faithful Citizenship* the U. S. bishops offered Catholic voters a nuanced explanation of how to hold together the priority of issues such as abortion and euthanasia, which involve the direct and intentional destruction of human life, while at the same time taking into account the importance of issues such as racism, the death penalty, torture, poverty, and so forth, which are serious threats to human life and dignity. They presented this complex question in terms of avoiding two temptations regarding the dignity of human life:

> Two temptations in public life can distort the Church's defense of human life and dignity:
>
> The first is a moral equivalence that makes no ethical distinctions between different kinds of issues involving human life and dignity. The direct and intentional destruction of innocent human life from the moment of conception until natural death is always wrong and is not just one issue among many. It must always be opposed.
>
> The second is the misuse of these necessary moral distinctions as a way of dismissing or ignoring other serious threats to human life and dignity. Racism and other unjust discrimination, the use of the death penalty, resorting to unjust war, the use of torture, war crimes, the failure to respond to those who are suffering from hunger or a lack of health care, or an unjust immigration policy are all serious moral issues that challenge our consciences and require us to act. These are not optional concerns which can be dismissed. Catholics are urged to seriously consider Church teaching on these issues. Although choices about how best to respond to these and other compelling threats to human life and dignity are matters for principled debate and decision, this does not make them optional concerns or permit Catholics to dismiss or ignore Church teaching on these important issues. Clearly not every Catholic can be actively involved on each of these concerns, but we need to support one another as our community of faith defends human life and dignity wherever it is threatened. We are not factions, but one family of faith fulfilling the mission of Jesus Christ.

The Vatican Congregation for the Doctrine of the Faith made a similar point:

> It must be noted also that a well-formed Christian conscience does not permit one to vote for a political program or an individual law

which contradicts the fundamental contents of faith and morals. The Christian faith is an integral unity, and thus it is incoherent to isolate some particular element to the detriment of the whole of Catholic doctrine. A political commitment to a single isolated aspect of the Church's social doctrine does not exhaust one's responsibility towards the common good.[20]

Building a Culture of Life

To challenge the "culture of death" Pope John Paul II urged building "a new culture of life." This culture of life would be new because it would have to address "today's unprecedented problems affecting human life," such as cloning and stem cell research. The culture of life would be new in its scope, which would be ecumenical and interfaith (*The Gospel of Life*, 95).

The starting point of this cultural transformation would be "in forming conscience with regard to the incomparable and inviolable worth of every human life" (96). The culture of life would include "the courage to adopt a new lifestyle consisting in making practical choices—at the personal, family, social, and international level—on the basis of a correct scale of values: the primacy of being over having, of person over things" (98). This is a tall order for a materialistically centered culture.

This distortion of having over being was discussed in chapter 1, and it emerges here as well as part of analyzing the underlying assumptions of the culture of death. Accumulation of possessions does not lead to life. In fact, that attitude can lead to death.

Amy, a fifteen-year-old, had always earned straight A's in school, so her parents were extremely upset when a B appeared on her report card. "If I fail in what I do," Amy wrote to her parents in her suicide note, "I fail in what I am." Dr. Darold Treffert of the Winnebago Mental Health Institute in Wisconsin explained Amy's behavior and attitude with his theory called "the American Fairy Tale." This theory is based on two principles: first, more possessions mean more happiness, and second, a person who does or produces more is more important.[21] In Amy's framework, her life was of less value because she had not produced enough.

This attitude distorts the thinking not only of our teens, but of all ages in society. It is part of the reason why millionaire George Eastman put a bullet through his heart at age seventy-eight. He believed his productive days were over and he was ill, so life had lost its value. Mr. Eastman was not an idiosyncratic exception to the rule. The highest suicide rates are among males who are eighty to eighty-five years old. These men, who no longer feel valued, find it difficult to face the dependency of old age.

A Firm Foundation

A recent document from the New York State Catholic Conference, *Pursuing Justice*, points out how the dignity of the human person becomes the basis for the Catholic involvement in the spectrum of social issues:

> Our belief in the sanctity of human life and the inherent dignity of the human person is the foundation for all of the principles of our social teaching. We believe that every person is precious, from the moment of conception to the moment of natural death; that people are more important than things; and that the measure of every institution or policy is where it enhances the life and dignity of the human person.

- It is this firm foundation that solidifies the Church's opposition to abortion, euthanasia, assisted suicide and other direct attacks on human life.
- It is the reason we work toward the abolition of capital punishment.
- It is the impetus behind our advocacy for adequate health care for poor mothers, children, people with HIV/AIDS and the elderly.
- And it is why we reject embryonic stem cell research and human cloning, procedures which destroy developing human lives and reduce the creation of human life to manufacture of a product.
- The sacredness and dignity of human life is shared by all, regardless of sex, race, ethnicity, religious belief, disability, economic status, age or sexual orientation.
- Thus respect for human life lies at the heart of the Church's opposition to racism, discrimination and violence of all kinds.
- It is likewise the basis for our support for adequate food, shelter and clothing for the poor, just wages with decent working conditions, and health care and education for immigrants.[22]

The New York bishops note that "the Church works proactively to enhance human life by supporting alternatives to abortion such as subsidized prenatal care and adoption; alternatives to assisted suicide such as palliative care and hospice options for the terminally ill; and measures to reduce gun violence, prevent drug abuse and rehabilitate prisoners."[23]

Some Hopeful Signs

There is some good news to report on the human dignity front. There are hopeful signs that the U.S. population is becoming more respectful of the life of the pre-born. In preparation for the thirtieth anniversary of *Roe v. Wade* on January 22, 2003, the bishops noted some hopeful signs:

- Today fewer abortions are being done each year, and fewer doctors are willing to be involved in abortion.
- More Americans identify themselves as pro-life, while the numbers of those saying they are "pro-choice" have declined significantly.
- Ultrasound and other medical advances have made possible a greater appreciation of the humanity of the unborn child.
- In these three decades thousands of pro-life groups, individual parishes, Catholic social service agencies, and pregnancy resource centers have provided practical assistance and support to thousands of women facing difficult pregnancies.
- Most state legislatures have enacted measures to restrict or regulate the practice of abortion and reduce its incidence.
- Above all, the pro-life movement is brimming with the vibrancy of youth.[24]

I had the grace of experiencing some of that "vibrancy of youth" when I traveled from Rochester, New York, to Washington, D.C., to participate in the March for Life on the thirtieth anniversary of *Roe v. Wade*. As we marched down Constitution Avenue in the nation's capital in the cold January air, you could hear the shouts of high school students as they chanted, "Hey, hey! Ho, ho! *Roe v. Wade* has got to go!" These chants drowned out the middle-school children who were walking arm-in-arm a few feet away singing, "Jesus loves the little children, all the children of the world." Their song blended with the group that was praying the rosary and following the statue of Our Lady of Fatima and the gold–plated processional cross. All of these Christians were expressing their spirituality, their convictions, and their hopes.

The day began with a 7:30 a.m. mass at the Basilica of the National Shrine of the Immaculate Conception, which rooted the activism and witness in a sacramental and spiritual framework of carrying on God's concern for the weak and vulnerable. This liturgy was the highlight of the day for John, who brought his four teenage children to the March for Life. The liturgy connected the advocacy efforts with his faith. "When it comes right down to it, what makes it all meaningful is that life is a gift from God. The Mass really elevates the issue from the human to the divine."[25] A few hours after the mass our contingent from Rochester was in Senator Charles Schumer's office to write down our concerns about the senator's pro-choice stance. Later in the afternoon, Senators Clinton and Schumer held an open forum to hear the opinions of our delegation. Senator Schumer expressed his respect for the group by listening, even though he did not agree with the marchers' desire to overturn *Roe v. Wade.*

While this was my first March for Life in Washington, many of the young people in our group had been here many times before. Fifteen-year-old Sarah has spent many of her birthdays participating in the March for Life with her brothers, sisters, and parents. Her birthday is on January 22, the anniversary of the *Roe v. Wade* decision by the Supreme Court. Sarah said she didn't mind spending her birthdays in Washington because it is a cause she believes in. "I don't think anybody has the right to end the life of any child."[26] The issue of abortion is very clear for Sarah and her friends in the march, and their conviction is obviously shared by the beliefs of their parents, but it also may be rooted in their understanding of the value of embryonic life.

The teens of today are the "ultrasound kids." Many of them have seen the ultrasound pictures of themselves in their mother's uterus. Some of them have those ultrasound pictures in their baby photo album, right next to the pictures of their birth and their baptism. Technology has helped them understand that human life is a continuum that does not begin at birth, but at the moment of conception. They have a concrete image of their own pre-birth existence, and they want all unborn children to have the right to life.

Sarah, John, and three hundred others from the Rochester Diocese have internalized the Church's teaching about the sacredness and dignity of life and they are witnessing to that faith in the public arena, both in the streets and in the congressional offices.

The teaching of the Church on the dignity of the human person challenges Catholics across the political spectrum to be attentive to the full
range of life issues. As Archbishop Bernardin noted, "Those who defend
the right to life of the weakest among us must be equally visible in support
of the quality of life of the powerless among us: the old and the young, the
hungry and the homeless, the undocumented immigrant and the unemployed worker." He went on to say:

> The consequences of a consistent ethic is [sic] to bring under re-
> view the positions of every group in the Church which sees the
> moral meaning in one place but not the other. The ethic cuts *two*
> ways, not one: It challenges pro-life groups, and it challenges justice
> and peace groups. The meaning of a consistent ethic is to say in the
> Catholic community that our moral tradition calls us beyond the
> split so evident in the wider society between moral witness to life
> before and after birth.[27]

The dignity of life means advocacy for the value of every life, even of
those who have taken the life of another person. The issue of the death
penalty is an example of a Church teaching where many Catholics do not
agree with the pro-life vision of their bishops and popes.

The Death Penalty

A 2010 Pew survey reports that Americans continue to express support
for the death penalty for persons convicted of murder. Currently 62% favor
the death penalty, while 30% oppose it. This is lower than in 1996 when
78% favored the death penalty and just 18% were opposed. That is a 16%
drop in support for the death penalty in the last fourteen years. If the trend
continues, by the year 2020 we could expect fewer than 50% will support the death penalty. White Catholics support the death penalty at 68%,
a slightly higher rate than the general population while support among
Hispanic Catholics is 43%. The support among Protestants is divided as
follows: white evangelicals (74%), white mainline Protestants (71%),and
black Protestants (37%).[28] A 2005 Zogby poll showed a greater drop in
support of the death penalty in that year. It showed that less than half of
adult Catholics (48%) supported the use of the death penalty. Catholics
cited "respect for life" as their primary reason for changing attitudes.[29]

As with other life issues, the attitudes of people in the pews do not
always align with Church teaching. Only 17 percent of Catholics report

that their religion is the most important influence on their thinking about the death penalty. They cite their education, the media, or personal experience as important influences as well. Pope John Paul II and the U.S. bishops have been very clear that the magisterium does not support the death penalty.

According to historian James Megivern, Pope John Paul II "had more to say about capital punishment than any previous pope in a comparably authoritative document. His spirited repudiation of death as a punishment was all but total, to the consternation of many."[30] In the *Gospel of Life* Pope John Paul II teaches that "not even a murderer loses his personal dignity, and God himself pledges to guarantee this," as can be seen by God's protection of the murderer Cain (9). Later in the letter, after quoting from the 1992 version of the *Catechism of the Catholic Church*, he all but closes the door on capital punishment, stating that "punishment . . . ought not to go to the extreme of executing the offender except in cases of absolute necessity . . . such cases are very rare if not practically nonexistent" (56).

John Paul II argues that if there are bloodless ways in which society can protect itself from violent criminals then those methods such as lifetime sentences without the possibility of parole must be used. The exceptional case may occur where a society does not have a way of protecting itself from a violent criminal; then capital punishment may be justified as a necessary option. Such a possible exemption might be if a murderer were stalking a nomadic community. But, as the pope notes, "such cases are very rare if not practically nonexistent."

Under the pope's leadership the *Catechism* was revised in 1997 to reflect his teaching in *The Gospel of Life*. The revised text reads:

> Today, in fact, as a consequence of the possibilities which the state has for effectively preventing crime, by rendering one who has committed an offence incapable of doing harm—without definitely taking away from him the possibility of redeeming himself—the case in which the execution of the offender is an absolute necessity "are very rare, if not practically nonexistent" (2267).

Pope John Paul II brought this message directly to the United States when he visited St. Louis, Missouri, on January 27, 1999:

> The new evangelization calls for followers of Christ who are unconditionally pro-life: who will proclaim, celebrate and serve the Gospel of life in every situation. A sign of hope is the increasing recognition that

the dignity of human life must never be taken away, even in the case of someone who has done great evil. Modern society has the means of protecting itself, without definitively denying criminals the chance to reform. I renew the appeal I made most recently at Christmas for a consensus to end the death penalty, which is both cruel and unnecessary.[31]

During that visit to St. Louis the Holy Father met with Governor of Missouri, Mel Carnahan, and asked him to commute the death sentence of Darrell Mease who was scheduled to be executed in the next weeks. Carnahan was moved by the pope's appeal for mercy and granted the pope's wish. The pope had not requested a reevaluation of the merits of the condemned man's case. Rather, he presented a simple and straightforward petition for mercy. The sentence was changed from death by lethal injection to life imprisonment without parole. This decision protected the safety and common good of society and saved a human life.

Archbishop Wilton Gregory of Atlanta acknowledged the ongoing debate about the death penalty in Catholic circles. "Much of our attention continues to focus on deterrence since that aspect of the debate continues to be central to the public debate." He added that the

bishops conceded the death penalty defends society from the particular prisoner who committed the grave offense for which capital punishment was prescribed, yet registered serious doubt as to the deterrence value of executions in relation to those who might commit heinous crimes in the future. We bishops have also pointed out the alarming number of mistaken convictions of men and women on death row who were later exonerated. . . . We [U.S. bishops] are on record to say that the argument that executions deter potential offenders from capital crimes lacks empirical support.

When asked why more Catholics still have not embraced the pope's teachings on the death penalty, Archbishop Gregory responded, "I take the responsibility (in North Georgia) . . . in teaching, and I have not been universally successful and have not moved the hearts of the faithful."[32]

Archbishop Charles J. Chaput of Denver also recognized that not all Catholics support the Church's position on the death penalty. He calls Catholics to a higher ethic:

We should remember that Catholic teaching on the death penalty flows from the sanctity of the human person. All life is sacred. Every person, even the convicted murderer, is created by God with God-given dignity. . . .

[T]he Church has repeatedly called us to a higher road over the past five decades as an antidote to the growing culture of death around us. We don't need to kill people to protect society. We don't need to kill people to punish the guilty. And we should never be in a hurry to take anyone's life. As a result, except in the most extreme circumstances, capital punishment cannot be justified. In developed countries like our own, it should have no place in our public life. . . .

[W]e need to think carefully about the kind of justice we want to witness to our young people. Most American Catholics, like the vast majority of their fellow citizens, support the death penalty. That doesn't make it right. But it does ensure that the wrong-headed lesson of violence "fixing" the violent among us will be taught to another generation. As children of God, we're better than this, and we need to start acting like it. We need to end the death penalty now.[33]

To mobilize support to end the use of the death penalty the Catholic bishops invited Catholics to join them in an ongoing "Catholic Campaign to End the Use of the Death Penalty."[34]

Sister Helen Prejean

What moved a forty-one-year-old nun from Louisiana who had been the religious education director at St. Frances Cabrini Parish in New Orleans and the formation director for her religious community to become an internationally recognized activist against the death penalty? How did Sister Helen Prejean find the courage to load her personal possessions into a small brown truck in 1981 and move into the St. Thomas housing project in the inner city of New Orleans?

Some years later, Sister Prejean answered those questions. "When I started out as a young Catholic nun, I had no idea that I would walk this path into America's death chambers. My Catholic faith has been the catalyst to inspire me to follow the way of Jesus, who sided with the poor and dispossessed and despised."[35]

But it wasn't just an individual response. Her entire religious community, the Sisters of St. Joseph of Medaille, made a commitment in 1980 to "stand on the side of the poor." This was not an easy decision. The Sisters

struggled with their role in social justice issues and engaged in heated debates over what their mission should be.[36] Prejean reluctantly agreed with
that commitment by the Sisters. "I resisted this recasting of the faith of my
childhood, where what counted was personal relationship with God, inner peace, kindness to others, and heaven when this life was done. I didn't
want to struggle with politics and economics. We were nuns, after all, not
social workers. . . ."

The Sisters of St. Joseph explored the meaning of this commitment to
the poor by inviting Sister Marie Augusta Neal, a sociologist, who helped
them see the glaring poverty and injustice in the world in relationship to
their faith. This presentation was the turning point for Prejean. "I can remember the moment because it changed my life." It was as if Sister Neal
was speaking directly to Helen's hesitation and her desire to remain apolitical. Sister Neal pointed out that to claim to be apolitical or neutral in
the face of injustice would be, in actuality, to uphold the status quo, which
is a very political position to take. Sister Helen continues: "But it was the
way she presented the message of Jesus that caused the most radical shift
in my perspective."

> "The Gospels record that Jesus preached good news to the
> poor," [Neal] said, "and an essential part of that good news was
> they were to be poor no longer." Which meant they were not to
> meekly accept their poverty and suffering as God's will, but, in-
> stead, struggle to obtain the necessities of life which were rightly
> theirs. And Jesus' challenge to the nonpoor, she emphasized, was
> to relinquish their affluence and to share their resources with
> the dispossessed.[37]

Sister Neal was articulating a new understanding of poverty and the
church's role to work with the poor and be in solidarity with the powerless. This vision of walking with the poor emerged at the Second Vatican
Council (1962–1965), which had declared that "the joys and the hopes,
the griefs and anxieties of the men of this age, especially those who are
poor or in any way afflicted, these too are the joys and hopes, the griefs
and anxieties of the followers of Christ."[38] In 1971, a few years later, the
worldwide synod of Catholic bishops explained that "action on behalf of
justice . . . fully appear[s] to us as a constitutive dimension of preaching the
Gospel."[39] Thus, the message Sister Helen heard in 1980 had made its way
into the teachings of the church, and many religious congregations were
taking this new social consciousness very seriously.

The pieces came together for Helen: "Something in me must have been building toward this moment because there was a flash and I realized that my spiritual life had been too ethereal, too disconnected. I left the meeting and began seeking out the poor. This is what brought me one year later to the St. Thomas housing development."[40]

Her "enlightenment" continued as she ministered to and lived with the poor:

> In some mysterious way my living and working in St. Thomas is paring me down to essentials and liberating my spirit. Even living without air-conditioning is good for me. Intense heat slows you down. You choose essential tasks. You become grateful for small breezes and seek the company of trees. You appreciate a cool bath, ice water. Simple things. Good things.[41]

She crossed the racial divide by living within the black community.

> And for the first time in my life I have the opportunity to enjoy the friendship of black people. I realize how deprived my life was in the all-white-just-like-me social circles I used to frequent.... Even the way I pray is changing. Before, I had asked God to right the wrongs and comfort the suffering. Now I know—really know—that God entrusts those tasks to us.[42]

In the course of her work she was invited to become a pen pal with Elmo Patrick Sonnier, a man on death row, and she agreed. Sonnier and his brother had abducted a teenage couple, David LeBlanc and Loretta Bourque, in 1977. They raped the girl and then forced the couple to lie face down and shot them in the head. After a few months of writing to Sonnier, Prejean admitted that "the sheer weight of his loneliness, his abandonment, draws me. I abhor the evil he has done. But I sense something, some sheer and essential humanness, and that, perhaps, is what draws me most of all."[43] She served as his spiritual advisor for the last two years of his life.

Sister Prejean was present at his execution on April 5, 1984, in Louisiana's Angola prison. After sharing in "the joys and hopes, griefs and anxieties" of Patrick Sonnier and the LeBlanc and Bourque families, she told of her ministry in a best-selling book, *Dead Man Walking*. The book has been translated into ten languages and made into a movie, an opera, and a play.

As her ministry took her deeper into the flawed judicial system, she wrote a second book, *The Death of Innocents: An Eyewitness Account of Wrong-*

ful Executions in which she tells the story of two men she accompanied to their executions. One of them, Dobie Gillis Williams, had an IQ of 65. Less than two years later the Supreme Court ruled it unconstitutional to execute a person so mentally disabled. The second man was Joseph Roger O'Dell who tried for twelve years to have forensic testing on evidence that he claimed would exonerate him. But the courts refused, and after his execution the state, Virginia, destroyed the evidence. In this way the conviction of O'Dell could never be scrutinized.[44] Sister Prejean believed that both men were innocent.

Her second book examines the American sense of justice. "In these pages I tackle head-on the spirit of vengeance—a wrongful death can be set right only by killing the perpetrator—that has dominated the religious, political, and legal discourse of our country during the past twenty-five years."[45]

Her work highlights the sacredness of life and the dignity of each human being, even those who have committed terrible crimes. She explained her thinking in a talk given at an interfaith conference in Aachen, Germany, in 2003:

> We must help people to get past the visceral response of an "eye for an eye" vengeance. Transforming hatred of an enemy into compassion is what lies at the spiritual core of all religions. Certainly it is the energizing heart of the life and teachings of Jesus of Nazareth. Deep at the core of every religion is the belief in the sacredness of all life, the dignity that each being possesses, and that every human being is made in the image and likeness of God and possesses an inviolable dignity. And following the U.N. Universal Declaration of Human Rights and Pope John XXIII's encyclical, *Pacem in Terris*, we hold that this dignity belongs not only to the innocent but also to those guilty of terrible crimes. Our deepest spiritual traditions teach us that no human being should be killed or tortured, no matter what crime they have committed.[46]

For more than three decades this woman of faith has been defending the human dignity of prisoners on death row and fighting to abolish the death penalty. Her work and the work of other religious leaders, including the U.S. bishops, has brought about a change in attitude and the banning of the death penalty in a number of states. The most recent ban in Illinois was announced on Ash Wednesday, March 9, 2011.

Illinois is the fourth state to ban the death penalty since 2004, following New York, New Jersey, and New Mexico. The "land of Lincoln" had an especially poor record on capital punishment. Since 1977 twenty death-row inmates have been exonerated due to prosecutor and police misconduct, including confessions given under torture. Governor Pat Quinn said, "To say that this is unacceptable does not even begin to express the profound regret and shame we, as a society, must bear for these failures of justice."[47]

The Catholic bishops of Illinois thanked Governor Quinn and the legislators and advocates who had worked to repeal the death penalty and promote "a culture of life" in Illinois:

> As we begin the Lenten season on this Ash Wednesday, and we reflect on the crucifixion of Jesus and the mystery of His death and resurrection, there is no better time for this landmark law to be approved. The end of the use of the death penalty advances the development of a culture of life in our state. Furthermore, society will continue to be protected and those who commit crimes will still be held accountable through alternatives to the death penalty, including life without parole.[48]

In his remarks following the signing of the law, Governor Quinn acknowledged the influence of Cardinal Bernardin: "Cardinal Bernardin felt, as I do, that there are other means of punishing violent, evil people who commit heinous crimes, other than the state terminating their life."[49] The governor said that while he was mulling over his decision he read the Bible and Cardinal Bernardin's book, *The Gift of Peace*, co-authored by Father Alphonse Spilly. Though the book does not specifically mention the death penalty, it does tell of Bernardin's struggle with being falsely accused and facing his cancer diagnosis, "which ultimately was a death sentence."[50] When Father Spilly heard about the impact of the book and Bernardin's stand against the death penalty, he remarked, "Cardinal Bernardin is still touching people's lives in such a powerful way."[51] Even fifteen years after his death on November 13, 1996, Cardinal Bernardin's legacy of a culture of life is evident in this decision by the governor and legislature of Illinois.

Sex Trafficking

The Catholic Church's Respect Life program lifted up the issue of other victims of violence, those whose lives are subjected to human trafficking, in 2010–2011 by recalling a number of cases that were in the news:

Lena, a student from Eastern Europe, had dreams of visiting the United States and improving her English through a study-abroad program. When she arrived at the U.S. airport, she was told that her study placement had been changed. She was given a bus ticket to a different city. Upon arrival there, traffickers took her passport and enslaved her in the sex industry for almost a year.[52]

When Rosita was fifteen years old, a man walked up to her outside her school. He told her that she was pretty and that he wanted to be her boyfriend. He was a pimp. Over the next three years, Rosita endured an average of eight "customers" a day who were charged $1.50 each. All the money went to her pimp. "I just felt like I was put out to die," she said.[53]

These are just two stories of the tens of thousands of sex slaves in the United States. To the surprise of many, human beings continue to be bought, sold, and subjected to the dehumanizing conditions of bondage. Human trafficking is a high profit source of income for organized crime worldwide. Many of the victims are immigrant children and women.

To keep these women and children enslaved, traffickers may use beatings, rape, threats to family members, debt bondage, and threats of deportation or imprisonment. For a variety of reasons, victims rarely identify themselves. Often they are unable to speak English. They are full of fear and shame and unfamiliar with the protective U. S. laws. They may also be afraid of what will happen to their loved ones if they escape.[54]

They often feel trapped and hopeless because they are guarded by traffickers, mistrust local authorities who could help them, and they are unaware of how to get help. They do not realize that they can receive assistance and apply for immigration status as victims of the federal crime of trafficking.

Not all of the victims are immigrants. A large number of the children who are being exploited for commercial sexual prostitution are U.S. citizens and legal permanent residents. The average age of entry into prostitution in the United States is twelve to fourteen. Teenagers who run away from homes where they suffered sexual or physical abuse are lured by pimps with promises of love, security, and belonging. Sex trafficking survivors often suffer from HIV and other sexually transmitted diseases, mental health problems, drug and alcohol abuse, and problems related to pregnancy and forced abortions. The numbers are staggering:

- Worldwide 800,000 people are trafficked across international borders for commercial sex or forced labor. Eighty percent of these are women and children.
- In the last ten years 145,000 to 175,000 foreign nationals have been trafficked into the United States.
- At least 100,000 U.S. children are currently being exploited in the commercial sex trade in this country.
- In the United States, a sex trafficker can make over $200,000 per victim annually due to the high demand for sexual "services."[55]
- Annually pimps traffic thousands of under-age prostitutes at the Super Bowl.[56]

These few details make it obvious that sex trafficking is a horrific violation of human dignity. As a global institution, the Catholic Church is well-positioned to respond to human trafficking, and the Church has denounced this horrific crime because it constitutes an offense against human dignity and fundamental human rights. "The reality of thousands of our brothers and sisters laboring in modern day slavery compels us to act now to stop human trafficking and to serve the survivors of this crime."[57]

The United States Conference of Catholic Bishops' Department of Migration and Refugee Services (MRS) has organized a comprehensive response to sex trafficking that includes: (1) services for survivors; (2) training for social workers, religious communities, law enforcement, and medical and mental health professionals; (3) a national network linking services to refugee youth, children and their families; and (4) education and advocacy.[58] Finally, MRS organized the Coalition of Catholic Organizations against Human Trafficking, which is composed of more than twenty Catholic organizations. Each organization has its own network of concerned citizens who can work together to further the commitment to combat trafficking.[59]

Building a culture of life is an enormous undertaking. Such a task will only be accomplished by the work of God's Spirit alive in our hearts and permeating our vision and our actions. Come, Spirit of Life, empower your people!

Prayer for Life

Eternal God,
creator and sustainer of life,
bless us with the courage to defend all life
from conception to natural death.
Bless us with the strength to respect
all peoples from east to west, from north to south,
so that we may truly follow
the call of Jesus
to be neighbor.
We ask this in the name of Jesus,
who lives and reigns
With you and the Holy Spirit.
Amen.[60]

Prayer for Justice

You let your rain fall on the just and the unjust.
Expand and deepen our hearts
so that we may love as You love,
even those among us
who have caused the greatest pain by taking life.
For there is in our land a great cry for vengeance
as we fill up death row and kill the killers
in the name of justice, in the name of peace.
Jesus, our brother,
you suffered execution at the hands of the state
but you did not let hatred overcome you.
Help us to reach out to victims of violence
so that our enduring love may help them heal.
Holy Spirit of God,
You strengthen us in the struggle for justice,
Help us to work tirelessly
for the abolition of state-sanctioned death
and to renew our society in its very heart
so that violence will be no more.
Amen.[61]

Discussion Questions

1. The Catholic tradition teaches that "the dignity of the human person, realized in community with others, is the criterion against which all aspects of economic life must be measured." Give examples of how this teaching is both implemented and ignored.
2. Cardinal Bernardin saw the interrelatedness of diverse social problems, such as abortion and nuclear weapons. Do you agree with his approach? Explain why you agree or disagree.
3. Pope John Paul II believed that an excessive concern with efficiency is one of the causes of a "culture of death." What is he trying to say by the linking of excessive efficiency and a "culture of death"?
4. During the papacy of John Paul II, Catholic social teaching rejected the death penalty when a society can protect itself by bloodless means from violent criminals. Do you agree with this thinking? Explain.

4

Community, Family, Participation

As a young man Thomas Merton was a product of his times. Born in 1915, he fathered a child when he was a student at Cambridge. He "wantonly loved books, women, ideas, art, jazz, hard drink, cigarettes, argument, and having his opinions heard." Merton was on a fast track to becoming a wild man, high on drugs, perpetually on the road, writing in rebellion against the society of squares and men in gray suits. But God was not finished with him. Although Merton "came into the world, like everyone else, captive to a tainted ancestry of human selfishness, greed and violence," conversion was possible. At age twenty-three he was baptized a Roman Catholic; three years later he decided to become a Trappist monk, to the consternation of his friends.

> By a committed life of prayer and work he would learn the right means to root out the thicket of Western culture's materialism lodged within him. He would discover for himself and for others reading over his shoulder a traditional road toward selflessness, generosity, and nonviolence. . . . Merton would become another witness for his generation of the way out of self-defeating individualism by tracking anew the boundaries of that ancient other country whose citizens recognize a hidden ground of unity and love among all living beings.[1]

God invites all people to live in that "ancient other country whose citizens recognize a hidden ground of unity and love among all living beings." Merton was able to find his way, with God's help, to this "ancient other country," a place that we are all invited to as well.

As a Trappist monk Merton withdrew from the cares and confusion of modern life. He focused his heart and mind on God. But his contemplation and solitude led him back to the world, back to God's people. Merton scholar William Shannon explains: "Finding God in his solitude, he found

God's people, who are inseparable from God and who, at the deepest level of their being (the level that only contemplation can reach) are at one with one another in God, the Hidden Ground of Love of all that is."[2] As he stood on the corner of Fourth and Walnut, in the center of the shopping district in Louisville in spring 1958, Merton had an overwhelming sense of being part of humanity, and that his love of God and his search for holiness led him right back to humanity: "I was suddenly overwhelmed with the realization that I love all those people, that they were mine and I theirs, that we could not be alien to one another even though we were total strangers." He realized that he had been living under an illusion: "It was like waking from a dream of separateness, of spurious self-isolation in a special world, the world of renunciation and supposed holiness." He explained,

> The whole illusion of a separate holy existence is a dream. Not that I question the reality of my vocation, or of my monastic life: but the conception of "separation from the world" that we have in the monastery too easily presents itself as a complete illusion: the illusion that by making vows we become a different species of being, pseudo-angels, "spiritual men," men of interior life, what have you.[3]

Merton went on to express his delight at his discovery of the obvious.

> This sense of liberation from an illusory difference was such a relief and such a joy to me that I almost laughed out loud. And I suppose my happiness could have taken form in the words: "Thank God, thank God that I am like other men, that I am only a man among others." To think that for sixteen or seventeen years I have been taking seriously this pure illusion that is implicit in so much of our monastic thinking.[4]

He realized that even in his solitude the rest of humanity would be with him. "It is because I am one with them that I owe it to them to be alone, and when I am alone they are not 'they' but my own self. There are no strangers!"[5]

Thomas Merton's commitment to social issues flowed from a deep contemplative vision. Shannon points out that "we shall only learn to deal effectively with violence when we discover (or recover, for it is really always there) in ourselves that contemplative awareness that enables us, as it had enabled Merton, to see the oneness we share with all God's people—indeed with the whole of God's creation."[6]

This chapter begins with a reflection on God as the reason for our communal identity, looking at how God's work has been that of forming a covenantal community, through Moses and the prophets, through Jesus and the early church. Family is also examined as a complex and, at times, ambivalent symbol of the importance of the "domestic church." Finally, we will turn to the importance of participation as an expression of basic justice and as a way to prevent violence and establish peace.

The Community of the Trinity

As Thomas Merton discovered and the bishops have articulated, "our experience of the Triune God is also a basis for Catholic social thought." Catholic social thought is not some theological afterthought; instead it flows from the core understanding of the very nature of God. "In the coming of Jesus Christ, we understand the Trinitarian nature of God's own inner life. Jesus reveals God as Father and sends the Holy Spirit as his gift to us to dwell in our hearts and to form us into community." The bishops continue,

> God's nature is communal and social; therefore our nature, created in his image, is communal and social as well. We are communal and social because of the way we have been created and because of the One who has redeemed us. This is a very solid foundation for our Catholic social tradition—rooted in God's community of the Trinity and in our very nature, as created in God's image. For this reason the Task Force on Catholic Social Teaching and Catholic Education concludes that "We cannot call ourselves Catholic unless we hear and heed the Church's teaching to serve those in need, to protect human life and dignity, and to pursue justice and peace."[7]

Community goes to the heart of God, and to God's creative activity in the world, and community is at the heart of what it means to be human. As mentioned above, as Christians we believe in a God who lives in community: the community of the Trinity. We also believe, as John Coleman puts it, that God's "work," as revealed in the Bible, is creating, restoring when broken, and completing in the end time a covenant community whose main characteristics are peace and justice.[8]

That work was begun in God's covenants with the Hebrew community—through Noah, Abraham, and Moses. The prophets called the community back to the requirements of justice when greed and idolatry led them to disregard the requirements of the covenant. Jesus stood on the shoulders of the prophets and announced a new covenant that would be open to all people. It is the Spirit of God that pushes the church to be faithful to the covenant of Jesus in every age and in every circumstance.

The church's understanding of the centrality of covenant has always been strong, which is the reason the early church expanded. One author suggests that "the radical sense of Christian community—open to all, insistent on absolute and exclusive loyalty, and concerned for every aspect of the believer's life" is the single overriding reason that Christianity spread throughout the Roman Empire. "From the very beginning, the one distinctive gift of Christianity was this sense of community. . . . Christian congregations provided a unique opportunity for masses of people to discover a sense of security and self-respect."[9]

Moses Forms a New Community

The marvel of prophetic faith is that the imperial religion, the imperial economics, and imperial politics could be broken. Moses reveals a new god, a God who is free, namely, free to challenge the gods of Egypt and free to hear the cries of those who are exploited. This God is not a god of the "haves" but of the "have nots." This God that Moses announces is a God of freedom, a God who does not serve the interests of those in control of society, but those on the margins, those who are voiceless. This God of the Hebrews is present in the brickyards, hearing the cries of the Hebrew slaves and leading them out with justice and compassion. The narrative of liberation for Israel begins with their groaning for liberation—not unlike the groans for liberation of the American slaves: "And the people of Israel groaned under their bondage, and cried out for help, and their cry under bondage came up to God. And God heard their groaning, and God remembered his covenant. . . . And God saw the people of Israel, and God knew their condition" (Ex 2:23–25).

Moses formed a new community that would not follow the Egyptian model, a community that attempted to live an economics of equality and a politics of justice. This new way of being a community lasted about two hundred and fifty years. But eventually the old ways returned as the Jewish economic system and political order began to reflect the patterns of the neighboring countries. The economic prosperity and affluence in Israel was not democratically shared. King Solomon brought in the trappings of empires, including a standing army, central taxation, and forced labor as he tried to secure his wealth and control.[10] By the time of King Solomon, two hundred and fifty years after the Exodus, Israel is beginning to resemble the oppressive policies and practices of Pharaoh's Egypt.

King Solomon had undermined the covenant commitment to "right relationships" that is the basis of peace and justice. "He had traded a vision of freedom for the reality of security. He had banished the neighbor for the sake of reducing everyone to servants. He had replaced convenanting with consuming, and all promises had been reduced to tradable commodities."[11] So, God sent prophets to speak out against the violations of God's covenant.

The Prophetic Task

The prophet has two tasks: first, to call people back to the covenant community envisioned by Moses, and, second, to imagine a different kind of a future than the current reality. As the prophet criticizes the present injustice and grieves with the community, the words of the prophet Jeremiah come to mind: "A voice is heard in Ramah, lamentation and bitter weeping. Rachel is weeping for her children; she refuses to be comforted for her children, because they are no more" (Jer 31:15).

Grief and tears are an expression of solidarity in pain when no other form of solidarity remains. Tears can break barriers like no harshness or anger can. We know that Jesus, in keeping with this dimension of prophecy, wept over Jerusalem (Lk 19:41). He also taught that those who mourn will be comforted (Mt 5:4). Jesus knew that weeping permits the reign of God to begin. Such weeping is a radical criticism, a dismantling of the old order and the old relationships, and the beginning of new relationships.

We know this is true from our own experiences of loss and death. Through grieving and tears we weep over what was lost, but our grief opens the door to something new. We weep over being fired, a broken marriage, and the death of a loved one, but that painful experience may open us up to new job possibilities, a more selfless way of loving, or a new relationship "in the spirit" with our deceased loved one. The prophetic vision is often the boldest when the situation seems utterly hopeless—"the deeper the crisis, the bolder the vision."[12] When the community faces difficult times it is then that it needs a vision of hope and justice.

The second task of the prophet is to imagine a different kind of a future. "The prophet does not ask if the vision can be implemented, for questions of implementation are of no consequence until the vision can be imagined. The *imagination* must come before the *implementation*." The creative energy of the prophet is to call the community to a new vision of reality. "It is the vocation of the prophet to keep alive the ministry of imagination, to keep on conjuring and proposing future alternatives to the single one the king wants to urge as the only thinkable one."[13]

In the face of injustice and oppression the community may be tempted to despair. Prophetic consciousness, on the other hand, speaks and acts a message of hope. "Hope is the decision to which God invites Israel, a decision against despair, against permanent consignment to chaos (Isa 45:18), oppression, barrenness, and exile."[14] This hope is rooted in the assurance that God does not quit even when the evidence is not hopeful.

"The hope-filled language of prophecy, in cutting through the royal despair and hopelessness, engages the community in new discernments and celebrations just when it had nearly given up and had nothing to celebrate." One powerful expression of hope is to give praise to God and to utter thanksgiving even when all is not well—just as Jesus did at the Last Supper, before being betrayed and executed. Doxology, the act of giving praise, makes us aware of God's presence even in the places that seem godless.[15] By offering hope, the prophet energizes the community and in turn the community becomes prophetic.

Jesus as Prophet

Jesus clearly identified with the prophetic tradition and the new consciousness the prophets announced. At the beginning of his ministry Jesus prophesized that a new age was beginning: "The Spirit of the Lord is upon me, because he has anointed me to bring good news to the poor. He has sent me to proclaim release to the captives and recovery of sight to the blind, to let the oppressed go free, to proclaim the year of the Lord's favor" (Lk 4:18–19). Jesus claims this message as his ministry by telling those in the synagogue: "Today this scripture has been fulfilled in your hearing" (Lk 4:21). As Jesus carried out his ministry of healing outcasts and calling for justice in the overturning of the money changers in the Temple, the religious and political leaders realized that Jesus was a threat to the survival of the order that Rome had imposed. The high priest Caiaphas realized that Jesus had to die to protect the status quo.

Jesus expresses his solidarity with the people through his compassion— a compassion that announces that the hurt of the marginal and powerless is being taken seriously. Jesus' response of compassion is both a personal emotional reaction and also a public criticism of the present order. Jesus has compassion on individuals and on whole populations who were "harassed and helpless": "And Jesus went about all the cities and villages, teaching in their synagogues and preaching the gospel of the kingdom, and healing every disease and every infirmity. When he saw the crowds, he had compassion for them because they were harassed and helpless, like sheep without a shepherd" (Matt 9:35–36). Jesus also showed compassion for the rich and powerful who were attracted to his message: Matthew the tax collector, the rich man Zacchaeus, and Nicodemus, a member of the Sanhedrin. They left behind their old ways to become his disciples.

Compassion is the ability to stand with those who are suffering. Compassion reaches out to the vulnerable, including the unborn. Standing with the poor and vulnerable means more than works of charity. It means confronting the unjust laws, policies, and practices that prevent the poor and vulnerable from flourishing. There will always be resistance by those who currently benefit from the unjust and violent situation. This was the experience of Jesus. This was the experience of Sister Dorothy Stang in the rain forest of Brazil (as noted in chapter 2). This was the experience of Archbishop Oscar Romero who stood with the poor and the four American women who were martyred for their solidarity with the poor of El Salvador.

The church is charged with preaching the good news to the poor and exhibiting the same compassion and the justice of the prophets, a compassion that opens the door for hope and a new beginning. The early church struggled to be the compassion of Jesus and to continue God's work of building a covenant community committed to biblical justice and peace. Early Christians protected all human lives, especially the lives of the poor and vulnerable. They spoke out against the taking of life, whether in war or through abortion.[16]

The early church challenged the idolatry of Rome and struggled to live an alternative consciousness where the economics of equality and the politics of justice were expressed in a religion that celebrated God's freedom. But as the church gained acceptance by the Roman emperor Constantine, it gradually shifted its stance. When Rome "fell" in 467, church leaders became more responsible for the social order. As it developed a hierarchical structure, the church itself took on some of the cultural trappings of power and authority of Rome. The pattern was beginning to repeat itself as it had in the time of Solomon.

However, the radical voice of the gospel still echoed in the monastic traditions and in vigilant church leaders. St. Basil is an example of a leader who continued to respond to God's call for compassion and justice.

St. Basil Focuses on Community

Basil (329–379) came from a family of rich landowners in Caesarea in Cappadocia (modern-day Kayseri, Turkey). After his studies and influenced by the radical asceticism of the monks of Egypt, he distributed all his possessions among the poor. Basil visited different monasteries and then joined one near his home city. He drew up a rule that had a revolutionary influence on the development of monasticism. Unlike the early monks whose spirituality focused on individual feats of asceticism, Basil stressed the importance of community.

For Basil the monastery was to model the ideal community, a community where the love of God and the love of neighbor could be cultivated side by side. He believed that the monastery should be integrated into the life of the church and society. Rather than existing in isolation, the monastery should welcome guests, it should include orphanages and schools, and it should be a center of service and a center for the works of mercy. "For Basil the monastery did not exist for the sanctification of its members alone, but for the entire wider community."[17] Basil made the connection between love of God and love of neighbor as the unified vision of contemplative life—a tradition that Thomas Merton would echo sixteen hundred years later. In seeking the isolation of the monastery the monk is led back to the service of God's people in the world.

As Bishop of Caesarea in Cappadocia, Basil translated the social demands of the gospel into action by setting up a large welfare center at the gates of the city for the poor, the old, and the sick, together with a hospice for penniless travelers. Welfare centers of this kind also came into being in other cities in his diocese.

Although a famous preacher, Basil was better known for his emphasis on the social aspects of the gospel. He organized soup kitchens, personally waiting on the hungry. He established a hospital for the sick poor that was described as one of the wonders of the church. And Basil went beyond the traditional exhortation to charity by calling for a basic redistribution of wealth as a requirement of justice. In effect, he taught that the needs of the poor held a social mortgage on the surplus holdings of the rich. He challenged the well-to-do in his community with blunt language: "You refuse to give on the pretext that you haven't got enough for your own needs. But while your tongue makes excuses, your hand convicts you—that ring shining on your finger silently declares you to be a liar! How many debtors could be released from prison with one of those rings?"[18]

He preached a famous sermon on the rich farmer (Lk 12:18) in which he called the man who could help the needy but keeps his possessions to himself a "robber and a thief":

> Are you not a robber, you who consider your own that which has been given you solely to distribute to others? This bread which you have set aside is the bread of the hungry; this garment you have locked away is the clothing of the naked; those shoes which you let rot are the shoes of him who is barefoot; those riches you have hoarded are the riches of the poor.[19]

Basil left a lasting legacy in the Eastern church. To this day monastic life in the East is based on the ideals he set forth in his monastic Rule. His emphasis on community in monastic life, his preaching, and his direct action to serve the needy shaped the early church's understanding of its mission to build community. The early church realized that all of God's people had a right to participate in the resources of the Earth. That community-focused message and community-related principles are at the heart of the Catholic social tradition as they were at the time of Jesus. They are still controversial in our day.

The Principles of Catholic Social Teaching

Michael was persistent. He had already spoken to the two priests of the parish about his concerns. Now, after the 11:00 mass he was talking with our pastoral administrator, Anne-Marie, about the church's social teaching and advocacy efforts. He did not support the petition that we were asking people to sign after mass that called for subsidies for child care and transportation for low-income workers. Anne-Marie suggested that he speak with me.

Michael is a senior at the University of Rochester majoring in finance who would like to get a job on Wall Street or "Teach for America." Michael does not believe it is the role of government to take care of poor people. He believes it is actually counterproductive to do so as it creates cycles of dependency and lessens the incentive to work. He believes that the church should not support minimum-wage laws as many studies point out that there are fewer jobs for low-income workers because of the minimum-wage law. The church should serve the needs of the poor as it has done for centuries through voluntary charitable contributions rather than relying on government support through taxation.

While I did not agree with Michael that our taxes should not be used to help the poor, I did listen carefully to what he was saying and I told him that I respected his intelligence and passion for his beliefs. I said that it is important for the church to have forums of dialogue so that people in the pews and economists (and other experts) can be consulted as the church formulates its teaching and advocacy positions. After the conversation I wondered if Michael had ever studied Catholic social teachings. I wondered how he understood the Eucharist that we had just celebrated, which challenges us to live the message of Jesus and the teachings of the church.

Michael is an example of why Catholic social teaching has not taken root in our society. As sociologist John Coleman, S.J., notes: "Many ethicists or political philosophers in the United States favor a view of the unencumbered individual as an autonomous chooser, cut off from essential relationality. This is, of course, diametrically opposed to the Catholic understanding of the human person as profoundly, and *essentially*, relational." This means that "strong notions of solidarity and communitarianism do not resonate as well in the United States as they do in papal social teaching."[20]

While the dominant culture in the United States focuses on the rights of individuals and autonomous decisions, the Catholic tradition stresses community and solidarity as well as the freedom and dignity of each person. This means that the common good is on a par with the individual good. In fact, an individual cannot develop or flourish without a supportive community. The principle of the common good and the virtue of solidarity mean that individuals have an obligation to contribute to the needs of others in a variety of ways.

We contribute to the community and common good through our jobs, volunteering, paying taxes, contributing to charities, and becoming politically active. The common good is served when, for example, a retired couple with no children of their own pay their tax bill to support public education and when they volunteer in the school by mentoring students. They are contributing to the common good by helping children to receive an education. As the bishops at the Second Vatican Council noted: "Citizens, for their part, should remember that they have the right and the duty, which must be recognized by civil authority, to contribute according to their ability to the true progress of their community" (*Gaudium et Spes*, 65).

Pope John Paul II noted how the virtue of solidarity and the common good are linked when he described the virtue of solidarity as "*a firm and persevering determination* to commit oneself to the *common good*; this is to say to the good of all and of each individual because we are *all* really responsible *for all*."[21]

In Catholic social thought the government has a positive role to play in promoting the common good. As the *Compendium of the Social Doctrine of the Church* puts it: "The responsibility for attaining the common good, besides falling to individual persons, belongs also to the State, since the common good is the reason that the political authority exists" (168). This does not mean that everything should be done by the government. "While it is not always immediately clear which level applies best to a given task, the rule of thumb laid out in Catholic social teaching is to rely as much as possible on those solutions that are closest to the people affected and to employ the smallest groupings and mechanisms that are still effective."[22]

This principle of subsidiarity stresses the importance of grassroots groups, including families, neighborhood groups, community organizations, and voluntary associations in responding to the needs of the common good. In the words of Pope John Paul II: "[A] community of a higher order should not interfere in the internal life of a community of a lower order, depriving the latter of its functions, but rather should support it in case of need and help coordinate its activities with the rest of society, always with a view to the common good" (*Centesimus Annus*, 48).

This kind of thinking is not foreign to the American tradition, which is rich in volunteer organizations. President Abraham Lincoln commented on the role of government in a similar vein: "The legitimate object of government is to do for a community of people whatever they need to have done, but cannot do at all, or cannot so well do, for themselves—in their separate, and individual capacities."[23]

Common Good and Solidarity in Action: Hurricane Katrina

"These people blow my mind," said Deanna Misko, volunteer coordinator in the Diocese of Biloxi, Mississippi. "I had no concept of someone that says, 'Hey I'm going to take a week off to go to this mosquito infested land and work like a fiend for people I've never seen before, all the while possibly dodging alligators.'" Misko's sense of humor helps her stay balanced while she organizes volunteers who help gut homes and prepare them for rebuilding after Hurricane Katrina. In Mississippi more than 65,000 homes were destroyed or severely damaged. More than 1,500 volunteers removed debris, tore down damaged infrastructure, and performed mold abatement so that other crews could come in and rebuild them.[24]

Jennifer L. Dyer, from Catholic Charities, the Diocese of Camden, reflected on the six hundred people from her diocese who volunteered to work in New Orleans. This work provided "concrete opportunities for parishioners to live out their call to solidarity and demonstrate their belief that 'we are one': one people, one community and one human family." Work provided "concrete transformative opportunities for individuals to come together as teams to live out some of the most important concepts and beliefs of Catholic social teaching." Upon their return, participants were encouraged and expected to share their experiences with others in their parish as a way of engaging and educating persons who may not have been able to participate. Additionally, post-trip reflections were coordinated to assist participants as they began to focus on the systemic injustices that not only cause poverty, but keep so many families in poverty and actions that they could take to become more involved in working for change.[25]

Participation in Community

While the early church preachers and bishops like St. Basil focused on the right to participate in the bounty of the Earth, later church teaching added the right to participate in the political process. In 1971 Pope Paul VI noted that participation and equality are two fundamental aspirations of humanity. They are also a way to promote human dignity and human freedom. Pope Paul VI recognized that people today expect "a greater sharing in responsibility and in decision making." He said that sharing in responsibility and in decision-making in the social and political arenas "must be established and strengthened."[26]

The U.S. bishops picked up the theme of participation in their 1986 pastoral letter on the economy, *Economic Justice for All.* They moved beyond affirming it as a fundamental aspiration to calling it a demand of basic justice: "Basic justice demands the establishment of minimum levels of participation in the life of the human community for all persons." They explained that "The ultimate injustice is for a person or group to be treated actively or abandoned passively as if they were nonmembers of the human race."

The bishops pointed out that the lack of participation or exclusion happens in the political and economic spheres in both wealthy and poor nations. "These patterns of exclusion are created by free human beings. In this sense they can be called forms of social sin." The bishops teach that it is a sinful situation when we do not change policies and practices that continue to exclude people, socially, politically, and economically. "Acquiescence in them or failure to correct them when it is possible to do so is a sinful dereliction of Christian duty" (77).

In the next paragraph the bishops repeat their understanding of the importance of participation:

> Recent Catholic social thought regards the task of overcoming these patterns of exclusion and powerlessness as a most basic demand of justice. Stated positively, justice demands that social institutions be ordered in a way that guarantees all persons the ability to participate actively in the economic, political, and cultural life of society. The level of participation may legitimately be greater for some persons than for others, but there is a basic level of access that must be made available for all. Such participation is an essential expression of the social nature of human beings and of their communitarian vocation (78).

These strong convictions are a judgment on the policies of society and church whenever they resist expanding the legitimate arenas of participation in decision-making or economic opportunity.

In his 1985 World Day of Peace Message Pope John Paul II pointed out that the denial of participation often leads to violence and injustice:

> It is essential for every human being to have a sense of participating, of being part of the decisions and endeavors that shape the destiny of the world. Violence and injustice have often in the past found their root causes in people's sense of being deprived of the right to shape their own lives. Future violence and injustice cannot be avoided when the basic right to participate in the choices of society is denied.[27]

Promoting the right to participate is, therefore, a way to work for peace and the reduction of violence.

Political Participation: Faithful Citizenship

Every four years when the presidential election rolls around, the U.S. bishops remind Catholics of their duty to participate in the political process and they provide guidelines for our political involvements: "In the Catholic Tradition, responsible citizenship is a virtue, and participation in political life is a moral obligation. This obligation is rooted in our baptismal commitment to follow Jesus Christ and to bear Christian witness in all we do" (13).[28]

They also point out that public service can be a worthy vocation. "The Catholic call to faithful citizenship affirms the importance of political participation and insists that public service is a worthy vocation" (14). All segments of society and all people have a duty to participate.

> Building a world of respect for human life and dignity, where justice and peace prevail, requires more than just political commitment. Individuals, families, businesses, community organizations, and governments all have a role to play. Participation in political life in light of fundamental moral principles is an essential duty for every Catholic and all people of good will (57).

How the church enters public life is a crucial question. The bishops note that the church does not impose a sectarian doctrine, but acts out of moral convictions, sharing its experience of serving the poor and vulnerable, and participating in the dialogue about our nation's future. Three principles are offered to guide the church's political involvement:

1. The Church is involved in the political process but is not partisan. The Church cannot champion any candidate or party (58).
2. The Church is engaged in the political process but should not be used. We welcome dialogue with political leaders and candidates; we seek to engage and persuade public officials (59).
3. The Church is principled but not ideological. We cannot compromise basic principles or moral teaching. We are committed to clarity about our moral teaching and to civility (60).

The bishops added:

In light of these principles and the blessings we share as part of a free and democratic nation, we bishops vigorously repeat our call for a renewed kind of politics:

- focused more on moral principles than on the latest polls,
- focused more on the needs of the weak than on benefits for the strong,
- focused more on the pursuit of the common good than on the demands of narrow interests (61).

This kind of political participation reflects the social teaching of our Church and the best traditions of our nation (62).

Aly May, a fourteen-year-old from St. Jude of the Lake parish in Mahtmedi, Minnesota, knows that participation in political life does not have to wait until she is twenty-one years old and able to vote. She was part of a six-bus caravan from the Archdiocese of St. Paul and Minneapolis for the January 24, 2011, March for Life in Washington. Even though she is confined to a wheelchair due to her condition called spinal muscular atrophy, she did not let that stop her from participating in the March for Life for the last two years. "We went to the White House," she said. "We and a bunch of my friends made a sign that said, 'St. Jude is pro-life.'"[29] No doubt, Aly has grown up in a family that nurtures the value of all of life and the importance of participating in the public arena.

"Family" plays a central role in the church's understanding of society. It is interesting to note how the early church understood family in light of the reign of God and to compare that understanding with that of Pope John Paul II and the role family plays today in shaping citizens and addressing social concerns.

Teachings on Family in Early Christianity

While the church has unflinchingly taught the importance of community as essential for Christian life, it has a mixed history on stressing the importance of being part of a biological family. The church has always recalled the importance of the Holy Family—and every family—as a vehicle of God's grace, but it has also maintained that not having a family and remaining celibate can be an effective form of discipleship. This ambivalence about family is found in the very words of Jesus. Luke's account records: "Then his mother and his brothers came to see him, but they could not reach him because of the crowd. And he was told, 'Your mother and brothers are standing outside, wanting to see you.' But he said to them, 'My mother and my brothers are those who hear the word of God and do it'" (Lk 8:19–21). On another occasion his relatives and family tried to restrain Jesus because they were "convinced he was out of his mind" (Mk 3:21).[30]

Jesus said that his message was a "sword of division" setting family members against one another: "I have not come to bring peace, but a sword. For I have come to set a man against his father, and a daughter against her mother, and a daughter-in-law against her mother-in-law; and one's foes will be members of one's own household" (Mt 10:34–36). The radical edge of Jesus' message is that we are to love him more than our family members: "Whoever loves father or mother more than me is not worthy of me; and whoever loves son or daughter more than me is not worthy of me" (Mt 10:37).

Jesus also preached of a "new age" that would exclude marrying: "Jesus said to them, 'Those who belong to this age marry and are given in marriage; but those who are considered worthy of a place in that age and in the resurrection from the dead neither marry nor are given in marriage'" (Lk 20:34–35). As ethicist Margaret Farley notes: "All family bonds and responsibilities were relativized in favor of an imminent realm of God in which the unity with God and all persons would transcend the special human relations that were in place before its coming."[31]

God's "new era" relativized all human institutions, including marriage and family. At the same time, the followers of Jesus became the new family for those without a family—the poor, the orphan, and the widows. "If any believing woman has relatives who are really widows, let her assist them; let the church not be burdened, so that it can assist those who are real widows" (1 Tim 5:16). For those who had to leave their birth families because of the gospel, the church became their new community of brothers and sisters—their new family. This new family of the church offered a membership that abolished all barriers of nation, gender, or economic status. Here there "is neither Jew nor Greek, there is neither slave nor free, there is neither male nor female; for you all are one in Christ Jesus" (Gal 3:28). While this was the framework of the age to come, it also could be experienced in the here and now.

In its response to "family," the church rejected family ties as the highest bond and substituted the church as the new family. But, in time, the church reaffirmed family ties as important, so as not to appear too radical in the Greco-Roman world. While we have the radical "egalitarian" statement of Galatians stated above, a few years later we find in Ephesians the traditional hierarchical framework wherein wives are instructed to be "subject to your husbands as you are to the Lord" (Eph 5:22). The radical teaching of Jesus on family ties was softened so that the church was seen in a more positive light by the surrounding cultures. These later writings in the New Testament tried to adhere to the spirit of Jesus even as they affirmed traditional relationships. A new spirit was brought to the relationships within the family, even as the patriarchal structures remained in place.

The same could be said of the relationship of servant and master. Paul sent the runaway slave, Onesimus, back to his master Philemon with the instruction that the latter should treat his slave as a brother. Paul addressed Philemon, saying, "Perhaps this is the reason he was separated from you for a while, so that you might have him back forever, no longer as a slave but more than a slave, a beloved brother" (Phil 15–16).

Although social institutions were not overturned, they were challenged to be transformed by the love and equality of God's realm. A remnant of the radical vision of equality remains, even as the church accepted traditional hierarchical relationships of males over females and masters over slaves. There is a hint in Paul's advice to the Corinthians of overturning the societal norms that tolerated inequality in marriage: "the husband rules over his wife's body and that the wife rules over her husband's body" (1 Cor 7:4).

However, the teachings of the early church on family remained ambiguous. In the third century the church rejected the extreme anti-family, anti-marriage teaching of some Gnostic sects. "Marriage was affirmed as good by the Christian church, as part of creation, though celibacy was considered better."[32] This view of marriage and family continued through the centuries, more or less in place until the fourteenth century, when the humanists in the Renaissance proposed a change from otherworldliness to social responsibility, from renunciation and withdrawal to self-discipline and achievement in a world where family and productive labor were combined. The Protestant Reformation in the sixteenth century built on these new orientations and shifted the focus away from the monastery and the sanctuary to the marketplace. The Christian vocation "in the marketplace, behind the plow, and in front of the stove" was extolled.[33]

Family Since Vatican II

The Roman Catholic tradition resisted the "this worldly" focus until the Second Vatican Council (1962–1965), which ethicist Farley calls "a quantum leap in the church's positive affirmation of the family."[34] The documents of Vatican II and subsequent documents hail the family as the foundation of society and the "domestic church."[35] Alongside this positive view of family, Pope John Paul II reaffirmed the historical understanding of the "superiority of this charism [of celibacy] to that of marriage, by reason on the wholly singular link which it has with the kingdom of God."[36]

Today, Catholic theology and spirituality do not view the love of another human being as detracting from our love of God. In fact, love of a spouse and child is viewed as participation in divine love. Sexuality is viewed in more positive terms as a gift of God to be enjoyed and celebrated within committed love and it is not simply tolerated for the sake of procreation. These positive themes provide the starting points for a reinterpretation of marriage and family within the Catholic tradition. The magisterium remains committed to the traditional understanding of marriage and resists efforts to redefine marriage. The U. S. bishops explained "marriage must be defined, recognized, and protected as a lifelong commitment between a man and a woman, and as the source of the next generation and the protective haven for children."[37] Pope Benedict XVI said this is not negotiable.[38]

There is an ongoing discussion of how to understand the equal dignity and responsibility of men and women in marriage and family. Pope John Paul II spoke of the "complementarity" of men and women. While this is an improvement over the overt inequality of past thinking, Margaret Farley fears that this means that "the gendered hierarchy of roles and separation of spheres [public and private] remains entrenched in the tradition."[39] On the other hand, Pope John Paul II's insistence on the value of the stay-at-home mother has resonated well with those who believe society undervalues the importance of parents who stay at home to nurture their children.

Pope John Paul II's most distinctive contribution is his teaching that the Christian family is the "domestic church." This term had been used in the Vatican II document *Lumen Gentium*.[40] In a church that had often emphasized the primacy of discipleship through celibacy, this concept of family as the domestic church helped to highlight "the notion that the Christian couple and their children participate in an ongoing sacramental reality through which they are sanctified and invited to participate actively in the outward mission of the church, especially through service and hospitality."[41]

The understanding of family as the "domestic church" fits well with the church's principle of subsidiarity wherein the smaller, local associations are linked with the larger institutions, but are also relatively independent. This is true for the family as it relates both to the larger church and to the state. The family is a sacrament of God's love when parents and children imitate Christ's self-giving love. The family is "a saving community" as it reflects and communicates Christ's love to others. The love between husband and wife and among family members participates in "the prophetic, priestly, and kingly mission" of Christ and the church. In this way the Christian family is a gospel community, a community in relation to God, and a community of service to others. According to Pope John Paul II, the family also plays a vital role in society:

It is from the family that citizens come to birth, and it is within the family that they find the first school of the social virtues that are the animating principle of the existence and development of society. Thus, far from being closed in on itself, the family is by nature and vocation open to other families and to society, and undertakes its social role.[42]

Thus, the family is "the most effective means of humanizing and personalizing society"; it is "the first and irreplaceable school of social life, and example and stimulus for the broader community of relationships marked by respect, justice, dialogue and love."[43]

John Paul II encouraged families to work for structural reform, claiming that the Christian family "is not closed in on itself, but remains open to the community, moved by a sense of justice and concern for others, as well as by a consciousness of its responsibility toward the whole of society." The family's commitment to the hungry, the poor, the old, the sick, the disabled, drug victims, ex-prisoners, and those without families, especially abandoned children and orphans, leads it to social action and "active and responsible involvement in the authentically human growth of society and its institutions," extending even to the international level.[44] Our Catholic tradition is sprinkled with socially conscious families who lived out those social virtues that help our society develop. I met the mother of one of those families who taught by her example. Her name was Esperanza.

The Grandmothers for the Common Good

Esperanza, who could not speak much English, slept at our house just one night, but she made a big impression. Esperanza is a short, Mexican-American widow from Waukegan, Illinois, where she raised eleven children. All of her children graduated from college. Now at the age of seventy years, it's time to relax, right? Not for Esperanza and the eleven other members from her parish and small Christian community in northern Illinois. They climbed onto the buses in Chicago as part of a nine-day journey to Washington D.C. and New York City to demonstrate on behalf of recent immigrants whose rights and dignity are not being recognized.

Esperanza was part of a national campaign, Immigrant Workers' Freedom Ride—Legalization and a Road to Citizenship, which brought seventeen buses full of immigrant workers and their supporters from nine cities across the country. Esperanza was one of 142 riders on the three buses from Chicago. Fifty-two of the riders stayed in homes while the others stayed in a Super 8 motel. Esperanza and her friends, Juanita and Alicia, stayed at the Mich home. The night before, they had slept on camping pads and blankets on the floor of a church basement. They appreciated being able to sleep in a bed.

Esperanza and her 141 companions embody the theme of this chapter. Here is a Catholic woman who raised her family and is deeply concerned about her community of immigrants, new and old, who are trying to participate in the U.S. economy. She participates in her parish as a member of a small Christian community that nourishes her faith and encourages her to work for a more just society. She is one of the unnamed heroines of our church who has a sense of justice and lives it out with her other grandmother friends in Waukegan.

Families as "the Salt of the Earth"

Esperanza's activism is an example of what the bishops and Pope John Paul II have been teaching, that the family is the place where the work of pro-life and social justice witness begin. The U.S bishops admit that "the most challenging work for justice is *not* done in Church committees, but in the secular world of *work, family life and citizenship*."[45] The parish as a whole, through its worship and preaching, through its faith-formation programs, through its sacramental life, helps us to be agents of gospel values at home, at work, and in the community.

"Our parishes are clearly called to help people live their faith in the world, helping them understand and act on the social dimensions of the Gospel in their everyday lives."[46] "Living our faith in the world" is the challenge for all Christians. The bishops continue: "[P]arish committees can be useful, but they are not substitutes for everyday choices and commitments of believers—acting as parents, workers, students, owners, investors, advocates, policy makers and citizens."[47]

Living the faith begins in our homes, carries forth into the workplace, and is visible in our interactions in the marketplace and government. It can be as simple as honesty and fairness. Parents need to live with integrity and honesty as our children learn from us. What lesson does a parent communicate who says to a fourteen-year-old child at the box office, "Don't say anything because I am going to try to get you in as a child"? Or the parent who is upset when the son's pencil is stolen at school, but who has no problem taking pens and pencils from his or her workplace.

Our daughter who was about to begin her second year of college took me (and my credit card) shopping for clothes on the Labor Day weekend before she headed back to school. While at J. C. Penney's she picked up a belt, slippers, and a purse. I bought a pair of shoes. We paid our bill and wandered down the mall to another clothing store. I started thinking about the bill. I knew everything was on sale and that there was no sales tax on clothing that week, but how could we get everything for seventy-one dollars? I looked at the receipt. The clerk had forgotten to include my shoes, but had scanned the purse twice. I said that I needed to go back. My daughter thought we should just keep going, that it was the clerk's mistake. I said that once we realized the mistake, it was comparable to stealing and that I needed to go back. When I returned to the store the sales clerk was very appreciative and said that a lot of people do not come back. She rang up the shoes and gave me an additional ten percent discount for coming back. I am sure my nineteen-year-old daughter was watching my actions. I hope she learned something about the Seventh Commandment during our shopping excursion.[48]

The document *Communities of Salt and Light* offers eight concrete ways in which parishes can help their members to live the Gospel in the world of family, work, and citizenship:

1. Building and sustaining marriages of quality, fidelity, equality, and permanence in an age that does not value commitment or hard work in relationships.
2. Raising families with Gospel values in a culture where materialism, selfishness, and prejudice still shape so much of our lives.
3. Being a good neighbor, welcoming newcomers and immigrants, treating people of different races, ethnic groups and nationalities with respect and kindness.
4. Seeing themselves as evangelizers who recognize the unbreakable link between spreading the Gospel and work for social justice.
5. Bringing Christian values and virtues into the marketplaces.
6. Treating coworkers, customers and competitors with respect and fairness, demonstrating economic initiative and practicing justice.
7. Bringing integrity and excellence to public service and community responsibilities seeking the common good, respecting human life, and promoting human dignity.
8. Providing leadership in unions, community groups, professional associations, and political organizations at a time of rising cynicism and indifference.[49]

Many of these ideas are being put into practice in parishes around the country. For example, St. Martha's Parish in Akron, Ohio, has eighteen Vocation Reflection Groups organized by occupation, educators, lawyers, journalists, and so on. They meet monthly to reflect on their work and to discuss how they can apply their beliefs and values in their workplaces. The pastor helps the lay facilitators from each group plan their monthly meetings. The Sunday liturgies are also used to recognize the different professions and bless them during the liturgy when the readings focus on a specific profession.[50]

God is at work in the world lifting up witnesses and prophets of God's covenant community, a community of justice and peace. They are, for example, the members of Esperanza's small Christian community in Waukegan who climb the buses and demonstrate for justice for immigrant workers, or the parishioners at St. Martha's who discuss how they live their Christian values as citizens and in the marketplace. God is inviting all to hear the call to build a community of peace and justice. God is inviting all to participate, economically, politically, and socially in the resources of creation and human community.

One of the more complex questions is how Catholics should participate in political life, both as voters and politicians, especially when social policy is not in accord with the Catholic moral tradition. However, as members of our family and our community we are called to participate in society as citizens, workers, and as Christians. Through our jobs, our parenting, through our political participation we must always seek to serve the needs of the poor and vulnerable and work to create a society that respects the dignity of every life and more closely reflects the compassion, justice, and peace of the reign of God.

Prayer for Community

Embracing God,
We praise you for the communities of life which sustain us:
creation, family, church, and the community of all people.
May we learn from your Son Jesus to love our neighbors more deeply,
so that we may continue your work of creating a community
of justice and peace in our world.
May that same love of neighbor fill us with creative energy to
overcome the obstacles of intolerance and indifference and to
build inclusive communities in our neighborhoods, nations,
and among all your children.
Amen.[51]

Discussion Questions

1. Why did the prophets of the Hebrew Scriptures speak out against the growing power and wealth of King Solomon?
2. The creative energy of the prophet is to call the community to a new vision of reality. Who are the prophets of our time? Describe their new vision of reality.
3. Discuss the implication of these statements from *Faithful Citizenship*:
   a. the church is involved in the political process but is not partisan, and
   b. the church is principled but not ideological.
4. "Basic justice demands the establishment of minimum levels of participation in the life of the human community for all persons." Cite examples of how this principle is violated in church and society.

5

Option for the Poor

Donna Ecker was a model Catholic suburban parishioner. She was a lector, active in a Bible study group and involved in the family ministry program. Despite her involvement, Donna sensed there was something more she could be doing. "I felt there was someplace else that I had to be that I hadn't gotten to yet."

In response to that yearning, she volunteered at Bethany House, a Catholic Worker home for homeless women and children—including many victims of domestic violence. By the end of the second day she realized that this was "where I needed to be."[1]

That was eighteen years ago. Since then Donna has been the full-time, unpaid co-director of Bethany House—a home that provides food, clothing, and temporary housing for women and children who suffer from unemployment, substance addiction, domestic abuse, and many other problems. "What we're trying to do here is create an atmosphere where everyone who comes here feels cared for and supported." The compassion is the one thing that makes Bethany House work: the compassion of the staff and volunteers, compassion for the residents. The eight-bed home is run with volunteer, around-the-clock, unpaid help. In the Catholic Worker tradition, Bethany House is supported only by donations and not by any government funding. The house operates solely on private donations from individuals and parish tithing committees. Food and donations come in month by month, trusting that "God will provide."

With the decision to work for no pay, Donna and her husband Tom, who is a permanent deacon, had to simplify their lives. Tom, who fully supports and works with Donna, explained: "We don't live the high life or fast life. But I don't feel that we gave up anything." The Eckers have made an option for the poor, an option that is rich in human rewards. Donna believes that Bethany House has made her rich in ways that can't be measured. The "assets" in her bank account include the many lives she has been able to touch and the little moments of joy that her guests experience in her presence. Sometimes, just having a birthday party for a guest who has never had a birthday party brings a deep joy.

In living out her option for the poor Donna is supported by her spouse and by a community of prayer. Tom and Donna minister as a married couple, and Donna credits Tom for sustaining her ministry. "There's no way this could have happened if he was not as supportive as he is." Tom has recently retired and is happy to be able to spend more time at Bethany House. He assists in many ways, including leading weekly prayer services. Donna sought out a community of prayerful women to be part of her spiritual and moral support, which led her to become a lay associate of the Sisters of Mercy. Donna explained that the Mercy Sisters offer more than spiritual support in that some members also volunteer at the house. In December 2002 Donna was honored with the Mercy Action Cunningham Award, a national award along with a five thousand dollar donation to Bethany House. The Sisters of Mercy offer their prayers, their time, and their financial support.

Under Donna's guidance, Bethany House has served over twelve hundred people in the last ten years. Besides providing a safe place to sleep and eat for a few months, Donna and the staff give unconditional love. One graduate of Bethany House, Philomena Allen, said, "That to me was a basic need at that time because I'd never had it before." Donna explained the importance of compassion for her guests at an evening of reflection that she led for the Social Ministry Committee of St. Mary's Church, one of the parishes that support Bethany House. She said that the guests are "blown away" by the unconditional love of the volunteers. Some of the guests, as Philomena pointed out, never received that kind of love before, even from their own families, and when it is offered by the staff and the volunteers, the guests are sometimes surprised and shocked. Receiving such unconditional love is part of the healing process and the road to recovery for many women.

Donna said that working with homeless women and children for eighteen years has changed her views about homelessness and success. In the beginning she thought homelessness would be eradicated by society in a few years, but she is far less optimistic now. These days, she takes delight in smaller successes. For some residents, success might mean three months of living free from drug use, while for others it might mean emotionally reconnecting with their children.

"What brings me back every day is the women and children. Watching them in their struggles to do better, to love their children, to get on their feet. It takes a lot of courage and tenacity. . . . That's something a lot of people don't get to see. . . . Why wouldn't I come back?" asks Donna Ecker.

An Ancient yet New Teaching

Although God's option for the poor is well established in the biblical record, the phrase "option for the poor" has appeared only recently in the lexicon of Catholic social teaching. This concept was given the clearest articulation by the church of Latin America, especially by the theological movement known as liberation theology.

The "preferential option for the poor" is a central theme in both the Hebrew and Christian scriptures. The foundational event in the history of the Hebrew community was God's response to the cries of the oppressed in Egypt: "I have heard the cry of my people and I see how they are being oppressed" (Ex 3:9). God instructs Moses, "Go to Pharaoh and tell him that Yahweh says, 'Let my people go'" (Ex 8:1). This event reveals what kind of God Yahweh is and what kind of people Israel is to become. As Jorge Pixley notes "the correct referent [for God] is always that God who redeemed Israel from slavery in Egypt. Any god who is not the savior of the poor and oppressed cannot be the true God of Israel." He continues in language that could be applied to today's use of religion to justify slavery and oppression: "A god who legitimates the oppression of peasants, no matter how solemn its cult, is not the true God of Israel, for the true God is only that One who hears the cries of the oppressed and frees them from their oppressors."[2]

The Exodus experience of God liberating the oppressed is foundational to biblical faith. The very identity of Israel as a people was that of a community liberated from slavery and oppression by Yahweh (Dt 26:6–9): "This awareness of being a poor and oppressed people who struggle for life with the help of Yahweh is basic. Yahweh is the true God who hears the cries of those who are oppressed and Israel is the people of Yahweh that depends on Yahweh for the success of its struggles for liberation."[3]

By Yahweh's power and intervention, Moses did indeed lead the Hebrew slaves of Pharaoh out of their captivity, through a time of testing in the desert, and into a new land of their own. For a few hundred years the covenantal vision of liberation, equality, and participation was partially implemented in the economic arrangements and the political and social structures of Israel. But before long greed, injustice, and oppression became visible in the community. Now the oppressor was not the Egyptian Pharaoh but those who had emerged from the Hebrew community as the new elite, with power and resources. Through the prophets, God protested against the social injustices, the bribery, and the arrogance of the rich (see Am 2:6, 4:1, 5:12; Is 3:14–15, 10:1–2; Jer 22:3). Through the Torah, the law of the land, God called for protection and justice for the poor, the indebted, the widows, the resident foreigners, the domestic and wild animals, and even the Earth itself (Lev 19:33, 25:10–16; Ex 15:12–15, 22:21; Deut 23:12, 25:4).

The Hebrew Scriptures contain a consistent and insistent message that God watches over the poor, especially widows and orphans. The people of Israel were to imitate God by treating the aliens, widows, and orphans as God had treated them (Ex 22:20–22). Many of the psalms call out to the Lord from foreign lands where they were an oppressed people. They proclaim God as a "stronghold for the oppressed" (Ps 9:9).

The prophets of Israel were powerful champions of the poor. "According to the prophets of Israel, the law of justice stands to serve all, middle-class merchant and farmer as well as the widow, orphan, and alien (1 Kings)."[4] The Hebrew Scriptures regarded the poor as favored by God because they were victims of injustice. The Hebrew faith community believed that God intervened on behalf of the poor. "It is Yahweh who makes a man poor or rich, who brings down or raises up, who lifts up the weak from the dust and raises the poor from the ash heap" (1 Sam 2:7–8).

God's identification with the poor and the outcast is clearly evident in the Christian Scriptures when God chooses a poor, young, single woman to be the bearer of the Christ child. The message and action of Jesus continues the tradition of social justice proclaimed in the Hebrew Scriptures. Jesus stands on the shoulders of the prophets and the psalmists who proclaim God's love for the poor in many words and actions:

- Jesus came to bring good news to the poor, to proclaim liberty to captives (Lk 4:18–21).
- Jesus proclaimed that the poor and the hungry are blessed by God (Lk 6:20–21).
- Jesus has a special concern for the rejected and outcasts of society, including lepers, prostitutes, tax collectors, and those disturbed in mind and spirit.
- Jesus did not endorse the idea that prosperity was a sign of God's favor, but spoke out on the dangers of riches (Mt 6:19, 24, 13:22, 19:24; Lk 6:24, 12:20, 16:22–23).
- Jesus reversed Cain's question as he teaches that not only are we our brother and sister's keepers, but that we also are to love our enemies.

- Jesus identified with the poor and neglected: "Whatever you did to the least of these brethren, you did unto me" (Mt 25:40).
- He taught that the rich man is condemned, not only for abusing the poor man, but for ignoring him.
- Jesus taught that women are not second-class members of the human family; they are examples of loyal and valued disciples and, even in the case of Mary Magdalen, an apostle to the apostles.
- Children were not pushed aside by Jesus but were welcomed and set up as examples of open and trusting discipleship.
- Those ostracized because of illness are offered healing and inclusion in the community.
- Social pariahs like tax collectors of the colonizing Roman government and prostitutes are given a privileged place among his followers.
- In the end, Jesus was rejected and put to death by the authorities because they, rightly, perceived that his message was undermining their power.
- The followers of Jesus took seriously his word to care for the poor and the alienated.
- James chided his community when they offered only kind words to the poor with no action to lift a hand in help.
- Luke describes the Christian community in Jerusalem as a place where "there was no needy person among them, for those who owned property or houses would sell them, bring the proceeds of the sale, and put them at the feet of the apostles, and they distributed to each according to need" (Acts 4:34–35).
- The early Christian community took seriously the needs of the widows in their community, who had no other means of support. The Acts of the Apostles (6:1–7) tells us that food was distributed every day to the widows. But inequalities crept into the distribution, so the Greek-speaking widows needed advocates to receive the support they deserved. The community appointed Greek-speaking "ministers" to distribute the food to their needy sisters.[5]

Jesus was a creative religious genius. Steeped in the biblical and religious tradition of his faith community, he gave a personal interpretation of the tradition that often challenged the orthodox teaching of the religious leaders. His central conviction was God's love of the poor. From this belief Jesus taught that care of the poor takes precedence over the law and every form of tradition. For this reason, he rejected the religious leaders' obsession with proper ritual. It was more important to purify the heart than to perform ritual washings before eating. In keeping with the teaching of the prophets he taught that sharing one's bread with the poor was more important than fasting. In short, the law of God is summarized in love of God and love of neighbor.

Jesus' freedom from ritualism and his capacity to reach out to each people in need attracted many followers, and he followed up his words with actions: "He taught with authority" in comparison with other religious leaders. People saw in Jesus the values of God's reign and they were pulled into this vision, experiencing the freedom that he offered. He removed from his disciples the yoke of suffocating religious traditions, social conventions, and the barriers of fear by focusing on what was truly important: the double commandment to love God and to love the neighbor. Those who live in the Spirit of Jesus live in this radical freedom.[6] All are invited to this way of living. Our tradition is rich with men and women who have lived this radical freedom and who are living it today.

Martin de Porres

Born out of wedlock in Lima, Peru, to a Spanish knight and a black, freed slave named Ana, Martin de Porres started out on the wrong side of the tracks. Because he inherited his mother's features and complexion, his father did not acknowledge his mulatto child until many years later. At his baptism, he was registered as the "son of an unknown father" and was considered illegitimate. This standing placed him at considerable social and economic disadvantage in sixteenth-century Lima. Martin was apprenticed to a barber, a profession that in those days included hair-cutting as well as surgical and medical skills. Martin excelled in these skills and at the age of fifteen applied for the lowliest position as a *donado* or lay helper at a Dominican monastery. His work included sweeping the cloister and cleaning latrines. When the brothers recognized his medical skills, he was put in charge of the monastery infirmary.

Martin did not confine his healing ministry to the Dominican community. He cared for the sick and injured, especially the wretched poor who lived in the streets of Lima. Martin was apt to carry them back to his cell and lay them in his own bed. Although his superior told Martin not to bring the sick into the monastery, he did not follow those orders and, when confronted again, Martin answered by saying, "Forgive my mistake, and please be kind enough to instruct me. I did not know that the precept of obedience took precedence over that of charity." After that humble response, Martin was given liberty to act according to his own instincts.

"Martin's charity was poured out on all those who were counted as nothing—Indians, the poor, the sick. He had a special ministry to African slaves, to whom he would deliver gifts of food and drink, healing their sick, consoling them in their miserable bondage."[7] Martin died on November 3, 1639, when he was sixty years old. Pope John XXIII canonized him in 1962 and named him the patron saint of race relations and those who work for social justice. Here was a simple man who lived the option for the poor in the fifteenth century.

Latin American Roots of the Option for the Poor

In 1968 the bishops of Latin America met in Medellín, Colombia, to examine the situation in their countries in light of the new approaches of the Second Vatican Council. The bishops came face to face with the growing poverty in Latin America and decided to shift their support to the poor: "It is necessary that small basic communities be developed in order to establish a balance with minority groups, which are the groups in power. . . . The church—the people of God—will lend its support to the downtrodden of every social class so that they might come to know their rights and how to make use of them."[8]

With this decision, the bishops confirmed a new direction for the church in Latin America. The Medellín documents "provided legitimation, inspiration, and pastoral plans for a continent-wide preferential option for the poor, encouraging those who were already engaged in the struggle and exhorting the entire church, both rich and poor, to become involved."[9]

While many Christians identified with the poor and tried to reshape their societies, others in the church and society in Latin America attacked this new identification with the poor. "Some members of the upper classes, convinced that the church had been infiltrated by Marxists and furious at what they perceived to be the treason of an old ally, lashed out at progressive elements in the church."[10] This lashing out led to the persecution and martyrdom of Latin American Christians, beginning in the late 1960s through the present. This persecution against fellow Christians was unprecedented in their continent. Many Christians were singled out as dangerous subversives who paid with their lives for their adherence to the gospel. Archbishop Dom Helder Camara of northeastern Brazil, one of those accused, ironically quipped: "When I feed the poor they call me a 'saint.' When I ask 'why' the poor are hungry, they called me a 'Communist.'" While in the United States in 1976 for the Eucharistic Congress in Philadelphia, he added, "I don't need communism, I have the gospel."

The Latin American bishops reaffirmed the centrality of social reform and the church's preferential option for the poor in their meetings at Puebla, Mexico in 1979 and in Aparecida, Brazil in 2007[11] Tension remains high in the Latin American church regarding social reform, the role of the church in society, and how the church is to live out its preferential option for the poor. Not surprisingly, a similar resistance is at work in the United States. Throughout its forty-year history the Catholic Campaign for Human Development has been attacked again and again for supporting the empowerment of the poor through community organizations and economic development.

(CH)
attacked
from/by
where whom

Liberation Theologian: Gustavo Gutiérrez

Peruvian theologian Gustavo Gutiérrez points out that while the term "preferential option for the poor" comes from the Latin American church, "the content, the underlying intuition, is entirely biblical. Liberation theology tries to deepen our understanding of this core biblical conviction." According to Gutiérrez the preferential option for the poor "has gradually become a central tenet of the church's teaching." Father Gutiérrez examines each word in this controversial phrase:

[Poverty] The term *poverty* refers to the real poor. This is not a preferential option for the spiritually poor. After all, such an option would be very easy, if for no other reason that there are so few of them! The spiritually poor are the saints! The poverty to which the option refers is material poverty. Material poverty means premature and unjust death. The poor person is someone who is treated as a non-person, someone who is considered insignificant from an economic, political, and cultural point of view. The poor count as statistics; they are the nameless. But even though the poor remain insignificant within society, they are never insignificant before God.

[Preferential] God's love has two dimensions, the universal and the particular; and while there is a tension between the two, there is no contradiction. God's love excludes no one. Nevertheless, God demonstrates a special predilection toward those who have been excluded from the banquet of life.

[Option] In some ways, option is perhaps the weakest word in the phrase. In English, the word merely connotes a choice between two things. In Spanish, however, it evokes the sense of commitment (*compromise*). The option for the poor is not optional, but is incumbent upon every Christian. It is not something that a Christian can either take or leave. As understood by Medellín, the option for the poor is twofold: it involves standing in solidarity *with* the poor, but it also entails a stance *against* inhumane poverty.[12]

This twofold stance of being against inhumane poverty and standing in solidarity with the poor is often filled with conflict. Such a stance is resisted by those who benefit from the present unjust and oppressive order. This solidarity with the poor unfortunately comes at a great price, including the price of martyrdom, for some.

Maura, Ita, Dorothy, and Jean

The history of the church is written in the blood of martyrs. But these four women represented a different kind of martyrdom, increasingly common in our time. Their murderers dared to call themselves Christian, indeed defenders of Christian values. And they died not simply clinging to the true faith but for clinging, like Jesus, to the poor.[13]

The "four women" Robert Ellsberg refers to are the four American women who were murdered in El Salvador in 1980: Maura Clarke and Ita Ford, two Maryknoll Sisters; Dorothy Kazel, an Ursuline Sister; and Jean Donovan, a lay missionary from Cleveland. Maura and Ita had spent many years as missionaries in Nicaragua and Chile. Sister Dorothy Kazel had worked the longest in El Salvador. Jean Donovan, at twenty-seven, was the youngest of the four.

Jean, who came from a background of privilege, had earned a degree in business. She contemplated the possibility of marriage and a lucrative career. The Donovan family had asked Jean to come home when the situation became more dangerous in El Salvador, and especially after the assassination of Archbishop Oscar Romero while he had been celebrating mass just nine months earlier. Two weeks before her death, Jean wrote of her decision to stay in El Salvador: "Several times I have decided to leave—I almost could except for the children, the poor bruised victims of adult lunacy. Who would care for them? Whose heart would be so staunch as to favor the reasonable thing in a sea of their tears and loneliness? Not mine, dear, not mine."[14]

Their work to support the church of El Salvador involved ministering to the needs of the refugees caused by the civil war. They delivered supplies and comforted terrified religious leaders and catechists in the rural areas. "The women's work confronted them with scenes from hell." They saw villages where the Salvadoran Army had committed massacres and then refused to allow the survivors to bury the dead. Sister Maura wrote, "The other day, passing a small lake in the jeep I saw a buzzard standing on top of a floating body. We did nothing but pray and feel." Each of these women had made a preferential option for the poor, "believing that the effective witness to the gospel was inseparable from the witness to life and solidarity with the oppressed. In El Salvador this was enough to label one a subversive."[15]

These four saw the hope and the spirit of the El Salvadoran people, even in those horrendous times. They had a reason for living, for sacrificing, and for dying. Sister Ita Ford captured something of the spirit of the people in a letter she wrote to her niece.

> This is a terrible time in El Salvador for youth. A lot of idealism and commitment are getting snuffed out here and now. The reasons why so many people are being killed are quite complicated, yet there are some clear, simple strands. One is that people have found a meaning to life, to sacrifice, struggle, and even to die. And whether their life spans sixteen years, sixty or ninety, for them their life has had a purpose. In many ways, there are fortunate people.
>
> Brooklyn is not passing through the drama of El Salvador, but some things hold true wherever one is, and at whatever age. What I'm saying is that I hope you can come to find that which gives life a deep meaning for you, something that energizes you, enthuses you, enables you to keep moving ahead.[16]

Ita knew the risk they faced by keeping their commitment to the poor. On the night before their death, she quoted their deceased and much-loved Archbishop Romero. "One who is committed to the poor must risk the same fate as the poor. And in El Salvador we know what the fate of the poor signifies: to disappear, to be tortured, to be captive, and to be found dead."[17]

On December 2, 1980, Dorothy and Jean went to the airport to pick up Maura and Ita, who were returning from a meeting in Nicaragua. The four never made it home. Two days later a few peasants alerted church leaders and led them to the shallow grave in a cow pasture. Two had been raped and each shot in the head at close range.

The death of the four women had an enormous effect on the North American church. It helped to galvanize opposition to U.S. funding for the Salvadoran government. Their deaths also brought a defensive backlash by those who defended the U.S. policy in Central America. One American official shot back that "the nuns were not just nuns, the nuns were also political activists . . . on behalf of the Frente [the insurgents]."[18] In truth, the women were not "political activists on behalf of the Frente, except that standing with the poor put one in opposition to those who defended the current political oppression: "You say you don't want anything to happen to me. I'd prefer it that way myself—but I don't see that we have control over the forces of madness, and if you choose to enter into other peoples' suffering, or love others, you at least have to consent in some way to the possible consequences."[19]

The Option for the Poor Articulated in Catholic Social Teaching

In 1971, writing three years after Medellín, Pope Paul VI picked up the language of the Latin American bishops in his apostolic letter *Octogesima Adveniens* (*A Call to Action*) when he said: "[I]n teaching us charity, the Gospel instructs us in the preferential respect due to the poor and the special situation they have in society: the more fortunate should renounce some of their rights so as to place their goods more generously at the service of others" (23).

The U.S. bishops agreed with their counterparts to the south that we must make an option for the poor. In 1986 in their pastoral letter on the economy, *Economic Justice for All*, they taught:

> Such perspectives provide a basis today for what is called the "pref-erential option for the poor." Though in the Gospels and the New Testament as a whole the offer of salvation is extended to all peo-ples, Jesus takes the side of those most in need, physically and spiri-tually. The example of Jesus poses a number of challenges to the contemporary Church.

- It imposes a prophetic mandate to speak for those who have no one to speak for them, to be a defender of the defenseless, who in biblical terms are the poor.
- It also demands a compassionate vision that enables the Church to see things from the side of the poor and powerless, and to assess lifestyle, policies, and social institutions in terms of their impact on the poor.
- It summons the Church also to be an instrument in assisting people to experience the liberating power of God in their lives, so that they may respond to the Gospel in freedom and dignity.
- Finally, and most radically, it calls for an emptying of self, both individually and corporately, that allows the Church to experience the power of God in the midst of poverty and powerlessness.[20]

Again and again the U.S. bishops returned to the central theme of "option for the poor" in their letter on the economy:

- Decisions must be judged in light of what they do *for* the poor, what they do *to* the poor, and what they enable the poor to do *for themselves* (24).
- *The obligation to provide justice for all means that the poor have the single most urgent claim on the conscience of the nation* (86).
- As individuals and as a nation, therefore, we are called to make a fundamental "option for the poor" (87).

The bishops believe that this option for the poor implies "the obligation to evaluate social and economic activity from the viewpoint of the poor and the powerless." This obligation "arises from the radical command to love one's neighbor as one's self. . . . The prime purpose of this special commitment to the poor is to enable them to become active participants in the life of society. It is to enable *all* persons to share in and contribute to the common good" (88).

The needs of the poor are considered "the highest priority":

The fulfillment of the basic needs of the poor is of the highest priority. Personal decisions, policies of private and public bodies, and power relationships must all be evaluated by their effects on those who lack the minimum necessities of nutrition, housing, education, and health care. In particular, this principle recognizes that meeting fundamental human needs must come before the fulfillment of desires for luxury consumer goods, for profits not conducive to the common good, and for unnecessary military hardware (90).

The U.S. bishops restated the option for the poor and claimed it was the litmus test for the justice of the community. "At a time when the rich are getting richer and the poor are getting poorer, we insist the moral test of our society is how we treat and care for the weakest among us." Later in the document the bishops state unambiguously that "Our parish communities are measured by how they serve 'the least of these' in our parish and beyond its boundaries—the hungry, the homeless, the sick, those in prison, the stranger."[21]

Pope John Paul II has echoed the preferential option for the poor in his writing and speaking. He has used the phrase "preferential love of the poor" and has interpreted the last one hundred years of Catholic social teaching as evidence of the church's option for the poor even before this phrase was coined. Later Pope John Paul II characterized the preferential option for the poor as a "call to have a special openness with the small and the weak, those who suffer and weep, those that are humiliated and left on the margin of society, so as to help them with their dignity as human persons and children of God."[22]

Option for the Poor by the Poor

When we speak of an option for the poor we usually mean a choice freely made by the non-poor. It is a choice that can be made by individuals, by the local faith community, or even by the continent-wide church, as in the case of Latin America. When Christians become aware that they are relatively wealthy and privileged, they can decide to relinquish some of their privilege and wealth to identify with those who do not have wealth and privilege.

The poor can also make an option for the poor: a choice to be in solidarity with other underprivileged people rather than trying to exploit them and join the aspirations of the materialistic culture. In Rochester, New York, I witnessed a small example of how the working poor give expression to their option for the poor.

One September afternoon three buses of immigrant workers from Chicago stopped in the parking lot of the Church of the Nativity in Brockport, a town in the heart of the apple orchards of western New York.

The 142 riders were part of the Immigrant Workers' Freedom Ride, which was bringing immigrant workers and their supporters from nine major cities to Washington D.C. and New York City to demonstrate and lobby for more humane and just policies toward immigrant workers. The riders were immigrant workers who had found jobs as cleaners in the hotel industry and entry-level, low-income jobs in retail chain stores such as Walmart and Target. Many of the riders were originally from Latin America. As the rally in the parking lot unfolded, a group of farm workers arrived with their crew leader, driving their van straight from the fields. They had not cleaned up or put on their good clothes. As they greeted each other through the chants, waving flags, and speeches, the riders experienced a powerful sense of solidarity. The immigrant workers from Chicago and the immigrant workers from Brockport looked into each others' eyes and shared their common struggle. The workers from Chicago spontaneously took up a collection for their fellow workers in upstate New York. They shared of the little they had with those who were newer immigrants. The $150 collected was not as important as the powerful message this gave to all of us. There is solidarity in the struggle, and the poor often shame us by their generosity.

A Religious and Political Option

For Christians, the option for the poor is a deeply religious choice with serious political ramifications. The *religious* foundations sustain the option, while the *political* implications are more controversial and conflictual. The option for the poor presupposes that one has become aware that in society as a whole and in most organizations people "at the top" have opportunities and power and those "at the bottom" have little or no power and few opportunities. "To make an option for the poor is to choose to disengage from serving the interests of the powerful and instead to take the side of those who are relatively powerless."[23]

The option for the poor links the religious insight of the Judeo-Christian tradition (that God has made an option for the poor) with the political arena as a space where this option can become a reality. This linkage between faith and politics contradicts the liberal Western tradition that religion is to be relegated to the private, personal spheres of individual and family affairs. The option for the poor says that Christianity has direct political implications. (The word "political" in this context does not refer to political parties, but to how a society organizes its political power.) Choosing an option for the poor means that we acknowledge that our faith has political implications. Even those who try to privatize religion and keep it out of the public arena are not really eliminating religion's political implications; instead, they are making an option to continue the current arrangement of power. The option for the poor teaches that we cannot be neutral. Being neutral means opting for the current realities, which, from the perspective of the poor, are unjust.

Neutral

Father Donal Dorr believes that the option for the poor involves an experiential aspect and a political aspect, and that both are important. The experiential dimension means a deliberate, personal choice to enter to some degree into the world of the powerless. It means to share in a significant way their experience of poverty, alienation, or mistreatment. This stance is rooted in compassion, which is a willingness to suffer with those who are on the margins of circles of wealth and power: "By entering the world of deprived people one begins to experience not only their pain and struggle but also their hopes and their joys."[24]

Making an option for the poor breaks through the "them" and "us" attitude toward the poor. Rather, we begin to identify with the poor in our very lifestyle and attitudes. The poor are not objects of sympathy or paternalistic help. Rather, we are one in solidarity, working to change society and doing it in a way that values and needs everyone's gifts.

Our option must also be accepted by the poor. It is not in my power to be fully in solidarity with a particular group of marginal people. All I can do is *offer* to be in solidarity with them. This offer is not made in words, but in the attitude with which we see the group and relate to them. In response, the marginal ones may choose to offer me the gift of their solidarity, which takes time. It is up to the poor to accept our option for them.

up to the poor to accept our opt"

A second aspect of our option for the poor is its *political* dimension, meaning the willingness to take action to overcome systemic injustice. Dorr suggests four steps in this process of taking action:

1. Careful analysis of the situation to understand the root causes of injustice.
2. Avoiding collusion with those groups or individuals benefiting from the current system. This may mean not accepting funding from certain sources.
3. Planning effective challenges to the unjust order.
4. Designing realistic alternatives.[25]

For example, in solidarity with those who work in sweatshops, we can:

1. Analyze the situation to understand the reasons for sweatshop exploitation.
2. Join boycotts of the most notorious sweatshop products.
3. Make our voices known to the corporate leadership and government leaders, challenging current practices.
4. Support Third World and local alternatives to sweatshop clothing.

Every Christian can make an option for the poor, in decisions large and small.

Rhetoric or Reality?

The pope, the bishops, and the rest of the church can proclaim that the church has "opted for the poor" or is "a church of the poor," but those words do not make it a reality. One pastoral leader, Denis Murphy, who lives in Manila and works with the Urban Poor Associates, believes that those phrases "have the appeal of a vision, though the realization of such an abstract vision seems impossible to anyone who considers it seriously."[26]

Although he is writing about the Philippines, the question applies to the whole church. He explains the reason for his sanguine remarks:

There was a time during the years 1960 to 1980 when people believed Philippine society could accept a real church of the poor, that is, a church where the poor had pride of place, and social change was expected to come from the organized movements of the poor. It was in keeping with the national resistance to the tyranny of martial law. But now times are different.[27]

Most parishes in Manila are characterized by a mix of well-off people and poor people, and the priests usually spend most of their time with the well-off parishioners. By tradition, lifestyle, education, and many other cultural bonds that are centuries old, the church has been and still is linked to the upper classes. According to Murphy, "Few priests have made any serious study of the social and religious problems of the poor, and most share the anti-poor prejudices of the upper classes."

The seminarians seem to follow that linkage to the upper classes. When Murphy asked a class at the major seminary about the church's commitment to become the church of the poor, of imitating the poor Christ, taking up his cross and finding Christ in the suffering poor, the seminarians were honest enough to say that those words no longer meant very much. Murphy claims that "a church of the poor has a chance when large sectors of the society are struggling for change and social justice. It has little chance in a society committed to the values of the marketplace."[28]

Even as Denis Murphy was lamenting the situation in the Philippines, he found reasons to be hopeful. Four parishes with their priests from Quezon City held a demonstration at the mayor's office asking the mayor's help in getting government land for the poor. At first, the mayor resisted but the parishioners would not leave. Eventually, he promised to help twenty thousand families get land. The people broke into song and dance to celebrate their achievement. Actions such as this align the church with the poor and not only with the interests of the well-off. Murphy concludes, "Such priests and poor people are enough to begin with. As the founder of the Highlander movement, Myles Horton, said, 'We make the road by walking.'"[29]

Catholic Campaign for Human Development

Throughout history the church has made an option for the poor, a commitment to the poor. This option for the poor is seen in the works of charity of our parishes, the great work of religious orders in serving the poor, in the programs of Catholic Charities and Catholic Relief Services. The Catholic Church also funds programs that help the poor and powerless to speak for themselves and to organize themselves to bring about change in their communities. This effort is the Catholic Campaign for Human Development (CCHD), an initiative that really takes the option for the poor to heart. Here are some examples of groups that receive CCHD support.

Farm Worker Pesticide Project (FWPP)

When female farm workers in Washington state spend long hours in orchards and fields without adequate gear to protect them from pesticides, their health—and for pregnant workers, that of their unborn children—can be endangered. Farm workers who experience nausea, vomiting, headaches, and burning eyes are trying to improve worker conditions through the Farm Worker Pesticide

Project of southeast Washington. The FWPP, a group newly funded by CCHD, trains farm workers as advocates, publishes reports, and empowers workers to test pesticide levels at work and in homes where dangerous residue has also been found. Thanks to FWPP, the lives of farm workers, their families, and their unborn children, are seeing greater attention.

Faith and Action for Strength Together (FAST)

To address the growing problem of a lack of affordable housing for low- and middle-income persons in Pinellas County, Florida, this group of 34 churches prayed, organized, and invited public officials to meetings where 2,500 members were gathered to challenge those officials to support policies that benefit poor people. Their efforts resulted in an affordable housing trust fund that directed $19 million toward housing for low-income persons, and new legislation to guarantee development of 3,000 units over the next three years for families with incomes under $42,000 a year. One thousand units have already been built.[30]

CCHD and the Option for the Poor

Programs sponsored by the CCHD encourage the poor themselves to be their own advocates, which recognizes the dignity and gifts of the poor to be leaders themselves and not simply dependent on the leadership of others. Groups receiving grants from the CCHD must show that 50 percent of their board or leadership team is composed of low-income people, a distinctive feature of the CCHD. A second requirement is that the group or community organization must be addressing systemic change, for example, establishing a housing trust fund in Pinellas County, Florida. This is a systemic change that will help many people.[31]

The Catholic Church has made a strong option for the poor through CCHD-funded programs, but an option for the poor cannot be satisfied by an initiative like CCHD alone, even if it is successful. It must be taken up by every Christian and every faith community.

Farmworkers and Immigrants

Another example of the church's option for the poor is in its commitment to seek justice for farmworkers and immigrants—another controversial issue. Each year thousands of migrant workers move into upstate New York to work in the apple orchards and vegetable farms. Some are undocumented and fearful of Immigration and Customs Enforcement patrols. While there was still some snow on the ground in early Spring, the JustFaith group from St. Mary's and Blessed Sacrament parishes visited migrant camps near Elba, New York—about an hour west of Rochester. These "muck" farms are great for growing onions. We entered a run-down mobile home filled with well-worn furniture and beds where eleven men were living. The men were caught in limbo. They had decided to stay over through the winter rather than return to Mexico or Central America because they might not be able to get back into the United States to work. Afraid to go out of their ten by forty foot trailer home into the nearby towns because of immigration raids, they were waiting for the snow to melt so they could start planting onions. We shared a meal with them and tried to communicate in our halting Spanish or through our interpreter.

In a second camp six men were living in a dingy cinder-block house whose walls and ceiling were covered with years of grease and dirt from cooking. After we had asked all of our questions, we asked the farmworkers if they had any questions for us. One of the young men, Geraldo, looked in our eyes and asked, "Do you ever think of us?" We wanted to say "yes," but the truth is, they are hidden from us as are most of the working poor. I think he was asking us to remember him and the others after we left the camp. When I got home, I noticed that the bag of onions in our pantry had come from Elba, New York.

Geraldo's question lingered in Bill's mind and heart after that visit. One of the parishioners, Bill has since become active with Rural and Migrant Ministry, an interfaith program that educates and advocates on behalf of farmworkers. Geraldo also has been active trying to defend the rights of farmworkers in New York State. He has traveled to Albany to speak with legislators in support of the Fair Labor Practices Act, which would give agricultural workers some of the rights enjoyed by other workers, such as the right to a day of rest, overtime pay, workers' compensation, and the right to collective bargaining. The bill has passed the Assembly but has not passed the Senate after many years of lobbying, rallies, marches, and petitions. The New York State Catholic Conference brought the growers, the Farm Bureau, the workers, and their advocates together to work out a compromise, but the bill has not yet been approved by the Senate. Of course, the issues in New York State are multiplied by forty-nine other states in the country.

The Pew Hispanic Center estimates that at least twelve million un-documented immigrants live and work in the United States today.[32] The motivations pushing immigrants to risk unauthorized entry into America are varied, but most come with the hope of reuniting with family members already here or to find work that will provide support for their family back home. The existing immigration system has resulted in a growing number of persons in this country in an unauthorized capacity, living in the shadows as they toil in jobs that would otherwise go unfilled. The Catholic Church believes that current immigration laws and policies have often led to the undermining of immigrants' human dignity and have kept families apart. It should be no surprise that the U.S. Catholic bishops are calling for comprehensive immigration reform. The Catholic Church has a history of being a church of immigrants.

The U.S. bishops have taken the gospel teachings and the teachings of the popes and applied it to the immigration reality in the United States. In January 2003 the U.S. bishops issued the pastoral letter *Strangers No Longer: Together on the Journey of Hope* to articulate the five principles that govern how the church responds to public policy proposals relating to immigration.

1.   *Persons have the right to find opportunities in their homeland.* This principle states that a person has a right *not* to migrate. In other words, economic, social, and political conditions in their homeland should provide an opportunity for a person to work and support his or her family in dignity and safety. In public policy terms, efforts should be made to address global economic inequities through just trade practices, economic development, and debt relief. Peacemaking efforts should be advanced to end conflicts that force persons to flee their homes.

2.   *Persons have the right to migrate to support themselves and their families.* When persons are unable to find work and support themselves and their families, they have a right to migrate to other countries to work. This right is not absolute, as stated by Pope John XXIII, when he said that this right to emigrate applies when "there are just reasons for it." In the current condition of the world, in which global poverty is rampant and political unrest has resulted in wars and persecution, migrants forced to leave their homes out of necessity and seek to survive and support their families must be given special consideration.

3.   *Sovereign nations have a right to control their borders.* The church recognizes the right of the sovereign to protect and control its borders in the service of the common good of its citizens. However, this is not an absolute right. Na-

tions also have an obligation to the universal common good, as articulated by Pope John XXIII in *Pacem in Terris*, and thus should seek to accommodate migration to the greatest extent possible. Powerful economic nations, such as the United States, have a higher obligation to serve the universal common good, according to Catholic social teaching. In the current global economic environment, in which labor demands in the United States attract foreign laborers, the United States should establish an immigration system that provides legal avenues for persons to enter the nation legally in a safe, orderly, and dignified manner to obtain jobs and reunite with family members.

4.   *Refugees and asylum seekers should be afforded protection.* Persons who flee their home countries because they fear persecution should be afforded safe haven and protection in another country. Conflict and political unrest in many parts of the world force persons to leave their homes for fear of death or harm. The United States should employ a refugee and asylum system that protects asylum seekers, refugees, and other forced migrants and offers them a haven from persecution.

5.   *The human rights and the human dignity of undocumented migrants should be respected.* Persons who enter a nation without proper authorization or who overstay their visas should be treated with respect and dignity. They should not be detained in deplorable conditions for lengthy periods of time, be shackled by their feet and hands, or abused in any manner. They should be afforded due process of the law and, if applicable, allowed to articulate a fear of return to their home before a qualified adjudicator. They should not be blamed for the social ills of a nation.[33]

From these five principles the bishops recommend three broad policies that are part of a nationwide advocacy campaign. Catholics are asked to sign postcards to send to their U.S. senators and members of Congress. The postcard petition reads:

Dear Senator :
    I am a concerned constituent and agree with the U.S. Catholic bishops that the U.S. immigration system is broken and is in need of repair. I ask that this year you support immigration reform legislation that
- keeps immigrant families together,
- adopts smart and humane enforcement policies, and
- ensures that immigrants without legal status register with the government and begin a path toward citizenship.
Our families and communities cannot wait![34]

The Catholic bishops are speaking out for comprehensive reform and urging the people in the pews to support this work for the good of the country and to address the needs of the poor on both sides of the border.

Elizabeth Ann Seton's Option for the Poor

Elizabeth Ann Seton made an option for the poor at a very young age and followed that commitment throughout her life (1774–1821). Her parents were well-connected Episcopalians in colonial New York. As a child she was nicknamed "the Protestant Sister of Charity" because of her great love of the poor. After her marriage to William Magee Seton, a successful merchant, she continued her work with the poor, becoming one of the founders of the Society for the Relief of Poor Widows and Small Children. But soon she became one of those "poor widows" herself.

When her husband lost his fortune, suffered ill health, and died, Elizabeth was widowed at age twenty-nine with five children to raise. She decided to join the Catholic Church despite the great opposition of her family, friends, and spiritual advisor. When she joined the Catholic Church she was almost completely ostracized by her family and friends. In 1809 Elizabeth and four companions started a religious community, the Sisters of Charity. They also started a school for poor children near Emmitsburg, Maryland, which was the beginning of the Catholic parochial school system in the United States.

Elizabeth trained teachers, wrote textbooks, translated French religious books, and wrote spiritual essays. This was the first religious community formed by Americans for Americans. In 1975 Pope Paul VI canonized her as the first American-born saint.[35] Our Catholic tradition is filled with like-minded men and women who have also made "an option for the poor."

How Do We Make an Option for the Poor?

The Catholic social tradition can become a living reality in the lives of the many saints among us who live out their commitment to the gospel. We are invited to join that living tradition. Here are some suggestions of small steps to take to move in the direction of solidarity with the poor.[36]

Connect with the poor. Michael asks for money for food as I come out of our Catholic Charities office. On my way to my car, I said I would buy him lunch at the nearby diner. He ordered two cheeseburgers and two orders of fries. When I asked if he could eat all of that, he assured me he would and even asked for some food for breakfast the next day. (I drew a line with the cheeseburgers!) As we waited for his food, I learned that he has emphysema and lives in a flophouse hotel. I gave him a little bit of my time and a meal. In the process we connected as two human beings. He was no longer a pesty beggar. He was Michael who lived near my office.

There are many ways to connect: visit folks in a nursing home who don't get any visitors, tutor a fifth-grader in an inner-city school, serve and eat lunch with the guests at a soup kitchen. Don't stay in the kitchen behind the protection of the pan of lasagna you are dishing out. Pull up a chair next to the guests to connect with them—if they are open to connecting with you.

Ask questions and search for answers. Face-to-face contact may stimulate questions and concerns. We may ask: Why are there so many people at the soup kitchen who are the working poor? Read about social issues in a diocesan newspaper or magazines like *U.S. Catholic*, *America*, or *Sojourners*. Connect with the diocesan social ministry office and talk with people who have been working in social ministry for a long time. Sign up for courses, workshops, or retreats that focus on social justice concerns and pro-life issues.

Advocate. While we continue to work in the soup kitchen and donate to the food pantry, we may want to work with Bread for the World and other hunger-related advocacy groups to address the systemic issues that prevent a better distribution of food. We may want to work with urban agricultural projects that are growing food in vacant city lots and bringing fresh vegetables to "food deserts" in urban areas.

Work with the poor as they empower themselves. As we become advocates for the poor we also want to help them find their own voice and not simply depend on us as their "advocates." We may want to join our own community organization to give voice to our concerns for our community. We can connect with local Catholic Campaign for Human Development projects, which are working to empower people.

Use your resources for others. A mature, well-considered dedication to the poor often leads to a simpler life, with fewer things and less preoccupation with money, status, and possessions. We may realize that we don't "need" another pair of shoes when we work with people who only have one pair. The resources of money and time can be used to support the works of charity and justice and pro-life projects.

The experience of being in solidarity with the needy and vulnerable should help us develop both the virtue and the spirituality of solidarity.

How a Parish Lives Out Its Option for the Poor

A parish can become a community that makes an option for the poor in ways large and small. *Tithing* of parish income and investments is a good way to support efforts that provide both direct service and empowerment of the poor. *Twinning* with a "sister parish" within your diocese or in a developing country is a way to build relationships and not simply provide financial support. Find ways to *involve a wide range of parish members*. Some will serve as leaders of projects and on committees and others will be "doers" for one-time activities. Home-bound persons may commit to pray for specific individuals in need or knit prayer shawls for the ill; children can help with many activities. The aim is that the parish's outreach effort become a ministry of the entire parish. Similarly, members can join a legislative *advocacy* network that acts on public policy issues, or organize a meeting between members of the parish and local elected officials to discuss issues affecting the working poor, the unborn, and the vulnerable.[37]

The biblical record and the life of Jesus clearly show that God chooses to stand with the poor. The church, if it is to be faithful to the God of the Bible, also has to choose the poor, not only by its words, but by its deeds. Our eternal destiny depends on this option: "A basic moral test is how our most vulnerable members are faring. In a society marred by deepening divisions between rich and poor, our tradition recalls the story of the Last Judgment (Matt 25:31–46) and instructs us to put the needs of the poor and vulnerable first."[38]

Prayer for the Poor

God of Justice,
Thank you for the gift of your Son Jesus who taught us:
to open our eyes
to see you in the face of the poor.
to open our ears
to hear you in the cries of the exploited.
to open our mouths
to defend you in the poor and vulnerable in the public squares
as well as in our private deeds.
May we always remember that we find you in "the least of these."
Amen.[39]

Discussion Questions

1. Why are the Hebrew Scriptures concerned with the lives of orphans, widows, and resident aliens?

2. Archbishop Dom Helder Camara from Brazil said: "When I feed the poor they call me a 'saint.' When I ask 'why' the poor are hungry, they call me a 'Communist.'" Why does the option for the poor often involve conflict and controversy?

3. For Christians, the option for the poor is a deeply religious choice with serious political ramifications. What does that mean?

4. The U.S. bishops teach that "decisions must be judged in light of what they do for the poor, what they do to the poor, and what they enable the poor to do for themselves." Give examples of work done "for the poor," "to the poor," and "to enable the poor to do for themselves."

6

Rights and Responsibilities

In the Catholic tradition protecting human rights and responding to our responsibilities are the roadmap to creating healthy individuals and communities. Respecting our human rights and living out our responsibilities are the way human dignity is enhanced. When human rights are not protected and responsibilities to each other are ignored, the human community is destroyed and our dignity is threatened. Philomena's story is an example of rights and responsibilities gone amok.

Philomena had lived in thirty-five foster homes since she was ten years old. She had two children by the time she was eighteen, little self-worth, and a long history of run-ins with the law. She left her hometown of Utica, New York, to escape "bad relationships." She ended up on the streets of Rochester and finally in the county jail for abusing drugs. While she was in jail she met Amy, who was sentenced to thirty days in the Monroe County jail for participating in an anti-abortion "rescue" or blockade at a Rochester hospital. Somehow these two women from two different worlds became friends. When Amy left the jail she did not forget her new friend, and Philomena did not forget Amy.

Four years later, Philomena found herself in jail again, and this time she was pregnant. When she called Amy for assistance, Amy responded by helping her get into Bethany House, a Catholic Worker house for women and children, after her release. Philomena gave birth to her third child, a daughter, Bena, while at staying at Bethany House. Eventually, the staff of Bethany House helped her find an apartment and she got a job.

Philomena pointed out the priceless gift she received while at Bethany House. "They gave me unconditional love. That to me was a basic need at that time because I'd never had it before." This unconditional love led to friendship between three women: Amy, Philomena, and Donna, the co-director of Bethany House, and both Donna and Amy became godmothers to two of Philomena's children. Philomena, who has been clean and sober for a decade, now works in a family support program for the mentally ill through Monroe County's Mental Health Office. She points to Donna, the staff, and the volunteers at Bethany House as instrumental in turning her life around. "She just is very welcoming and nonjudgmental. Even if a resident relapses into bad habits, Donna still welcomes you and looks at you with the same eyes."[1]

Donna's look communicates her respect for Philomena even when things are not going well. Philomena did not lose her dignity when she was in jail or when she had a relapse. She still remained a child of God, with dignity, rights, and responsibilities. Donna's look of unconditional love communicates that message to all the desperate women of Bethany House.

Philomena's story is a story of hope and recovery, but it is also a story about the redemptive power of love.

> The Catholic tradition teaches that human dignity can be protected and a healthy community can be achieved only if human rights are protected and responsibilities are met. Therefore, every person has a fundamental right to life and a right to those things required for human decency. Corresponding to these rights are duties and responsibilities—to one another, to our families, and to the larger society.[2]

Philomena, like every human being, has "a right to those things required for human decency." Being loved by those who raise us is something required for human decency, yet Philomena claims she had never experienced that kind of love. She realized how essential it was for her healing. One could say, "See how these Christians around Bethany House love one another!" Human rights and responsibilities—abstract notions—start with the very concrete experience of being loved.

This chapter begins an examination of what we mean by "rights and responsibilities" today by looking at biblical perspectives on justice. As we shall see, the Catholic tradition was slow to embrace the modern meaning of individual human rights and it wasn't until the papacy of Pope John XXIII that a modern understanding of human rights became part of the tradition.

Biblical Perspectives

The Bible is replete with teachings about rights and responsibilities, even though our notion of individual human rights is not present. Scripture scholar Father John Donahue explains:

In contrast to modern individualism the Israelite is in a world where "to live" is to be united with others in a social context either by bonds of family or by covenant relationships. This web of relationships—king with people, judge with complainants, family with tribe and kinfolk, the community with the resident alien and suffering in their midst and all with the covenant God—constitutes the world in which life is played out.[3]

Rights and responsibilities were viewed in the context of these overlapping relationships in the community. Rights were not viewed as individual rights, but rather as duties and responsibilities that were lived out in relationships. The word that best describes "fidelity to the demands of a relationship" is the biblical notion of justice. Rights and responsibilities were not identified as the inalienable rights of each person, as in the U. S. Declaration of Independence; instead, they flow from the relationships that are part of living in community.

Just relationships are the heart of the covenant that God established with the Hebrews and all people. The Hebrew word that is used to express that aspect of the covenant is *sedaqah*, which is translated as justice or righteousness, certainly a dominant message of the Bible. "There is absolutely no concept in the Old Testament with so central a significance for all relationships of human life as that of *sedaqah* [justice/righteousness]."[4]

The Ten Commandments are given and interpreted throughout Jewish history as a way of living out the meaning of justice—fidelity to the demands of relationships with God and within the community. The most important relationship is with God, hence the first three commandments assert the absolute holiness of God. God should not be used to reinforce any political or economic system, and the Bible points out the idolatry of giving ultimate value to any political or economic system: "Thus to 'love God' means to refuse every other ultimate love or loyalty."[5]

After the first three commandments that focus on "love of God," the remaining seven commandments focus on "love of neighbor." These seven commandments are practical teachings that focus on the basic needs of each neighbor, "including those who have no power to defend themselves or access to advocate their own interest." These guarantees "serve to protect the weak from the strong." The combination of the first three commands on the holiness of God and the last seven commandments on justice for the neighbor show that "God's holiness and neighbor love are of a piece in this revolutionary experiment in ancient Israel. Indeed, Israel has known from the beginning that love of God cannot be remote from love of neighbor (1 John 4:20), and that holiness and justice always come together."[6]

As we know from the Bible, Israel did not perfectly live out the justice called for in the covenant and the Ten Commandments. For example, while the Torah called for a limit on debt-slavery, the protection of the poor and the "resident alien," and a prohibition on bribes (which would bias justice toward the wealthy), the Torah also allowed compromises to serve the interests of the wealthy. For example, the same law that limits bondage for a debt (Ex 21:2, 4), also permits the break-up of a family of the indebted for the sake of economic gain. The creditor retains control of the wife and children while the man in debt is freed. The text even refers to the slave as the "property" of the owner, showing that even the Chosen People were corrupted by the attitudes of the Pharaoh, who treated the Hebrews as his property. The text reveals the struggle in ancient Israel between the egalitarian justice and the power of those who had economic control of society—a struggle of interpretation that continues in Jewish and Christian communities.

The Book of Deuteronomy also reveals Israel's ongoing struggle for economic justice. In Deuteronomy 15:1–11 the author envisions a time when the poor have been freed from poverty. The poor whose debts had been cancelled by the practice of Sabbath and Jubilee could reenter the economy with dignity and the possibility of economic viability. This teaching on freeing the poor from debt every seventh year is a powerful message in the Bible. It teaches that the creditor community has responsibility for the rehabilitation and restoration of those lost in the shuffle of economic transactions. The rules of economics are governed by the religious ethic: "Economics is understood as an instrument of a covenantal social fabric, and is not permitted to be a separate sphere with its own anti-neighbor procedures and laws."[7]

The social vision of Israel is rooted in its historical memory of a time when every family, clan, and tribe had its rightful place of power. Each family was to have enough to survive, access to public decisions, and fair treatment in court. Justice is present in the honoring of these relationships. When these social arrangements are ignored or distorted, injustice creeps in. Where there is injustice, the religious actions and pious practices of fasting or offering sacrifices to God are seen as morally bankrupt and powerful intervention is needed to restore justice.

Such intervening was the role of God's prophets who were sent to call the people back to the social vision of the covenant that linked love of

God and love of neighbor. The prophets were direct and concrete. They knew that injustice was not an accident but the result of human decisions and sin. The prophets "knew exactly what the causes were and who was responsible. They did not speak in abstraction. They knew what the oppression/injustice was, and who the oppressors were."[8] In the biblical perspective, "justice then is not a romantic social ideal for another world. It is the hard work of redeploying social power and the transformation of the social system."[9]

The Moral Outrage of Jesus at Rights Denied

Jesus, like the Hebrew prophets before him, also expressed moral outrage when the rights of the poor and day workers were trampled upon. Examples of his outrage in the face of injustice are seen in his reaction to the moneychangers in the temple and in his parable of the workers in the vineyard. (The parable of the workers in the vineyard is discussed in chapter 7).

Mark's account of the cleansing of the temple is as follows:

> Then they came to Jerusalem. And he entered the temple and began to drive out those who were selling and those who were buying in the temple, and he overturned the tables of the moneychangers and the seats of those who sold doves; and he would not allow anyone to carry anything through the temple. He was teaching and saying, "Is it not written, 'My house shall be called a house of prayer for all the nations'? But you have made it a den of robbers." And when the chief priests and the scribes heard it, they kept looking for a way to kill him. . . . (Mk 11:15–18).

Biblical scholars and preachers have a number of interpretations of Jesus' cleansing of the temple. A standard interpretation is that Jesus was angered over the cheating by the moneychangers. The people who came to offer sacrifice at the temple had to exchange their coinage to use temple money to buy their sacrifice. An uneducated peasantry could easily be taken advantage of by the unscrupulous moneychangers. "The action of Jesus is a spirited protest against injustice and the abuse of the temple system. There is no doubt that pilgrims were fleeced by the traders."[10]

While this is a fair interpretation of the text, Jesus is also challenging a deeper injustice. William Herzog argues that we cannot appreciate the meaning of Jesus' charge against the temple without some understanding of the economic role played by the temple in Jerusalem. "The temple cleansing cannot be divorced from the role of the temple as a bank."

In the time of Jesus the temple amassed great wealth because of the half-shekel temple tax assessed on each male. Historical evidence supports the fact that large amounts of money were stored in the temple. The temple then was able to make loans on behalf of the wealthy elites to the poor. If the poor were not able to pay their loans, they would lose their land. "The temple was, therefore, at the very heart of the system of economic exploitation made possible by monetizing the economy and the concentration of wealth made possible by investing the temple and its leaders with the powers and rewards of a collaborating aristocracy." As evidence of this role of the temple funds, Herzog notes, "It was no accident that one of the first acts of the First Jewish Revolt in 66 C.E. was burning of the debt records in the archives in Jerusalem."

The high priests and the lay aristocrats, such as the Sadducees, benefited from this system of exploitation. The high priests controlled the temple and all its functions, including the collecting of the temple tax. The temple was not only a religious and political institution; it was also a major economic force, controlling massive amounts of money while continuing to accumulate more. The temple had a large staff to assist those coming to offer sacrifices: the money-changers, the sellers who provided the unblemished sacrificial victims, and the oil, wine, and flour required for offering a sacrifice. The temple bureaucracy oversaw the temple's many functions, including its payroll, and the goods and services that defined the economy of Judea.

"When Jesus took action against the temple, therefore, he touched a raw nerve. . . ." We have "the match set to the barrel of gasoline." In Herzog's interpretation "the chief priests, the very paradigm of rectitude, are the social bandits creating havoc in the land." The money-changers were the street-level representatives of the banking interests and essential operatives in the collection of the temple tribute. Therefore, Jesus struck at the very heart of the temple's sacrificial system.

According to Herzog, Jesus shifted the focus of God's forgiveness away from the temple to himself. For example when he healed the paralytic he also forgave his sins (Mk 2:5). Jesus took on the role of being the agent of God's forgiveness, indicating that the temple was no longer necessary as the vehicle of forgiveness. Jesus rejected the temple and all it stood for, including the exploitation of the poor. For Jesus the temple was a symbol of economic exploitation that was taking place, and he rightfully called it a "den of thieves." Jesus was not only upbraiding the injustice of the money-changers, minor bureaucrats, but the entire economic system that impoverished the working classes. No wonder the text concludes with the observation, "And when the chief priests and the scribes heard it, they kept looking for a way to kill him. . . ."[11]

"You Always Have the Poor with You"

The background for the cleansing of the temple also helps explain the meaning of the text in Mark 14:7 where Jesus says, "for you always have the poor with you, and you can show kindness to them whenever you wish." Why is there always the poor? Because there is always a ruling class that takes advantage of the people of the land. Jesus offers a sad commentary on the persistence of greed and systemic exploitation that contribute to the persistence of poverty. Jesus interprets the message of Deuteronomy, which looks for the day when "there will, however, be no poor among you, because the LORD is sure to bless you in the land that the LORD your God is giving you as a possession to occupy, if only you will obey the LORD your God by diligently observing this entire commandment that I command you today" (Dt 15:4–6).

The elites have not obeyed the covenant that calls for justice for the poor and forsaking exploitation of the weak. Such systemic injustice violates the intention of God's covenant. Although God's plan is that "there will be no poor among you," the people have not kept God's covenant resulting in injustice and the violence of poverty.[12] By turning over the tables in the temple, Jesus expressed his outrage at the widespread disregard of covenantal justice.

Crystal

Each person has a responsibility to contribute to the common good in some way. Sometimes the small contribution of the "little people" embarrasses those of us with more resources. Crystal is one of those little people who makes a big contribution. Crystal is a seventy-five-year-old woman who is slightly developmentally handicapped, although she is spiritually and emotionally gifted. Crystal lives at a Catholic Worker homeless shelter; in fact, she has been there so long that she is now considered part of the staff. Her job at the shelter is to answer the door, which she does with her honest charm. She is good with names and remembers if you haven't been around for some time. She contributes regularly to the Catholic Worker community by simply doing what she can. Crystal lives a life of voluntary poverty, although it probably doesn't seem like poverty to her because she is surrounded by people who care for her, and her life has meaning and dignity. She has only one coat, one dress, and one blouse because she has given away the rest of her clothing to those in need.

When Crystal receives her Social Security check she immediately walks a mile and a half to give her tithe to her parish church. She doesn't wait until Sunday, but makes the monthly trip on whatever day of the week her check arrives. She gives of the little she has, like the parable of the widow's mite in the gospel story. By taking seriously her responsibilities to her Catholic Worker family and to her own faith community, Crystal inspires many others to live a life of simplicity, generosity, and joyful care for others.

The Church and Human Rights

In Western cultures few concepts carry as much passion and moral gravity as the question of human rights, especially when human rights are denied or violated. Western cultures, including the United States, have commissions and watchdog groups that alert us to human rights abuses in our country and around the world. Most Western democracies have learned to equate respect for human rights with respect for basic human dignity. Moral focus and passion for human rights are cherished and celebrated, both in civic and religious settings. While working to protect human rights is often seen as a contemporary project, there is clear evidence that this has been an issue in many cultures and historical settings. One of the most fascinating periods in the history of human rights is the struggle to appreciate the rights of the indigenous peoples in the New World.

Defender of the Rights of Indigenous People

The landscape of Christianity is sprinkled with pro-life martyrs and saints. One significant figure is a Spanish Dominican priest from the sixteenth century, Bartolomé de Las Casas (1484–1566). He was one of a number of Spanish friars who eventually defended the lives of the indigenous people of Central and South America from the rapacious violence of their fellow Spaniards.

As an eight-year-old, Bartolomé watched as Columbus returned to Seville from his first voyage to the New World. Bartolomé served in the military and went to Santo Domingo, Hispaniola (today, the Dominican Republic) when he was eighteen years old. As part of the conquering Spanish army he was awarded a plantation, known as an *encomienda*, complete with indigenous people as indentured laborers. At first he enjoyed the life of the colonial gentry as an *encomendero*, ignoring the spiritual care of the Indians charged to him. Later he became troubled by the Spanish exploitation of the indigenous people. When he brought his concerns to his confessor, Padre Pedro de Córdoba reminded him of the text from the Hebrew Scriptures: "A man murders his neighbor if he robs him of his livelihood, sheds blood if he withholds an employee's wages" (Sir 34:22). Padre de Córdoba refused him absolution, which was a drastic step and undertaken only when the penitent indicates no intention of changing his or her sinful ways. These words from the Bible stayed with Las Casas, leading to his moral conversion in 1514. He gave up his *encomienda* and began speaking out against the Spanish exploitation of the indigenous people. After returning to Spain, he joined the Dominican order, completed his university studies, and was ordained a priest.

While the search for gold was the main attraction for the Spanish in the New World, the conquest of the lands of the indigenous people was ostensibly justified by the desire to preach the gospel. The pope had authorized the subjugation of the Indian populations for the purpose of spreading the gospel and their salvation. Most of the Spanish conquistadors assumed they were superior to the pagan peoples, which allowed the Spaniards to exploit the indigenous people and the resources of the land. Las Casas cut through the rhetoric and noted the true religion of the conquistadors:

> In order to gild a very cruel and harsh tyranny that destroys so many villages and people, solely for the sake of satisfying the greed of men and giving them gold, the latter, who themselves do not know the faith, use the pretext of teaching it to others and thereby deliver up the innocent in order to extract from their blood the wealth which these men regard as their god.[13]

With Pedro de Córdoba's support, Las Casas returned to Spain to plead the cause of the indigenous people before the Spanish crown. He was able to gather support from humanists and religious leaders in the court of Charles V. In his treatise, *The Indians Are Free Men and Must Be Treated as Such*, he argued for eliminating forced labor and dismantling the *encomienda* system. In its place, he recommended the peaceful settlement of farmers, protection of the native populations, that land and animals be given to the indigenous people along with health care, basic education, and food supplies, and that the native population have legal rights and representation.

The court of Charles V agreed with the plan and named Las Casas "Protector of the Indians," with the responsibility of carrying out these reforms. His plan was to establish a number of conversion centers in South America that were intended to win over the Indians by peaceful means. He planned to bring farmers and skilled workers from Europe to introduce silk, spice, wine, wheat, and sugar production. Peaceful settlers would receive free passage, lands, animals, seeds, and tax abatements, working alongside free Indians. In 1520 the experiment began in Venezuela, but opposition from colonial authorities and the armed intervention of conquistadors against the indigenous population caused the downfall of the community in 1521.

While this experiment was resisted Las Casas did have many smaller victories in his fifty-two years of defending the rights and dignity of the Indians. While others claimed that Indians were a lesser race, he affirmed their full humanity and their entitlement to all human rights. His position was taken up by Pope Paul III, who declared the equality of indigenous people and Europeans in his 1537 papal bull, *Sublimus Deus*.

In 1544 Las Casas was named bishop of Chiapas in southern Mexico. He was shocked that the colonists were not respecting the rights of the indigenous people as described in the New Laws. He forbade his priest from giving absolution to any *encomendero* who would not free his indigenous slaves. This stance aroused hatred among the ruling class who denounced him as a "lunatic." Receiving numerous death threats and eventually expelled from the province, Las Casas returned to Spain. (In defending the rights of the indigenous people, Las Casas has been considered the patron saint of all who have done this work in Latin America, including modern-day saints like Archbishop Oscar Romero, the four women martyrs in El Salvador, and Sister Dorothy Stang.)

Las Casas returned to the New World in 1546 with additional authority, and at the first synod of bishops of Latin America he won support for the *Declaration of the Rights of the Indians*. This document established the rights of all people:

> All unbelievers, whatever their sect or religion and whatever their
> state of sin, by Natural and Divine Law and by the birthright of all
> peoples, properly possess and hold domain over the things they have
> acquired without detriment to others, and with equal right they are
> entitled to their principalities, realms, states, honors, jurisdictions,
> and dominions.[14]

By the time Las Casas died in 1566 major changes had taken place in the Spanish royal policy regarding the rights of Indians. Las Casas truly deserved the title of "protector of the Indians."[15]

Las Casas helped shape Spain's attitude toward the equality of all people, notions asserted 240 years later in the American Declaration of Independence. As Americans we are proud of our founding fathers' wisdom and courage in drafting the Declaration, which proclaims the dignity of every person, with the right to life, liberty, and the pursuit of happiness. As Roman Catholics, we can also be proud of the tradition of Bishop Las Casas. These Catholic activists and moralists in the sixteenth century made a great contribution to the emerging understanding of human rights and the role of the state in protecting those rights.

While the Catholic Church defended the dignity of the human person, as we saw in the work of Bartolomé de Las Casas, it did not support the "human rights" movement as it emerged in seventeenth-century Europe. Many of the secular movements promoting human rights had an anticlerical and anti-Catholic Church tenor. In France, Italy, Spain, Mexico, and other countries the Catholic Church was perceived as an enemy of both individual rights and the autonomy of the secular realm. The church of Rome reacted strongly to these movements.

The church rejected modern theories of rights as articulated by Thomas Hobbes, John Locke, and Immanuel Kant, which stressed *human rights as individualistic claims in competition*: individual against individual claiming their rights. In this competitive understanding of rights, a "social contract" was accepted as a way of balancing and curbing these competing claims to achieve some semblance of order. In contrast to this individualistic and competitive view of human nature, the Catholic tradition stressed the essential solidarity of each person with the human community. This was not a conflictual model of competing claims but an ethics of rights based on people's social nature. The Catholic vision stressed human rights in the context of community and a cooperative pursuit of the common good.[16] This understanding of rights is obvious in Pope Benedict's encyclical *Caritas in Veritate*, discussed at the end of this chapter.

It wasn't until the 1963 encyclical of Pope John XXIII, *Pacem in Terris*, that the Catholic Church accepted the notion of individual human rights, again, within the context of community. "While the nineteenth-century popes look on human rights with skepticism and rejection, John XXIII makes them the fundamental point of departure for his social and ethical argument."[17] With Pope John XXIII's writing, the implementation of human rights became a decisive criterion for evaluating the morality of a society. We read in *Pacem in Terris*:

> Any society, if it is to be well-ordered and productive, must lay down as a foundation this principle, namely, that every human being is a person, that is, his nature is endowed with intelligence and free will. By virtue of this, he has rights and duties, flowing directly and simultaneously from his very nature. These rights are therefore universal, inviolable and inalienable (9).

Among the individual rights that Pope John XXIII identified are:

- the right to life and to freedom from bodily harm,
- the right to those commodities necessary for an appropriate standard of living (food, clothing, a home, education, health care, unemployment aid, and help in old age),
- the right to freedom of opinion and information,
- the right to freedom of religion and conscience,
- the right to freedom to choose one's profession,
- the right to freedom of migration,
- the right to take an active part in public affairs, and
- the right to impartial legal protection of these rights.

Included in the rights to political participation are the rights to freedom of assembly and association.

These human rights are not simply to be guaranteed in theory, but a just society must work to actualize these rights.

> A well-ordered human society requires that men recognize and observe their mutual rights and duties. It also demands that each contribute generously to the establishment of a civic order in which rights and duties are progressively more sincerely and effectively acknowledged and fulfilled. It is not enough, for example, to acknowledge and respect every man's right to the means of subsistence. One must also strive to ensure that he actually has enough in the way of food and nourishment (*Pacem in Terris*, 31–32).

The Second Vatican Council confirmed the new direction taken by Pope John, signaling a consensus in the church on the importance of human rights. As the *Declaration on Religious Freedom* of Vatican II summarized it: "In the exercise of their rights individual men and social groups are bound by the moral law to have respect both for the rights of others and for their own duties toward others and for the common welfare of all" (7). Thus any discussion of rights in the Catholic tradition has two reference points: reciprocal duties and the common good.

Pope John Paul II was more detailed in delineating our human rights:

> Permit me to enumerate some of the most important human rights that are universally recognized:
> - the right to life, liberty and security of person;
> - the right to food, clothing, housing, sufficient health care, rest and leisure;
> - the right to freedom of thought, conscience and religion;
> - the right to manifest one's religion either individually or in a community, in public or private;
> - the right to choose a state of life, to found a family and to enjoy all conditions necessary for family life;
> - the right to property and work, to adequate working conditions and just wage;
> - the right to assembly and association;
> - the right to freedom of movement, to internal and external migration;
> - the right to nationality and residence;
> - the right to political participation; and
> - the right to participation in the free choice of the political system of the people to which one belongs.[18]

In this list of rights the church stresses not only individual civil rights but also economic and social rights. In the United States, we tend to put more emphasis on civil rights and give less attention to the protection and enhancement of economic and social rights, such as the right to a living wage, the right to adequate housing, or the right to health care.

The Right of Private Property

One of the more controversial teachings of the church concerns the right of private property. On the one hand, the church affirms the right of private property as Pope John XXIII stated: "[T]he right of private property, including that pertaining to goods devoted to productive enterprises, is permanently valid" (*Mater et Magistra*, 109). On the other hand, the church places conditions or limitations on that right: the right to hold property is not an absolute right, but a limited right. The needs of survival and the right of subsistence may override the right of private property. The right to life and the right to survival are more important rights than the right of private property. Pope Paul VI explained that "private ownership confers on no one a supreme and unconditional right. No one is allowed to set aside solely for his own advantage possessions which exceed his needs when others lack the necessities of life" (*Populorum Progressio*, 23). This teaching is rooted in the long-standing tradition of the Bible and the teachings of the early church that the goods of creation are meant for all people. Pope John Paul II explains:

> Christian tradition has never upheld this right (to ownership) as absolute and untouchable. On the contrary, it has always understood this right within the broader context of the right common to all to use the goods of the whole creation: The right to private property is subordinate to the right to common use, to the fact that goods are meant for everyone (*Laborem Exercens*, 14).

Thus, the Catholic tradition clearly holds that the basic needs of people or the needs of the common good supersede the right to private property. In other words, it may be necessary to override the right of private property to meet the needs of survival of individuals or to meet the demands of the common good.[19]

These words may be unsettling for some people because most Americans have a strong belief in the right of individual ownership with no strings attached. The church invites us to understand that there are "strings attached" to the right of private property. As noted in the chapter on creation, our "ownership" of property should be understood as a form of stewardship, because the goods of the Earth and all that is belongs to God.

Pope John Paul II offered another way of understanding the church's teaching by saying that "private property, in fact, is under a social mortgage": "The goods of this world are equally meant for all. The right to private property is valid and necessary, but it does not nullify the value of this principle. Private property, in fact, is under a social mortgage."[20] What this term "social mortgage" means is that we are not "free and clear" to ignore the needs of others in the use of our property. Catholic ethicist Thomas Massaro, S.J., explains that "our holding of property is strictly conditioned on fulfilling our social obligations to the rest of God's creatures."[21] Once again, church teaching situates this *individual right* within the context of the *needs of the community and the common good.* We are invited to recognize the social dimensions of the property within our care.

Civil Rights, Responsibilities, and Racism

The day after the election of President Barack Obama in 2008, second- and third-grade students on a school bus in Rexburg, Idaho chanted "assassinate Obama." In Standish, Maine, a sign inside the Oak Hill General Store read: "Osama Obama Shotgun Pool." Customers could sign up to bet $1 on a date when Obama would be killed. "Stabbing, shooting, roadside bombs, they all count," the sign read. At the bottom of the marker board was written, "Let's hope someone wins."[22]

In March 1997, Lenard Clark, a thirteen-year-old black boy from the south side of Chicago, wandered on his bicycle into a white neighborhood. He was savagely beaten by three white teenagers. He lingered in a coma, near death, for several days before making a gradual recovery.

On January 2, 1996, a black teenager, Cynthia Wiggins, from Buffalo, New York, was hit by a dump truck on a busy road as she struggled through the snow and cold. She was trying to get to her job as a cashier at the Walden Galleria Mall in suburban Cheektowaga. She died of her injuries. Cynthia was a serious and dedicated young person who had grown up poor but dreamed of becoming a doctor.

This may seem like an unfortunate accident, unrelated to racism, but wait. Why was Cynthia trying to cross a dangerous street after getting off the bus from Buffalo? Why didn't the bus stop at the mall? The truth is that the mall owners, the Pyramid Corporation, had refused to let Buffalo city buses pick up or unload on mall property. This policy was established to make it as difficult as possible for inner-city blacks to reach the mall.

The news of the beating of the thirteen-year-old and the overt racism expressed by the school children and the sign in the General Store is shocking. These are expressions of "hot" or overt racism. However, the "cold" racism of the Pyramid Corporation is also partially responsible for the death of Cynthia. The mall tried to impose segregation on the residents from black neighborhoods in Buffalo, and Cynthia died, in part, because of those racist policies.

Racism is a denial of human dignity and of basic human rights. It is present in overt and covert ways in the actions and attitudes of individuals as well as the policies, practices, and patterns of our institutions and our culture. This is true for society and for our religious communities. Bryan Massingale, a diocesan priest from Milwaukee and a professor theology at

Marquette University, has written a compelling book entitled *Racial Justice and the Catholic Church*. In it, he emphasizes the cultural and systemic dimensions of racism: "Racism is a cultural phenomenon, that is, a way of interpreting human color differences that pervades the collective convictions, conventions, and practices of American life."[23] As a cultural phenomenon, racism is learned when we are children through both spoken and unspoken understandings: "Even if a child is not told that blacks are inferior, he learns that lesson by observing the behavior of others. These tacit understandings, because they have never been articulated, are less likely to be experienced at a conscious level."[24]

One expression of such unconscious racism is the association of crime with people of color. This was very obvious during the reporting on Hurricane Katrina. Massingale recalls:

> The Associated Press published two photos of people in identical situations in the flooded waters of New Orleans. The first, of a black young man, carried the caption, "A young man walks through chest-deep water after looting a grocery store in New Orleans." The second showed two white men, with the caption, "Two residents wade through chest-deep water after finding bread and soda from a local grocery store after Hurricane Katrina came through the area of New Orleans." The people are engaged in identical actions, yet one is described as "looting," the other as "finding."[25]

The majority of white Americans are of two minds on eliminating racism: while we denounce blatant racial injustices, we tolerate and even support a situation of white social dominance and privilege. "To say it plainly, most Americans are committed to both interpersonal decency and systemic inequality. Racial equality encounters ongoing resistance because this nation is still committed to maintaining relationships of white cultural, political, and social dominance, that is to say, a culture of 'white supremacy.'"[26]

These attitudes of white superiority have deep roots in our country and in our church, and history does not reveal a flattering story of the Catholic Church on this issue. The history of American Catholics on the question of race is, in general, not exemplary. Religious orders and bishops kept slaves in this country. The Jesuits used African slaves as laborers on their four plantations in Maryland until 1837, and the Capuchins and Ursulines also used slaves on their plantations. The first bishop of Baltimore, John Carroll (1735–1815), had two black servants, one free and the other a slave.

African American Catholic theologian Jamie Phelps, O.P., describes the racism of those generations of Catholic theologians: "The silence of U.S. Catholic theologians about racism is parallel to the silence of leading German theologians and intellectuals during the Nazi atrocities and the prosecution of the so-called 'final solution' against the Jewish people."[27]

Jon Nilson, then president of the Catholic Theological Society of America, responded to Dr. Phelps's charge. "If ever there were a sentence that seems to come right off the page and seize the white reader by the throat, it is this one." He continues, "An initial reaction might well be to dismiss Phelps's claim as rhetorical overkill, a tactic to get whites to pay more attention to issues that she thinks important." But Nilson doesn't buy that argument.

> But that is a reaction born of ignorance. Her comparison of white Catholic theologians to the German theologians is
> - more than justified by Basil Davidson's conclusion that the slave trade "cost Africa at least 50 million souls";[28]
> - more than justified by the extremes of suffering endured by the kidnapped Africans and their descendants for the 244 years of legalized slavery;
> - more than justified by the 71 years of oppression and discrimination known as Jim Crow;
> - more than justified by the 51 of those same years during which one black person was lynched about every 2.5 days somewhere in the United States "at the hands of persons unknown";
> - and more than justified because racism continues to infect our country today.[29]

However, our history does tell stories of African American Catholics who confronted the violation of their human rights, and it also includes stories of their efforts to exercise their responsibility as members of society and the church. One stellar example is Daniel Rudd, who had two strikes against him: he was an African American and he was a layperson in the Catholic Church.

Daniel Rudd (1854–1933)

Daniel Rudd, the son of slave parents, was born and buried in Bardstown, Kentucky. He was the editor of the *American Catholic Tribune*, a paper published by and for African American Catholics. Rudd did more than just write about the issues of his fellow black Catholics; he organized a lay congress to bring the lay Catholic leadership together. In January 1889 Rudd convened the first of five Black Catholic Congresses in the basement of St. Augustine's Church in Washington, D.C. In the four succeeding years, other congresses followed in Cincinnati, Philadelphia, Chicago, and Baltimore.

These congresses served as forums "for black opinion, they voiced a desire for the spread of Catholicism within the African American community and sounded a clarion call to the American Church to change the racist policies so prevalent on the local level."[30] The participants at these lay congresses recognized that they shared the concerns of other immigrants in the Catholic community, especially the Irish, "who, like ourselves, are struggling for justice." They asked for schools and societies for African Americans as well as help in addressing racial discrimination by labor unions, employers, landlords, and real estate agents.

The lay leaders were addressing these issues because at this time the seminaries did not admit black candidates and thus there were no black clergy. The larger Catholic community was not ready for this strong leadership from the black community. The reaction from the hierarchy was based on a twofold concern: lay leadership and racism. The official church was concerned about the "militant" tone of these meetings and of the work of Daniel Rudd's paper. "That blacks were speaking for themselves, that they were calling the total Catholic community to just behavior, earned for them the epithet 'militant.'" Black historian Cyprian Davis notes that because of this label, "support dwindled. Rudd was pressured to move his paper to the East, where he could work under ecclesiastical supervision." When Rudd "tacitly refused to do so, another black Catholic paper was established." Both papers failed, and the embryonic movement died. But Davis notes that the movement started by Daniel Rudd "addressed critical issues and planted necessary seeds." These seeds would remain dormant for almost ninety-three years until the next National Black Catholic Congress was held in 1987.

According to Davis, "The black lay Catholic congresses were not a failure. In fact, they achieved what Rudd set out to do in calling the first congress." He believes that "They demonstrated beyond a doubt not only that a black Catholic community existed but that it was active, devoted, articulate and proud. It also demonstrated that given the opportunity, there was real leadership within the black community." As evidence of this leadership Davis points to the address of the IV Black Catholic Congress, published in the *Boston Pilot* on September 23, 1893, which he considers a "foundation of Black Catholic theology." They gave the black community and the larger church a sense of social mission, a focus on human rights, a theology of the priesthood of the faithful, and their rootedness in the African origins of the church.[31]

Church Teaching on Racism

The first step in addressing racism in society and in the church is to acknowledge its persistence in ourselves and our institutions and in cultural attitudes. The U.S. bishops explain, "Racism is a radical sin: a sin that divides the human family and violates the fundamental dignity of those called to be children of the same father."[32]

The Catholic Church has admitted that racism exists within the church and within society. In both settings it is sinful: "Racism is the sin that says some human beings are inherently superior and others essentially inferior because of race. It is the sin that makes racial characteristics the determining factor for the exercise of human rights. It mocks the words of Jesus: "Treat others the way you would have them treat you."[33]

Racism is contrary to the message of Jesus, as Archbishop Sean O'Malley explains:

> When asked for a definition of neighbor, our Lord answers with the parable of the good Samaritan. Jesus astonished his audience by making the Samaritan, the member of a despised minority group, the hero and protagonist of the story. In one fell swoop Jesus pops the bubble of ethnic superiority and at the same time challenges us to be a neighbor to all in need and to remove the barriers in our heart that prevent us from seeing our connectedness with every human being.[34]

A number of bishops have spoken out on racism, but the Catholic tradition has a long way to go. According to Father Massingale the church's past efforts to address racism have been impeded due to a *fundamental misunderstanding of racism*:

> Racism has never been principally about insults, slurs, or exclusion, as demeaning and harmful as these are. Racism entails more than conscious, deliberate, and intentional ill will or acts of avoidance, exclusion, or malice perpetrated by individuals. Individual bias and personal bigotry are real, but a limited slice of reality.

Massingale continues:

> Racism is an underlying cultural set of meanings and values, that is, a way of interpreting skin color differences so that white Americans enjoy a privileged social status with access to advantages and benefits to the detriment, disadvantage, and burden of persons of color. Racism, at its core, is a defense of racially based white social privilege.[35]

From his perspective as an African American

> [T]here are serious shortcomings and deficits in the dominant approach in U.S. Catholic social teaching on racial justice. This teaching is superficial in its social analysis of racism, naïve in its reliance upon rational persuasion, and blind to how the church's complicity in and bondage to a racialized culture compromises its teaching and identity. In short, Catholic reflection on racism is not radical enough to do justice to what the bishops themselves call a "radical evil."[36]

Massingale offers insights on how the Catholic tradition can move forward in a more constructive way. He urges the biblical tradition of lament. Laments are cries of anguish and outrage, groans of deep pain and grief, utterances of profound protest and righteous indignation over injustice. "Lamentation is a cry of utter anguish and passionate protest at the state of the world and its brokenness."[37] Laments and cries of personal and communal distress comprise fully one-third of the Book of Psalms. While lamentation is an *expression of complaint and grief*, it is also an *expression of hope* that God hears the cry of the afflicted and will respond compassionately to their needs.

Pope John Paul II provided an example of lament over racial injustice during a prayer service in St. Peter's Basilica during the 2000 Jubilee Year.

> Lord our God, you created the human being, man and woman, in your image and likeness, and you willed the diversity of peoples within the unity of the human family. At times, however, the equality of your sons and daughters has not been acknowledged, and Christians have been guilty of attitudes of rejection and exclusion, consenting to acts of discrimination on the basis of racial and ethnic difference. Forgive us and grant us the grace to heal the wounds

still present in your community on account of sin, so that we will all feel ourselves to be your sons and daughters.[38]

Fr. Massingale recommends that this papal lament needs to be made more specific and concrete by Catholics in the United States. Lament is rooted in the deep awareness that as a faith community we have betrayed our faith convictions through our participation in the sin of racism.[39] He believes that lament would be a good place to begin the work of racial reconciliation.

Linking Racism and Poverty

People of color have paid a price for the evil of racism that has excluded them from social, political, and economic opportunities. Racism is clearly linked with the problem of poverty. The national office of Catholic Charities has explored this linkage in its position paper *Poverty and Racism: Overlapping Threats to the Common Good*[40] and at its their annual conference in 2009. Catholic Charities leaders are convinced that poverty and racism

> are so intertwined that it is impossible to fully separate them. Racism, in both its individual and institutional forms, is a cause of poverty and at the same time an additional barrier for people of color seeking to escape poverty. We are convinced that without a conscious and proactive struggle against racism, our efforts to reduce the plague of poverty will be in vain.[41]

The paper presents a number of facts, noting that "while the majority of poor people in our country currently are white, a disproportionate number of poor people are persons of color. Consider the following facts cited in our 2006 statement":

- The highest rates of poverty are among children, especially children of color. The poverty rate for white children is 10 percent, while it is 28 percent for Latino children, 27 percent for Native-American children, and 33 percent for African-American children.
- African Americans, Latino Americans, and Native Americans are about three times as likely to live in poverty as are whites. While the poverty rate for non-Hispanic whites is 8 percent, the rate for African Americans is 24.1 percent, for Hispanics, 21.8 percent, and for Native Americans, 23.2 percent.[42]

The Catholic Charities position paper also points out important historical events that exemplify the link between race and poverty, "events that both burdened people of color seeking to escape poverty and eased the way for white Americans to advance their economic fortunes."[43]

- *The institution of slavery.* Slavery means exploited labor; the labor of enslaved Africans was essential for creating wealth for others from which they often derived no benefit. Slavery resulted in the creation of wealth not only for the white slave-holding elite, but for all who benefited from and participated in a "slavery-centered" economy (e.g., merchants, bankers, fishermen, ship-builders, traders, auctioneers, bounty hunters, and immigrant farmers).
- *The Indian Removal Act of 1830.* By this act of Congress, Native Americans were forcibly removed from their lands and resettled in territory that was of no interest to whites. Their property was then made available for white settlers. This stolen land became the basis for white economic enrichment that could be passed on as an inheritance to future generations. This economic disen-franchisement also led to the impoverishment of future genera-tions of Native Americans.
- *The exclusion of Asian Indians from eligibility for U.S. citizenship.* In 1923, the U.S. Supreme Court (*U.S. v. Bhagat Singh Thind*) ruled that while Asian Indians were indeed "Caucasians" by race, they could not be considered "white." The result was that many Asian Indians were stripped of their naturalized citizenship. This meant that they were unable to legally own property; many had their assets taken from them and given to whites.[44]

These decisions in the past created a legacy of discrimination that has affected generations of people of color and severely circumscribed eco-nomic opportunity. Such decisions have led to problems that continue today, such as the "exclusion of African Americans and other groups from the benefits of home ownership [that] creates an economic deficit and reduced access to social mobility that persists even today. Whites as a social group have the present advantage of decades of accumulated wealth and the opportunities it provides."[45] This legacy is visible in both the segrega-tion and the concentration of poverty in our cities, as well as in ongoing employment discrimination. The brief goes on to recommend measures to address these persistent problems of race and poverty.

The reality of poverty and racism reveals how far we are from honoring the rights of each person and how far we are from honoring our responsibility to each other as members of the one human family.

Economic Rights and Responsibilities amid Poverty

Every person has a right to sit at the table of life where, by our common labor, the basic hungers and needs of each person are met. It is a simple vision. As the U.S. bishops say in their letter, *A Place at the Table*, "This is not about having a new car or about how fast you can get on the Internet; rather this is about having a decent place to live, enough to eat, clean water in your village, and clean air in your community."[46]

The current realities reveal how far we are from the goal of protecting each person's dignity by meeting their basic needs. 43.6 million people in the United States live below the federal poverty level[47] and more than half of the world's population lives on less than two dollars a day. Eight hundred million people, most of them children, live with hunger or malnutrition, which means that "they die younger than they should, struggle with hunger and disease, and live with little hope and less opportunity for a life of dignity."[48]

The Catholic bishops offer the image of the table as a way to think about our response to poverty. "A table is where people come together for food. For many, there is not enough food and, in some cases, no table at all. A table is where people meet to make decisions—in neighborhoods, nations, and the global community. Many people have no place at the table. Their voices and needs are ignored or dismissed."[49]

For Catholics, the table recalls the Eucharistic Table, which expresses our New Covenant with God and the community of the faithful with whom we break bread. As we break bread at the table of the Lord, we are to feed the hungry in our world. As the *Catechism of the Catholic Church* insists, "The Eucharist commits us to the poor. To receive in truth the Body and Blood of Christ given up for us, we must recognize Christ in the poorest" (1397).[50]

The metaphor of the table also suggests the four legs, or institutions, that must take up their unique responsibility in addressing poverty. The table rests on (1) families and individuals, (2) community and religious institutions, (3) the private sector, and (4) the government. By identifying these four institutions, the bishops are spreading out the responsibilities among a diverse set of people and agencies, with each bringing something different to the table.

The bishops briefly explain the responsibilities of *families and individuals*. Every *individual* has a responsibility to respect the dignity of others and to work to secure not only his or her own rights but also the rights of others. The hard work of *parents*, their love and discipline, and their time and presence within their families are gifts not only to their children, but also to society and to the common good. They are also significant investments in avoiding or escaping poverty.

Community organizations and faith-based institutions also have a vital role to play in strengthening civil society and addressing poverty. "These institutions can confront structures of injustice and build community, and they can demand accountability from public officials."[51] The bishops know that faith-based institutions like Catholic Charities, Lutheran Social Services, and the Catholic Worker movement are essential expressions of faith and that "On the toughest problems, in the toughest, most desperate neighborhoods and villages, *religious and community institutions* are present and making a difference."

The *private sector* in the form of business, commerce, and labor "must be not only an engine of growth and productivity, but also a reflection of our values and priorities, a contributor to the common good." Employers and the labor movement must help the poorest workers to have a voice and a place at the table where wages and working conditions are set. The bishops note the centrality of "work" in providing for people's basic needs: "Parents need to be able to provide a life of dignity for their children by their work. Workers and farmers need living wages; access to health care; vacation time and family and medical leave; a voice and real participation in the workplace; and the prospect of a decent retirement."[52]

The fourth essential leg of the table is the role and responsibility of government. "In the Catholic tradition, government has a positive role because of its responsibility to serve the common good, provide a safety net for the vulnerable, and help overcome discrimination and ensure equal opportunity for all."[53] The bishops believe that government must act when the institutions mentioned above fall short in defending the weak and protecting human life and human rights.

The wisdom of the Catholic tradition is to recognize the *complementary responsibilities of individuals, families, communities, the market, and government to work together to overcome poverty and advance human dignity.*[54] This approach provides a "thick" description of rights and responsibilities in contrast to "thin" descriptions, which only emphasize one or two of these domains. A thick description is multileveled, avoiding ideological debates that place the blame and responsibility on the individual or, on the other hand, government and social structures. The Catholic tradition brings all of the players into the mix.

Subsidiarity

The framework of the four "legs of the table" establishes a complex network of interaction and assistance. For example, when confronting poverty and unemployment, the individual and family have their unique responsibility and realm of activity. But a family may not be able to pull itself up by the bootstraps; it may need "assistance" from the next layer of social institutions—the community organization, the faith community, business, or even the various levels of government.

Providing the appropriate assistance at the lowest level or the most basic unit of society is what the church means by "the principle of subsidiarity." The word comes from the Latin, *subsidium*, which means assistance or backup. "In Catholic usage the term means that larger organizational structures and higher authorities are by nature a backup form to supply what individuals and smaller or voluntary groupings cannot do."[55] This principle means that the larger institutions should not interfere on the local level when the local level can handle the need. However, because of the complexity of life and social problems, sometimes the local unit may not be able to adequately address the need. As the Task Force on Catholic Social Teaching put it:

> The Church vigorously defends the unique roles of families, community associations, and other intermediate institutions and insists their roles cannot be ignored or absorbed by the state or other large institutions. However, when the common good or the rights of individuals are harmed or threatened, society—including governmental institutions—has a responsibility to act to protect human dignity and rights.[56]

There is, of course, much debate about when the larger institutions should be involved. For instance, what is the role of the government in addressing the question of unemployment? Are we to rely on marketplace dynamics to resolve that problem? What role should the county, state, or the federal government play? Or, for example, in protecting our environment, when does the international level of governance need to be involved to address questions such as global warming or the use of international waters? At times, even the national level of government may not be able to address issues that are international in scope. Help may be needed from international organizations; however, these organizations should not overpower national or local agencies that can adequately address local aspects of the problem. This principle tries to guard against interference by government, but also to ensure that government provides enough help to promote the common good.

How to Respond as a Community

The bishops remind us that action is required for a Christian, as the Letter of James insists: "If a brother or sister has nothing to wear and has no food for the day, and one of you says to them, 'Go in peace, keep warm, and eat well,' but you do not give them the necessities of the body, what good is it? So also faith of itself, if it does not have works, is dead" (2:15–17).

Our action as a Christian community is multidimensional. The service and advocacy offered by the church must be rooted in prayer and worship and nourished and challenged by preaching the liberating Word of God. Our actions take place through our everyday lives, as consumers, parents, workers, and active citizens. Our faith will also lead us to serve those in need as "we house the homeless, feed the hungry, visit those in prison, welcome immigrants, and provide countless other services."[57] Through advocacy and community organizations, the Catholic community works with others to shape a culture of life and a more just and peaceful world.

Although rights and responsibilities are abstract notions, they have real urgency when we connect with real people whose rights are being denied. The teaching of the church encourages Catholics to stay in direct contact with those, like Philomena, who are not at the table of nourishment, health, housing, and quality education, or the table of economic and political power and decision-making. As we build relationships with those whose civil, economic, or political rights are denied, we will find a way make room at the table so that all of God's people may feast at the banquet of life.

Pope Benedict's Encyclical: *Caritas in Veritate*

On July 9, 2009, Pope Benedict XVI issued his first social encyclical *Caritas in Veritate* (*CV*). "Perhaps the principal service of the encyclical is to stimulate Christian readers at the level of their own global vision: to 'make sense' of our present challenging situation."[58] The pope believes that the best way to understand and address our social issues is to *remember who we are as human beings.*[59]

Benedict reaffirms the importance of interdependence: "As a spiritual being, the human creature is defined through interpersonal relations. The more authentically he or she lives these relations, the more his or her own personal identity matures" (53, also 55). He also teaches that authentic human development is a calling, a "vocation" from God. In responding to God's call to full human development we recognize "the astonishing experience of gift" (34). This is a new concept that Benedict brings to Catholic social teaching—the notion of gift or gratuitousness: "Gratuitousness is present in our lives in many different forms, which often go unrecognized because of a purely consumerist and utilitarian view of life. The human being is made for gift, which expresses and makes present his transcendent dimension" (34).

By lifting up these central dimensions of being human—the experience of interdependence and gift, the vocation to authentic development, and openness to God—the pope helps us find our bearings about what it means to "be human." Rooted in the church's understanding of who we are and what we are called to be will help us as we develop a Christian response to the issues of poverty, racism, globalization, and other serious social concerns.

The pope believes the poverty of the twenty-first century is unlike that of other times. In the past, poverty was the unfortunate result of natural scarcity, but today it results from a set of priorities imposed on world systems by rich countries and rich businesses. These market priorities have resulted in excessive inequalities that erode trust and the networks of relationships of trust, dependability, and respect for rules that are indispensable for any form of civil coexistence.

Pope Benedict sees in the current global crisis the collapse of solidarity and mutual trust. "*Without internal forms of solidarity and mutual trust, the market cannot completely fulfill its proper economic function.* And today it is this trust which has ceased to exist, and the loss of trust is a grave loss" (35). In response to this collapse of trust the pope urges the market to adopt relationships of trust and gratuity, suggesting a more human-oriented market that depends more on trust. For without trust, as the financial crisis has exposed, the market destroys itself.

The pope suggests that "gift" or gratuitousness is the heart of the Christian social vision. By "gift" he means freely giving and freely sharing for the good of all. The Christian vision of gift in the public sphere is rooted in God's love freely given to humanity (34). It is the gift of God's love that provides the framework for understanding the whole pattern of human experience. "It is the principle not only of micro-relationships (with friends, with family members or within small communities) but also of macro-relationships (social, economic and political ones)" (2).

In a globalized economy, Benedict argues that commercial relations must better embody "the principle of gratuitousness and the logic of gift as an expression of fraternity" (36). He continues:

> Today we can say that economic life must be understood as a multi-layered phenomenon: in every one of these layers, to varying degrees and in ways specifically suited to each, the aspect of fraternal reciprocity must be present. In the global era, economic activity cannot prescind from gratuitousness, which fosters and disseminates solidarity and responsibility for justice and the common good among the different economic players (38).

The pope believes that social responsibility across society, whether in business, politics, or civic society, arises only where there are underlying attitudes of giving and sharing. He is realistic enough to know that "the market of gratuitousness" does not exist, but he suggests that this is the way forward.

The rebuilding of trust and the instilling of attitudes of giving and sharing are essential in the marketplace as well as in civil society, which includes family, neighborhood groups, voluntary associations, parishes, schools, and so forth. Every parish, school, and non-profit organization can build the fabric of society by forging relationships of trust and by acting together to hold the state and the market accountable for serving the common good.

In commenting on the encyclical, Austen Ivereigh connected this work of rebuilding trust in society with a faith-based community organization in London. He explained that by listening to each other in one-on-one visits the people began to build relationships of trust. They also learn what is important to each person and discuss what issues are of greatest concern in the community. Through the skills and practices of listening to each other and developing realistic plans of action, people can establish relationships of trust across the diversity that divides the modern city.

> It is here that our common action can begin, here that we can strengthen civil society and accumulate the "social capital" praised

by Pope Benedict XVI (*CV* 32). From that invigorated civil society the state and the market can be infused by the spirit of gift, and human beings restored to their God-given dignity—precisely the vision of *Caritas in Veritate*.[60]

This chapter has reviewed the biblical understanding of rights and responsibilities in terms of biblical justice, of fidelity to one's relationships with God and the community. Pope Benedict has also drawn on this understanding by his use of the notion of "gift." God has gifted humanity with a covenant with its layers of relationships: with God, the community, and God's Earth. Benedict suggests this image of gift—freely giving and freely sharing for the good of all—as a way to restore the relationships in the marketplace, government, and civil society. What an attractive vision for understanding our rights and responsibilities! We are invited to freely give and freely share in imitation of God's gracious giving to us. While the concept of gift does not settle all of the thorny questions of racism and poverty, it does bring another resource to the table, also known as "grace."

Prayer for Basic Rights

God of freedom,
We praise you for the invitation to feast at your table,
both now and in the heavenly banquet.
With your grace, may we make room at all the tables our lives
for those who have been excluded from the feast of full human life.
Strengthen with hope and creative action
all people denied their basic human rights and freedoms.
May we who follow your Son
be empowered by your Spirit to continue your work in the world.
Amen.[61]

Discussion Questions

1. Compare biblical justice with the American understanding of justice as fairness and equality before the law.
2. What are the implications of the teaching of Pope John Paul II about private property when he says "The right of private property is subordinate to the right to common use, to the fact that goods are meant for everyone"?
3. The image of a table is offered in presenting a comprehensive approach to poverty. How are the four "legs" of the table helpful in discussing a Catholic response to poverty?
4. Give examples of "subsidiarity" in society and in the church.
5. Did you have a reaction to the section on racism? What are you feeling and thinking about the challenge of racial reconciliation in the United States?

7

The Dignity of Work and Workers' Rights

In February 2011 Governor Scott Walker of Wisconsin quickly became a national figure with his blunt calls for repairing the state budget by shrinking collective bargaining rights and benefits for public workers. Governor Walker proposed restricting the unions to bargaining over just one topic, base wages, while eliminating their ability to negotiate benefits such as health care, working hours, and vacations. He also wants to require unions to win an employee election every year to continue representing workers.

Union leaders responded by saying that several of Mr. Walker's proposals—including the one that would require elections each year to determine whether a majority of public employees want to keep their union—are really intended to cripple unions and not to balance the budget.[1] The controversy brought ten thousand protestors to Madison, Wisconsin's state capital, hoping to prevent the passage of the governor's legislation. Solidarity protests spread to other states and Ohio and Indiana passed similar legislation.

Catholic bishops weighed into the controversy, upholding the rights of workers and the value of unions. Archbishop Jerome E. Listecki, president of the Wisconsin Catholic Conference, issued a "Statement Regarding the Rights of Workers and the Value of Unions," which began:

> The Church is well aware that difficult economic times call for hard choices and financial responsibility to further the common good. Our own dioceses and parishes have not been immune to the effects of the current economic difficulties. But hard times do not nullify the moral obligation each of us has to respect the legitimate rights of workers.

He then quoted from Pope Benedict's encyclical, *Caritas in Veritate*:

> Governments, for reasons of economic utility, often limit the freedom or the negotiating capacity of labor unions. Hence traditional

networks of solidarity have more and more obstacles to overcome. The repeated calls issued within the Church's social doctrine, beginning with *Rerum Novarum*, for the promotion of workers' associations that can defend their rights must therefore be honored today even more than in the past, as a prompt and farsighted response to the urgent need for new forms of cooperation at the international level, as well as the local level (25).

Trying to find some middle ground, the Archbishop called for new forms of collaboration:

> It does not follow from this that every claim made by workers or their representatives is valid. Every union, like every other economic actor, is called to work for the common good, to make sacrifices when required, and to adjust to new economic realities.
>
> However, it is equally a mistake to marginalize or dismiss unions as impediments to economic growth. As Pope John Paul II wrote in 1981, "[a] union remains a constructive factor of *social order* and *solidarity*, and it is impossible to ignore it" (*Laborem Exercens*, 20, emphasis in original).
>
> It is especially in times of crisis that "new forms of cooperation" and open communication become essential. We request that lawmakers carefully consider the implications of this proposal and evaluate it in terms of its impact on the common good. We also appeal to everyone—lawmakers, citizens, workers, and labor unions—to move beyond divisive words and actions and work together, so that Wisconsin can recover in a humane way from the current fiscal crisis.[2]

The United States Conference of Catholic Bishops (USCCB) offered its support to the position taken by Archbishop Listecki and the Wisconsin Conference of Bishops. The chairman of the USCCB Committee on Domestic Justice and Human Development, Bishop Stephen E. Blaire, pointed out that

> Catholic teaching and your statement remind us these are not just political conflicts or economic choices; they are moral choices with enormous human dimensions. The debates over worker representation and collective bargaining are not simply matters of ideology or power, but involve principles of justice, participation and how workers can have a voice in the workplace and economy.[3]

As with other life issues and issues of social justice, the struggle to protect the rights of workers is often filled with passion, controversy, and conflict. The duties and rights of workers has a long tradition in Catholic social teaching, and labor has been a central concern for the Catholic tradition since the first papal social encyclical in 1891, titled *Rerum Novarum* (*The Condition of Labor*). The dignity of the human person is at stake in the way workers are treated, which is why the church has defended the rights of workers through the centuries.

Maria Moñtez is a senior citizen who has been working in a poultry processing plant for five years. She is friendly, though shy, and says a number of times that she is glad to have a job. She works hard using very sharp knives to cut up chicken carcasses as they whiz by at ninety chickens per minute. Señora Moñtez gets one bathroom break per shift and a short lunch break. If she doesn't keep up with the frenetic pace without complaining, she may be fired. Maria speaks of the pain and injury to her arms and hands, particularly the numbness in her arms and hands from the motions she repeats hundreds of time during her long shifts. The pain often keeps her awake at night, and she treats her numbness by using rubbing alcohol on her skin. Yes, the company has health insurance, but it is of no use to her, because the deductible is several hundred dollars, which she cannot afford on her wages. She has asked to be rotated to other tasks with different motions, but her supervisor told her she is too dependable in her job to be transferred.[4] Señora Moñtez works hard but her right to a healthy job environment and health insurance are not protected.

Life isn't that much better for the small farmers who raise the chickens. Because of vertical integration in the poultry industry, a large corporation usually controls the production and profits by contracting with the thirty thousand small farmers who raise chickens. The company owns the chickens, supplies the feed, slaughters the birds, and markets the meat. "Through these contracts farmers nearly always come up short," Father John Rausch explains. "The contracts give full control of the process to the firms, but full responsibility for any problems to the farmer. The mortgage debt incurred by contract poultry farmers keeps them serfs on their own land and intimidates them from speaking out, fearful of bankruptcy if the company cancels their contracts and stops delivery of young chicks."

The Catholic bishops of the south called attention to these abuses of workers and farmers in their pastoral letter *Voices and Choices*, released in November 2000. The letter recognizes the structural injustices in the industry, which tolerates low wages and allows only a meager return to farmers in order to maximize corporate profits and market an inexpensive product. When workers are paid a poverty wage, the poultry industry actually shifts certain costs to the public, including health care, supplemental food stamps for the working poor, and pollution of the environment. As Bishop John McRaith of Owensboro, Kentucky warns: "Somebody's paying the price, not only for bigness but for cheap food."[5]

The letter notes that 60 percent of the poultry companies surveyed were in violation of the Fair Labor Standards Act by failing to pay workers for job-related tasks such as clean up and necessary breaks for restroom use and by charging workers for their required protective gear. The bishops also pointed to the fact that poultry workers experienced repetitive motion injuries at a rate five times higher than workers in general manufacturing. Studies also show that real average wages for poultry workers declined from 1987 to 1997, while the "line speed" limit increased from seventy birds per minute in 1979 to ninety-one per minute in 1999. These factors produced very high profits for the chicken broiler industry, exceeding $1 billion in 1996. In 2011conditions have not improved.[6]

A review of the central issues involving the dignity of work and workers rights must begin with a brief structural analysis to determine who has the power in the workplace and how can workers give voice to their collective power. Subsequently biblical perspectives, which reveal the priority of people over profits, and the USCCB's ten principles of economic justice clarify rights and responsibilities in the economic arena. The chapter concludes with a discussion of living wage and worker rights within the church.

The Imbalance of Power

The bishops of the South quoted the 1986 pastoral letter of the U.S. bishops, *Economic Justice for All*, which addresses the imbalance of economic power in the United States: "The way power is distributed in a free market economy frequently gives employers greater bargaining power over employees in the negotiation of labor contracts. Such unequal power may press workers into a choice between an inadequate wage and no wage at all" (103).

Writing back in 1891 Pope Leo XIII could have been speaking of the situation of poultry workers and chicken farmers today when he argued: "As a rule, workman and employer should make free agreements, and in particular should freely agree as to wages; nevertheless . . . if through necessity or fear of a worse evil, the workman accepts harder conditions because an employer or contractor will give him no better, he is a victim of force and injustice" (*Rerum Novarum*, 6).

The issue is often missed today even by Catholic businesspeople and clergy, who tend to ignore or downplay the structural question of the *imbalance of power*. Instead, they usually translate the issue into a personal question of whether an individual boss or owner is fair. One pastor actually believes that the struggle for better working conditions by low-wage workers in a nursing home should be handled like marriage counseling. He maintains that if you put both parties in the room with a counselor, they can work out their differences. What he has missed in the analogy to marriage is the imbalance of power between individual workers and the management. An outspoken worker does not have equal power in that situation and could easily find herself or himself without a job.

The bishops of the South realized how difficult it is for workers to organize in order to bring their aggregate power to the bargaining table.

> Having a "voice" can lead to having a "choice" about wages, working conditions, job safety, medical care and other benefits. It is often difficult for workers to achieve this sharing of responsibility with owners and managers, which is why, for decades, the Church has supported the right of individuals to associate in groups organized to see that "voices and choices" become a reality.[7]

Organizing workers is never easy. In the poultry industry, as in migrant farm work, additional obstacles include a high turnover in the workforce, the vulnerable status of the workers, and the isolation of many of the workers. Juan Sanchez, a labor organizer, expresses the need to be organized: "People are tired, but they want to be organized. It's the only way to get the company's attention when they are abused by supervisors or overburdened with work. They want to protect themselves."[8]

Some people who work in the poultry industry do have more power to influence corporate policy and make changes. For example, John Stephens, senior manager in a poultry company, works to keep his operations profitable in the competitive business. His biggest challenge is employee turnover. As soon as people can find another job they are gone, so he hires immigrants, sometimes with questionable documentation. "The poultry industry in the U.S. is not an employment of choice for people," Stephens admits. "The work is very hard physically and repetitious—that's part of the problem."[9] Keeping a trained staff would be easier for managers like Stephens if there were industry-wide safety and health standards, improved working conditions, and just wages. These improvements usually come from collective bargaining, where the workers coalesce their power.

Changes can also be brought about by advocates outside the industry who bring their voice and power to bear when worker rights and dignity are threatened. In both strategies, the empowerment of workers and advocacy by outside voices, the church can play an important role.

Inequality of Wealth and Power

As many workers struggle for fair and living wages, the current reality in the United States is characterized by the ballooning salaries of chief executive officers, the stagnant wages of ordinary workers, and increasing economic inequality. The ratio between the highest-paid and the average-paid worker was 42 to 1 in 1980. By 2005 it had jumped to 411 to 1. The median American family made nearly $1,000 less in 2006 than in 2000, even though the U.S. economy had a healthy rate of growth during that period. Between 2002 and 2006, 75 percent of all income gains went to the top 1 percent, that is to households making more than $382,600 a year. According to the IRS, incomes rose fastest among the top 1 percent, and within that group, the biggest gain went to the richest one-tenth of 1 percent. These 145,000 taxpayers with reported incomes over $1.6 million saw their incomes rise by almost 10 percent from 2002 to 2003. The United States is now the third most unequal industrial society, after Russia and Mexico.[10]

What are the implications of this extreme inequality? First of all, the *concentration of wealth translates into concentrated political power.* Supreme Court Justice Louis Brandeis put it bluntly over a century ago: "We can have concentrated wealth in the hands of a few or we can have democracy. But we cannot have both." Judge Brandeis was writing in the context of the Gilded Age (1890–1915), which was also a time of extreme wealth inequality.[11]

Brandeis

Concentrations of wealth are a potential threat to democratic institutions, which in turn shape the rules of our economy and further increase concentrations of wealth, and so the cycle continues. Political scientist Samuel Huntington quipped: "Money becomes evil not when it is used to buy goods but when it is used to buy power. . . . Economic inequalities become evil when they are translated into political inequalities." In other words, as Chuck Collins and Mary Wright put it, "the problem is not how many yachts wealthy people buy, but how many senators." Collins and Wright note that "Our democracy is now at risk because of the enormous power of accumulated wealth in so few hands. The practices of government, legislating and administering for the common good, have been warped by the financial clout of the few against the interests of the many."[12]

Extreme inequality of wealth and income is destructive of our democracy. Many people who are not wealthy have become disillusioned with politics because their votes seem to have little impact in addressing their concerns. As a result, extreme economic wealth erodes the foundation of our political life and is also destructive of civic society.

> The civic life of an extremely unequal society resembles an apartheid society, with two or three Americas rather than one. People begin to live, work, worship, and socialize with people from only one sector of society and don't have deep connections with people from other sectors. This leads to distance, misunderstanding, distrust, and class and racial antagonisms.[13]

Hopeless
Anger
Shame

The distrust and misunderstandings lead to physical walls as well as economic and social walls. Over nine million households in the United States live behind walls that are similar to other polarized societies such as those of Mexico or Brazil. Sister Helen Prejean, as noted in chapter 3, recognized these separate worlds when she moved into the poor neighborhood in New Orleans. "Is this New Orleans?" she asked. "I feel like I'm in another country."[14] As she made friends with her new neighbors she realized how segregated and deprived her life had been: "And for the first time in my life I realized how deprived my life was in the all-white-just-like-me social circles I used to frequent."[15]

Intriguing new research shows that as the American economic system increases economic inequality, it also negatively impacts the *health of everyone within the society*. And it is not only health that is impacted by economic inequality but also the *quality of life*. This is true for all members of society and not just those at the bottom.[16]

The U.S. bishops wrote about the dangers of extreme inequalities of income and wealth in their pastoral letter on the economy.

> This duty [of establishing a floor of well-being] calls into question extreme inequalities of income and consumption when so many lack basic necessities. Catholic social teaching does not maintain that a flat, arithmetical equality of income and wealth is a demand of justice, but it does challenge economic arrangements that leave large numbers of people impoverished. Further, it sees extreme in-

equality as a threat to the solidarity of the human community, for great disparities lead to deep social divisions and conflict (43).

Biblical Perspectives

Because the Bible and the teachings of Jesus focused on issues of economic justice and income inequality, so must the church address these issues. In fact, in his preaching and teaching Jesus spent more time addressing the needs of the poor and economic issues than any other social issue. While studying in seminary, the Rev. Jim Wallis and his friends

> found several thousand verses in the Bible on the poor and God's response to injustice. We found it to be the second most prominent theme in the Hebrew Old Testament—the first was idolatry. . . . One of every sixteen verses in the New Testament is about the poor or the subject of money. In the first three (Synoptic) gospels it is one out of ten verses, and in the book of Luke, it is one in seven![17]

However, through the centuries the message of Jesus has been dulled or distorted as preachers reinterpreted the text. One example of Jesus' teaching is the Parable of the Laborers in the Vineyard in Matthew 20:1–16.

Jesus Gives Voice to Worker Complaints

When we hear this familiar parable we immediately identify God as the "generous" owner of the vineyard who pays the laborers who worked only one hour the same wage as those who had "borne the burden of the day and the scorching heat." This interpretation conveys a truth about God's reign: that those who come into the vineyard late are given the same reward as those who have been in the vineyard from the first call. The parallel is with the Jewish community who had been following God's invitation from the very beginning and the Gentiles who only recently have become part of God's covenant community. While this is a traditional reading of the parable, is it the only way Jesus intended for it to be read? Like most parables, it lends itself to different interpretations.

To hear the words in a new way, it's helpful to know something about the economic reality of the day laborers of Jesus' time. This interpretation is based on the insights of scripture scholar William Herzog as developed in his text, *Parables as Subversive Speech.*[18] At that time, like today, small farmers were losing land to the large estates because of accumulating debt. When they lost their land they were forced to work on the land as day laborers.

All they had to sell was their ability to work. Others joined this growing pool of unemployed because they were younger sons or daughters who did not inherit because the eldest son in the family was the sole heir. This class of peasants had a very grim existence. During the harvest they might find work, but even at harvest time there seemed to be more workers than jobs and the owners took advantage of this surplus of laborers. When there was no work the laborers were reduced to begging, hunger, and poverty, and many died within four or five years. The pay of a denarius a day was no more than a subsistence wage that barely covered one person's daily needs; it certainly could not provide for a family.

With that background, it is possible to see how the owner of the vineyard tried to keep the workers in their place when they spoke up against the injustice. He mocked their labor in the hot sun all day by giving the same amount to the ones who worked only an hour. To the wealthy owner, their day-long labor is worth only as much as he chooses to give. He is not generous, and the workers should react because their labor has been devalued.

The workers are complaining because they have been shamed. The landowner has deliberately insulted them and they react. By reversing the order of payment so that the last hired received a wage equal to that of the first hired, the owner has told them in effect that he values their day-long effort in the scorching heat no more than the brief labor of the eleventh-hour workers. If the workers consent to his judgment that their labor is worthless, then they have nothing at all left to offer. All they have is their labor, which he has mocked by his "generosity."

Rooted in human dignity, the workers must react. The owner responds, "Can't I be generous with what belongs to me?" Now the owner mocks God, for in the Jewish framework the land belongs to Yahweh and the Earth and its resources are meant for all. Jesus thus gives voice to the oppressed worker who confronts the greed of the elites. Jesus unmasks a situation in which the oppressed are condemned for speaking out.

A non-traditional interpretation of this parable paints a different picture. When we do not presume that we should identify God with the landowner we open ourselves to a new angle of understanding, seeing the world from the perspective of the oppressed day laborer. The parable interpreted in this way again shows a God who is on the side of the poor.

If it is faithful to the words and actions of Jesus, the church should look for ways to give voice to workers who bear the heat of the day, but who are not treated with dignity or paid enough to meet their basic needs. The Bible contains many texts like this parable that address the rights of workers, especially when they are trampled upon by the aristocracy.[19]

The Teachings of the Church

The Catholic Church has tried to keep the voice of Jesus alive in its social teachings. The parables of Jesus have been translated into principles to guide our reflection, our judgment, and our action.

The central principle is simple: the dignity of people must come before profit. The Second Vatican Council put it in these terms: "The social order and its development must constantly yield to the good of the person, since the order of things must be subordinate to the order of persons and not the other way around, as the Lord suggested when he said that the Sabbath was made for man and not man for the Sabbath" (*Gaudium et Spes*, 26).

Pope John Paul II spoke very clearly on the priorities of our faith tradition when he visited Toronto in 1984: "The needs of the poor take priority over the desires of the rich; the rights of workers over the maximization of profits; the preservation of the environment over uncontrolled industrial expansion; and production to meet social needs over production for military purposes."[20]

In 1986 the U.S. bishops published their lengthy pastoral letter on the economy, *Economic Justice for All.* Ten years later they put together a list of principles that can serve as the ten commandments of economic justice.

1. *The economy exists for the person, not the person for the economy.* This teaching echoes the words of Jesus on getting our priorities straight: "The Sabbath was made for humanity, not humanity for the Sabbath."
2. *All economic life should be shaped by moral principles.* Economic choices and institutions must be judged by how they protect or undermine the life and dignity of the human person, support the family, and serve the common good.
3. *A fundamental moral measure of any economy is how the poor and vulnerable are faring.* The Judeo-Christian biblical tradition forcefully teaches that the justice of the community is judged by how the community treats its widows, orphans, and resident aliens.
4. *All people have a right to life and to secure the basic necessities of life* (e.g., food, clothing, shelter, education, health care, safe environment, economic security).
5. *All people have the right to economic initiative, to productive work, to just wages and benefits, to decent working conditions, as well as to organize and join unions or other associations.*

6. *All people, to the extent they are able, have a corresponding duty to work, a responsibility to provide for the needs of their families, and an obligation to contribute to the broader society.* Pope John Paul II described our duty to work "both because the Creator has commanded it and because of his own humanity, which requires work in order to be maintained and developed" (*Laborem Exercens*, 16).

7. In economic life, *free markets have both clear advantages and limits; government has essential responsibilities and limitations; voluntary groups have irreplaceable roles, but cannot substitute for the proper working of the market and the just policies of the state.* This principle is very controversial. How do we find the proper role for the free market and the role of government? The principle of subsidiarity says "keep it as local as possible."

8. *Society has a moral obligation, including governmental action where necessary, to assure opportunity, meet basic human needs, and pursue justice in economic life.* This principle applies to providing an effective educational system. The church has recognized the need for governmental action to promote the common good when it is not achieved through market forces or intermediary institutions. In fact, the government loses its legitimacy when it does not promote the overall welfare of the community.

[margin note: Gov't loses its legitimacy]

9. *Workers, owners, managers, stockholders, and consumers are moral agents in economic life.* By our choices, initiative, creativity, and investment, we enhance or diminish economic opportunity, community life, and social justice. While structural and systemic forces limit personal freedom, that is not the whole story. Individuals still are responsible and can make choices that promote the greater good, just as they can make choices that are short-sighted, immoral, and corrupt.

10. *The global economy has moral dimensions and human consequences.* Decisions on investment, trade, aid, and development should protect human life and promote human rights, especially for those most in need wherever they might live on this globe.

How different our workplaces and lives would be if these principles were followed. While these principles may strike us today as unrealistic or utopian, there are businesses that incorporate these principles in their workplace and business model.

Focolare Movement

A network of businesses linked to the Focolare movement follows these principles. Focolare was founded in 1943 by Chiara Lubich, an Italian Catholic laywoman to promote the ideals of unity and universal brotherhood. The Focolare approach to business, called an "economy of communion," was referred to by Pope Benedict in his 2009 encyclical *Caritas in Veritate* (46). In 2009 750 businesses around the world were part of this network, including 36 in North America. John Mundell is the founder of one of these businesses, Mundell & Associates, which is a twenty-person firm specializing in environmental clean-up and design in Indianapolis.

Discovering Focolare in 1979, Mundell and his wife found it to be a concrete way of living out the gospel: "It's about infusing society with the gospel." A central tenet of the Focolare movement is that a portion of the profits is directed to other parts of the world through works of charity and empowerment of the poor. The "economy of communion" model also fosters a collaborative approach within the company, encouraging the staff to see other firms not as competitors but as colleagues in developing a strong sense of social responsibility in the local community.[22]

Stone Construction Equipment Company

Stone Construction Equipment Company is a medium-size manufacturing company that builds construction equipment in a small town in upstate New York. The CEO of the company, Bob Fien, is an active Catholic who has tried to put the principles of Catholic social teaching to work in his company. His industry, like many others, has seen an exodus from the United States in search of a labor force that would work for less money. However Fien did not follow the trend of moving to a developing country.

Instead, he called together the workers who made cement mixers to explain the situation to them and to ask for their input. Bob explained that with the procedures in place at the time it took ten hours to produce a cement mixer. How could they become more productive so as to compete with Mexican imports? The supervisors and workers took the challenge seriously, because they are not only employees of the company, but also its stockholders. Each worker receives company stock on an annual basis, so if the company does well their stock retains its value.

A worker with a high school education, such as a welder, who stays at Stone Construction for twenty-five years will receive a substantial amount on retirement (approximately $500,000) because the company is 100 percent employee-owned. As Fien notes, "When people feel like they are the owners, they react differently. They want to make sure they do things better, because it is their company."[23] The workers at Stone Equipment have a vested interest not only in keeping the shop open, but also in the company's thriving. The workers rose to Fien's challenge by streamlining the process of manufacturing cement mixers, reducing production time from ten hours to four hours. The company now can easily compete with another company that moved to Mexico.

The story of Stone Construction Equipment Company is a story of financial success and national recognition through treating workers with dignity and respect. Bob is now a nationally recognized advocate for a system of profit-sharing known as Employee Stock Ownership Plan (ESOP). He frequently travels around the country speaking to fellow CEOs about the advantages of treating workers with respect and giving them a share in the profits and ownership of the company.

Such companies are proof that the principles of Catholic social teaching can actually work. The concrete example of this manufacturing company moves from the realm of "wouldn't it be nice?" by demonstrating what can happen if workers and owners share in the wealth generated by their labor and are treated with respect. And, as Bob Fien explains, Stone Construction Equipment Company does more than profit-sharing:

> Profit sharing is nothing more than giving people a piece of the profits in any given year. In the course of a person's life that will end up being a relatively small sum. Wealth is generated when a portion of the profit is returned to the balance sheet. That strengthens the financial position of a company and increases the value of its stock. That is where the big bucks are, in owning stock. And that is the concept of ESOP: when you make the company profitable through your labor and a portion of that profit is returned to the balance sheet, you have generated wealth for the company by increasing the value of its stock. You should share in that wealth by owning stock yourself. It's the essence of *Rerum Novarum*.[24]

Global Working Conditions

Protecting the rights of workers in a global economy is a challenge. Because the United States has regulations to protect the safety and health of workers, higher wages and benefits, and the right to organize, it is often more efficient and/or cost-effective to move jobs to a country that does not have the same protections for workers.[25] While workers of all ages are exploited, the International Labor Organization estimates that 250 million children between the ages of five and fourteen work in developing countries—half of them on a full-time basis. In India it is estimated that between 60 million and 115 million children work; most work in agriculture while others work picking rags, making bricks, polishing gemstones, rolling cigarettes, packaging firecrackers, weaving silk saris and carpets, and as domestics.

A 2001 Human Rights Watch estimated that 15 million children in India worked in conditions of servitude in order to pay off debts incurred by their family. In exchange for a loan to their parents, these children earn so little they are never free from debt.[26] While conditions are not as severe in the United States, many children do risk their health and their lives by working in the fields as young as eleven and twelve years.[27]

Iqbal Masih from Pakistan was one of those bonded, child workers. Shortly after he was born in a small village in rural Pakistan, his father abandoned the family. Iqbal's mother struggled to support her children as a housecleaner, but could not. When he was four years old, Iqbal was sold for $16 into bonded labor at a carpet factory. He worked twelve hours a day and was horribly undernourished and beaten by the foreman many times. For the next six years he was shackled to a carpet loom and for twelve hours each day, six days a week, he tied thousands upon thousands of tiny knots, receiving three cents a day for his labor. Amazingly, Iqbal's spirit remained strong.

When Iqbal was nine years old, a local labor rights organization helped him escape the factory and found a place for him in a school for freed child laborers in Lahore where he would be safe. Iqbal began telling other child laborers about the law in Pakistan that made bonded labor illegal. The children had never before heard about the law. When children started to follow Iqbal's example, trying to escape from the factories, the owners threatened Iqbal and his family. He did not back down, and when he was only twelve he traveled to Sweden and the United States to speak out against child labor. When Iqbal returned to Pakistan on Easter April 16, 1995, he was shot and killed. Many believe he was killed by the "carpet mafia" whom he had defied. At his funeral, a young girl, Shenaz, who had been forced into bonded labor in a brick kiln, said, "the day Iqbal died, a thousand new Iqbals were born."[28]

A few days later on April 19, halfway around the world, another twelve-year-old boy was looking for the Calvin and Hobbes comic strip in his daily newspaper before heading off to school. On the front page of the *Toronto Star* Craig Kielberger was confronted by this headline, "Battled Child Labour, Boy, 12, Murdered." "It was a jolt. Twelve, the same age as I was. My eyes fixed on the picture of a boy in a bright red vest. He had a broad smile, his arm raised straight in the air, a fist clenched." Without reading his favorite comic strip, he spotted another story about another boy, Iqbal Masih, on the other side of the world. "I quickly read through the article, hardly believing the words before me. I turned to my mother. 'What exactly is child labour? Do you think he was really killed for standing up to this "carpet mafia," whatever that is?'"[29]

This story changed Craig Kielberger's life that April morning in 1995. With a small band of friends from school he formed a human rights organization called Free the Children. Before long he had convinced his parents to let him travel with a young Canadian human rights worker named Alam Rahman to see firsthand the working conditions of South Asian children. After the two of them visited the slums, the sweatshops, and the back alleys of India, Nepal, Thailand, Pakistan, and Bangladesh, Craig started an international network. "What started as a group of kids over pizza and pop dreaming of changing the world has grown to an ever-expanding network of young people in over twenty countries."[30]

With support from adults, Free the Children set up amazing programs, such as a rehabilitation and education center for children freed from working in the carpet and glass-blowing factories of India. At the center, one hundred children at a time learn basic reading, writing, and math, and receive professional counseling to help them recover from their abuse. They support projects that create alternative sources of income for families so that children can be removed from hazardous labor and sent to school.

One such project operates in two villages in the Tamil Nadu region of southern India. In these villages, many children work in the gem-cutting and polishing industry. The work causes severe eye strain and other health problems because of poor air quality and long hours in cramped conditions. Free the Children sends money to families to purchase goats and cows to provide milk and food for the family and any excess can be sold to gain some income. Each family that receives a milking animal must mate the animal and give the first calf to another family in the community to spread the benefits of the program.[31]

In helping others, young people can develop their own leadership skills. As they worked to free children in sweatshops, they also freed children and adults from the assumption that young people have to wait until they are adults to make a difference. Craig reports, "In our work with Free the Children we soon realized the need not only to free children from abuse and exploitation, but also to free children from the idea that they are powerless and have nothing to contribute to changing the world."

Free the Children continues to organize youth leadership sessions to help young people develop public-speaking, leadership, and research skills so they can draw attention to children's issues on a local and international level.[32] Free The Children empowers children in North America to take action to improve the lives of fellow children overseas. This initiative serves two communities: developing leadership and inspiring tens of thousands of youth in the United States and Canada and by developing over 650 schools and water projects in communities around the world.[33]

The Dignity of Work

A "theology of work" begins by recognizing that human beings share in God's creative power. "Work" is a form of co-creation with God that allows human beings to continue God's creative process using their human creativity and their hands. Human dignity is enhanced by participating in and contributing to the common good through our work.

The Catholic vision also maintains three basic points about the dignity of the worker. First, the dignity of the worker is more important than the product that is produced or the service that is delivered. Second, work must be done in a way that builds up a sense of community among workers. Finally, the work must be done in a way that gives workers a voice in what they are doing. Workers are to have a voice in conditions affecting their work, not only through grievance procedures but also in positive and constructive avenues as well: "This voice must not depend upon the willingness of superiors to listen but must be a structured means by which workers can make their voices heard."[34]

Giving voice to workers' concerns in a structured way is one justification for unions and for collective bargaining. However, listening to the concerns of workers should not depend on the virtue or benevolence of the managers and owners; it should be an expected part of the workplace. In addition, unions are not the only way to give workers a voice, as is demonstrated in the example of the Stone Construction Equipment Company.

Although a theology of work emphasizes the positive aspects of labor as continuing the creative work of God, work can be experienced and understood as drudgery. In the book of Genesis, God instructs Adam and Eve: "By the sweat of your brow, you will earn your bread." This dimension of work is seen as a penalty, something to be avoided if possible, done only under close supervision and with the threat of dire consequences if one fails to work. The Roman Catholic tradition, without denying that work too often is drudgery, promotes a positive understanding of work as the means to human fulfillment, both personal and communal.

Pope John Paul II was most articulate about the dignity of work, especially in his 1981 encyclical *Laborem Exercens*. First he connects human labor to God's creative work. Humanity "ought to imitate God both in working and also in resting, since God himself wished to present his own creative activity under the form of work and rest" (25). Then the pope points to the dignity of the worker as a person: "The basis for determining the value of human work is not primarily the kind of work being done, but the fact that the one who is doing it is a person" (6). Third, the pope focuses on the ethical meaning of work, namely, that work is a good thing for humanity because through work we not only transform nature, adapting it to our needs, but we also achieve fulfillment as human beings (9).

"Dirty Work"

While we may speak of the dignity of work, we have to be honest and admit that not all work has equal dignity in our culture. Feminist ethicists have focused on what we consider "dirty" work. Dirty work has many forms: farmers, miners, and construction workers, who are generally male, get dirty from their work and such dirt is almost a badge of honor. Other kinds of dirty work are seen as less honorable. The dirt and work that is associated with our bodies, especially work that involves contact with bodily fluids or waste products, has been the domain of women, often located in unpaid domestic households. Catholic ethicist Christine Firer Hinze summarizes our hierarchy of work as it relates to dirt:

> Dirty work carries connotations of work deemed distasteful, repugnant, and hence to be avoided whenever one has a choice in the matter. The less mediated by technology, by formal training and certification, or by controlled distance between the worker and others' bodily functions, fluids, and excreta, the more undesirable and dirty the work is apt to be considered. Comparing the work of a chef, professor, or surgeon on the one hand, to that of a

dishwasher, custodian, or nurse's aide on the other hand illustrates the point. . . . People performing work deemed dirty may find the repugnance dirt elicits rubbing off on them, rendering their social status and self-esteem at least threatened, and often harmed.[35]

In this framework, women who do unpaid domestic work are under-valued in the culture. Well-off women may choose to hire other women to take care of the dirty work. Barbara Ehrenreich notes that in twenty per-cent of U.S. households the family members do no domestic work at all.[36] Many of our most influential political, cultural, academic, religious, and business leaders identify their status in light of, among other things, escap-ing dirty work. These leaders reinforce the cultural linkage between dirty work and disrespect. This disrespect is translated into less status, power, and economic compensation. Why are home health aides or nurse's aides, often women of color, not paid a living wage?

Dr. Firer Hinze challenges our thinking: "To the extent that Christians continue to acquiesce, however unwittingly, in our culture's systemic deg-radation and devaluation of dirty work, we undermine the commitment to social and economic justice that is at the heart of our social mission." She points out that by actively ignoring the moral and economic import of bodily-related dirt, we fail to address people in the places where we really live. Our theology of work must correct this bias against "dirty work" by valuing all types of work and all workers, especially those who care for the needs of our children, the sick, and the elderly. "Correcting this omission will enhance the credibility and effectiveness of Christian ethical analysis and the churches' social ministry today."[37]

Worker Rights to Organize

> The economy must serve people, not the other way around. Work is more than a way to make a living; it is a form of continuing par-ticipation in God's creation. If the dignity of work is to be protected, then the basic rights of workers must be respected—the right to productive work, to decent and fair wages, to the organization and joining of unions, to private property, and to economic initiative.[38]

The Roman Catholic tradition speaks of the right to employment, and with the right to work comes a collection of other rights including: the right to a just wage, the right to rest, the right to a safe workplace, the right to join worker associations, the right to strike, and the right to health care.[39]

In his 1891encyclical *Rerum Novarum*, Pope Leo XIII recognized the right of workers to form unions or associations in order to bargain collectively for fair wages, benefits, and safe and healthy working conditions. As the bishops of the South recognized poultry workers, unions can be an effective strategy in addressing the inequality of power that exists between management and employees. Unions are also a way to establish solidarity and community among workers and to give a voice to workers in their workplace. Unions also contribute to the good of workers and the common good by offering ongoing education and training.

While unions are an effective means of achieving the above-mentioned goals, they are not the only means of accomplishing them. Each workplace situation must be evaluated individually, and the final decision rests with the workers to decide their approach without duress or intimidation from either union organizers or management. The Catholic tradition maintains that efforts by government and business to break unions and prevent workers from joining unions are not ethical. The U.S. bishops note, "No one may deny the right to organize without attacking human dignity itself. Therefore, we firmly oppose organized efforts, such as those regrettably now seen in this country, to break existing unions and prevent workers from organizing."[40]

As a major social institution, unions have obligations to society and must not only serve their own narrow self-interests. They must act in ways that benefit and empower workers *and* contribute to the common good.[41] At times unions are in an adversarial relationship with management, but often they work in collaborative ways with management and industry leaders. One area of collaboration is in the training and education of workers. Unions can also use their collective power to help establish social policy and funding streams that benefit the industry or service in which they work as well as the whole community. For example, unions that represent the staff in nursing homes and hospitals have lobbied *with* health care administrators to secure adequate funding for nursing homes and hospitals so they can more effectively serve their patients.

As Archbishop Listecki in Wisconsin noted "The Church fully supports the right of workers to form unions or other associations to secure their rights to fair wages and working conditions."[42] The Catholic tradition also recognizes that strikes may be used as a way to address labor grievances. Monsignor John Ryan sketched out the conditions for a justified strike in

1920: (1) if what is sought by the strike is just, (2) if all peaceful and less harmful means of bargaining have been exhausted, and (3) if the good to be attained outweighs the evil that may occur.[43]

Pope John Paul II outlined a nuanced position on the right to strike in *Laborem Exercens*:

> One method used by unions in pursuing the just rights of their members is the strike or work stoppage. . . . This method is recognized by Catholic social teaching as legitimate in the proper conditions and within just limits. In this connection workers should be assured the right to strike, without being subjected to personal penal sanctions for taking part in a strike. While admitting that it is a legitimate means, we must at the same time emphasize that a strike remains, in a sense, an extreme means. It must not be abused; it must not be abused especially for "political" purposes (20).

Just Wage

Church leaders have been wrestling with the meaning of a just way for more than 130 years. In Fribourg, Switzerland, lay leaders and clergy met for a month each year starting in 1885 to bring the best of the Catholic tradition to bear on the pressing economic issues of their day. This "Fribourg Union" was an early think tank of theologians and lay leaders who helped to give expression to emerging Catholic social thinking. Pope Leo XIII knew of their deliberations and asked for a full report as he prepared his 1891 encyclical *Rerum Novarum* (*On the Condition of the Workers*). The Fribourg Union (1885–1891) set forth the basic principles on work and wages that have shaped official social teachings, including the principle that a just wage is determined by the minimum necessary to maintain a family in ordinary circumstances.

Pope Leo XIII argued in *Rerum Novarum* that in justice the worker should "receive what will enable him, housed, clothed, and secure, to live his life without hardship" (51). And again, "Hence arises necessarily the right of securing things to sustain life, and only a wage earned by his labor gives a poor man the means to acquire these things" (62).

Papal documents since *Rerum Novarum* have deepened the church's commitment to the principle of a just wage. *The Catechism of the Catholic Church* summarizes this rich tradition by stating, "Everyone should be able to draw from work the means of providing for his life and that of his family, and of serving the human community" (2428).

The Catechism then elaborates on this basic right by quoting from
Gaudium et Spes (67):

> A just wage is the legitimate fruit of work. To refuse or withhold
> it can be a grave injustice. In determining fair pay both the needs
> and the contributions of each person must be taken into account.
> Remuneration for work should guarantee man the opportunity
> to provide a dignified livelihood for himself and his family on the
> material, social, cultural, and spiritual level, taking into account the
> role and productivity of each, the state of the business, and the
> common good (2434).

The right to a just wage is not an optional right in Catholic social
teaching. It is rooted in the dignity of the human person which, while it
is of eternal worth, is also realized concretely in the here and now. Each
person's dignity is lived out or denied within realities of life. If the lived
experience of people does not reflect and enhance human dignity, then the
social, economic, and political context must be changed to make it more
humane and protective of the person's dignity.

Western cultures have come to believe that the best way to protect human dignity is to guarantee human rights. In the human rights tradition,
each person, because of his or her dignity, has certain rights and duties that
are universal, inviolable, and inalienable. Human rights form "a constella-
tion of the conditions for the realization of human worth in action, in an
ordered arrangement."[44] No one right can be singled out without recognizing its relationship to other rights. The full web of rights guarantees the
full development of individuals and their communities.

Within this context of human rights, a just wage is connected to the
individual's right to work. When workers receive a just wage they are able to
achieve their other rights, such as the right to shelter, food, health care, education, support of their families, and the building up of the common good.

The right to a just wage also implies duties and responsibilities. Each
worker is responsible to work a full day and to respect his or her fellow
workers. For their part, employers have the responsibility to pay a just
wage, to respect the human limitations of the workers, to allow workers'
associations, to use all available technology prudently, and to make the
company competitive and profitable.

In the Catholic tradition, the just wage is linked to support for workers and their families. "All heads of households, whether female or male,
whether married or not, deserve a wage that enables them to provide suf-

ficiently for themselves and their dependents." Frank Almade points out six practical implications of the commitment to a just wage:

1. There is no single just wage; it depends on the circumstances in each region.
2. A just wage is at least a minimum to cover the needs of the worker.
3. A just wage is a family wage.
4. There should be a public system of employee administration which includes workers' participation and consultation, wage scales, job evaluation, opportunities for promotion and further training and education, signed agreements, grievance procedures, and an annual review of the whole system.
5. A just wage means equal pay for equal work. There can be no discrimination based on race, sex, national origin, age, or marital status. Benefits may be adjusted to support dependent family members.
6. A just wage is conditioned by the employer's ability to pay the wage, market forces, and the common good. A just wage is linked to other sectors of the society, which Pope John Paul II calls the "indirect employers," such as, governments, central banks, trade unions, and international trade agreements.[45]

Catholic social teaching is realistic about the living wage. It does not say that a company must pay employees in excess of a sustainable wage, that is, the wage should be consistent with sound financial management. The Catholic tradition does not expect a company to pay such high wages that it risks its economic viability. At the same time Catholic social teaching does emphasize the obligation in justice to create right relationships with employees and to work toward a living wage.

In the 1990s a living-wage movement developed in the United States around the moral propositions "first, that work should be rewarded, and second, that no one who works full time should have to live in poverty."[46] The Catholic Church has played a constructive role in this movement from the very beginning.

Living-Wage Movement

The modern living-wage movement was born in 1994 in the soup kitchens of Baltimore. One of those soup kitchens was at Blessed Sacrament Church. The pastor, Father Sam Lupico, in keeping with the church's tradition of the corporal works, offered meals for the poor on Wednesday evenings. He was surprised by the population who arrived for supper. He expected the usual soup-kitchen crowd: the homeless, the chemically dependent, and the mentally ill. He did not expect to see entire families searching for food. He learned that most of these families had at least one wage earner, but they were not able to live on those wages. "You can't support a family with the minimum wage. It's impossible. The numbers just don't add up," the priest noted, referring to the federal minimum wage of $4.25.[47] The injustice of the situation bothered Father Lupico. He, with other pastors and community leaders, began to explore the systemic problem of inadequate wages.

Father Lupico, other religious, and labor leaders discussed their concern about inadequate wages in the faith-based community organization called BUILD, the acronym for Baltimoreans United in Leadership Development. The fifty congregations who were part of BUILD studied the situation of low-income workers in Baltimore. They discovered that 40 percent of the people using their soup kitchens were employed at least part-time. Many of the members of their congregations were employed but were making poverty wages. "From this experience came the idea of addressing the issue of low wages."[48]

The coalition decided to focus on the idea of the living wage, namely, that any person who works full-time, year-round should make enough money to cover the necessities of life. The urban vicar of the Archdiocese of Baltimore, Bishop John Ricard, firmly supported the workers in their rights to organize and to receive a just wage. In December 1994 the Baltimore City Council passed a bill requiring companies that have service contracts with the city of Baltimore to pay workers $6.10 per hour, more than the federal minimum wage of $4.25. The bill included steps to increase the wage over a four-year period to $7.70 in 1999. The hourly living-wage rate of $10.59 will remain in effect through June 30, 2012.[49]

More than 150 cities and counties have passed living-wage ordinances. At the writing of this book in 2011, living-wage campaigns are underway in New York City and Sonoma County in California.[50] When a living-wage ordinance was passed in Rochester, New York, the Catholic Family Center, a regional office of Catholic Charities, voluntarily decided to pay a living wage to all of its employees. Catholic Family Center is not required by the ordinance to pay a living wage, but the president and CEO believed it was the right thing to do.[51] This is a good example of teaching the principles of Catholic social teaching by implementing them within a Catholic agency.

Living Wage in the Church

It is one thing to recommend a living wage for society and quite another thing to implement a living wage for church employees. The recommendation to pay a living wage would be seen as hypocritical if the church did not apply the same teaching to its own workers. For almost a century the church has stressed the importance of paying a living wage to its employees. In 1917 the *Code of Canon Law* instructed administrators to provide fair wages and decent working conditions to employees (1524). Unfortunately this canon wasn't automatically implemented. The *Revised Code of Canon Law* repeated and updated that teaching in 1983 (231 and 1286).

The most explicit statement on the church's responsibility to practice what it preaches is found in the 1971 document *Justice in the World* (41): "While the Church is bound to give witness to justice, she recognizes that anyone who ventures to speak to people about justice must first be just in their eyes." The document notes that all who serve the church by their labor—laity, religious, and priests—are to receive just remuneration (41). In addition to just wages, church workers are to benefit from all of the other rights that Catholic social teaching recognizes for workers, including the right to form a union. "All church institutions must also fully recognize the rights of employees to organize and bargain collectively with the institution through whatever association or organization they freely choose."[52]

Msgr. George Higgins

During the last half of the twentieth century the American Catholic Church was blessed to have the ministry of George Higgins, a powerful voice for worker rights within society and within the church. Few leaders have been as consistent on labor issues as Msgr. Higgins, a man who was not afraid to challenge big business, union leaders, or Catholic institutions. Higgins believed that

> In today's world, our large Catholic institutions have a glorious opportunity to set the example for the rest of the church and society in general. These institutions should not only follow legally established labor rules but should set the highest standard for fair treatment. Our role as Catholics is not only to respect workers' rights, but to be exemplary.[53]

George Higgins was a native of Chicago, where he was ordained in 1940. He completed his doctoral studies and began teaching in the economics department at the Catholic University of America in 1944. Ten years later he joined the Social Action Department of the National Catholic Welfare Conference, which would eventually become the National Conference of Catholic Bishops, now the United States Conference of Catholic Bishops. For thirty-six years he worked for the Bishops' Conference in various capacities related to social justice and labor. For thirty-five of those years he wrote a weekly column on social justice called "The Yardstick," which was reprinted in many diocesan weekly newspapers. Through this format Higgins helped Catholics understand how their faith is connected to the social issues of the day.

Higgins is remembered as well for his leadership in helping farm workers to win labor contracts in California. He did this by working with all the major players, as Gerard Sherry, a journalist for the *Central California Register* in Fresno, recalled:

> George educated the bishops' committee, but more important he facilitated the acceptance by the growers of a union and got them to accept the fact that the union wouldn't strain them. And he also got the farm workers to recognize the fact that to be successful in representing the workers they also had to be businesslike and that there had to be some give and take; that nothing was done by simply making demands.[54]

Monsignor Higgins also made a significant contribution to the church by his behind-the-scenes participation in the Second Vatican Council. His influence was especially evident in bringing two documents to successful completion. The first is the Declaration on Catholic-Jewish relations (*Nostra Aetate*), which repudiated anti-Semitism and the ancient charge of collective Jewish responsibility for the death of Jesus, and called for dialogue between Catholics and Jews. His connections within the American Jewish community allowed him to bring feedback to the bishops on how Jewish leaders perceived the various drafts. Higgins also was an important player in publishing the Council's *Declaration on Religious Liberty*. He worked with American bishops and Jesuit theologian John Courtney Murray to achieve a breakthrough in Catholic teaching on the right of religious freedom for all religions. The Council taught that religious truth can be found outside the Body of Christ, replacing the too-exclusive understanding of revelation as limited to "Christian revelation." The document also discarded the medieval teaching that "error has no rights."[55]

Even though Monsignor Higgins retired in 1980, he remained active in labor issues and was very outspoken in the tumultuous union struggles at California's Catholic hospitals during the 1990s. When the workers at Sacramento's Mercy General Hospital, which is part of the Catholic Healthcare West system, were battling to form a union, "a white-haired man of the cloth rolled his wheelchair through the automatic doors" of the hospital. He was there to chat with the delighted hospital service workers and, according to *The Sacramento Bee*, to "prick the hospital system's Catholic conscience." That white-haired man of the cloth was Higgins. The hospital administrators, who were opposing the workers' freedom to organize, reportedly greeted Higgins with "tight smiles." No wonder. As one theologian said, "It would be almost like bringing in Gandhi. He carries with him a long history and the respect of many people and he is well-known in the Catholic community."[56]

On August 9, 2000, at a White House ceremony presided over by President Clinton, Msgr. Higgins was honored with the Presidential Medal of Freedom, the nation's highest civilian honor. Msgr. Higgins was selected because of his nearly fifty years of service defending the rights of workers. His death on May 1, 2002, at the age of 86 left a huge hole in the leadership of the Catholic Church in the United States on labor issues.

A Just and Fair Workplace

As is obvious from the above descriptions of a just wage, justice in the workplace is more than a matter of adequate wages, although justice certainly includes wages. Over the last two decades administrators from Catholic health care institutions and leaders of labor unions have had candid and constructive dialogues about Catholic social teaching and the workplace. They produced a document called *A Fair and Just Workplace: Principles and Practices for Catholic Health Care*, released in November 1999, and a second document, *Respecting the Just Rights of Workers: Guidance and Options for Catholic Health Care and Unions*, in 2009.

Although written with health care workers in mind, these documents offer standards that apply to all workers: "Among the elements of a just and fair workplace are: fair wages, adequate benefits, safe and decent working conditions, and the right to participate in decisions which affect one's work, as well as opportunities for advancement, learning and growth." The 1999 document presents the components of a just workplace by asking:

- Does the institution provide a safe and healthful working environment?
- Do the lowest-paid workers receive wages sufficient to sustain themselves and their families?
- Is health care insurance provided, or are wages sufficient for a worker to both sustain a family and purchase health care insurance?
- Are work hours flexible so as to permit adequate rest, leisure time, educational opportunities, and quality family time?
- Are training and educational opportunities that will lead to advancement and promotions available to workers?
- What is the purpose of part-time or contract positions—to advance the institution and meet the needs of workers, or to avoid paying benefits?
- Do workers have easy access to written procedures that explain how to resolve disputes with supervisors or file a grievance to protect their rights or the rights of others?
- Do workers have avenues for meaningful input into decisions affecting the workplace?[57]

Ten years later leaders from Catholic health care, the labor movement, and the U.S. Conference of Catholic Bishops have agreed to another set of principles designed to ensure a fair process when health care workers are deciding whether to join a union. "The heart of this unusual consensus is that it's up to workers—not bishops, hospital managers or union leaders—to decide . . . whether or not to be represented by a union and if so, which union, in the workplace," said Cardinal Theodore E. McCarrick, retired archbishop of Washington and a participant in the consultations. The document calls on unions and employers to respect "each other's mission and legitimacy" and to pledge not to "demean or undermine each other's institutions, leaders, representatives, effectiveness or motives."[58] Furthermore, "All parties are committed to respecting each other's mission and legitimacy and (acknowledging) that a fair and just work place can exist in a unionized or non-unionized environment," Cardinal McCarrick added.[59]

The principles of Catholic social teaching are important, but they remain lifeless principles unless they take on human form. A fitting conclusion lies in the story of one individual who enfleshed these teachings in his organizing and in his spirituality as he stood up for the dignity and the rights of workers in the fields of America.

Cesar Chavez—Community Organizer

It is an old story: the young Chavez had to quit school to work in the fields full-time to help support his family because his father had lost the family farm during the Depression. He worked stooped over in the fields as his family followed the crops up and down the West Coast. As the son of migrant farm workers, Cesar Chavez had attended thirty-seven schools by the time he was in the eighth grade. Farm workers were (and are) notoriously the poorest and most exploited American workers. At the time they were unorganized and deliberately excluded from the labor laws that helped other workers.

In 1949 at the age of twenty-two he was married and living in a barrio of San Jose, California called "Sal Si Puede" (Leave, if you can!), which seemed to signal the desperate hope of many migrant workers. That same year he met a priest from San Francisco who helped him and his community find a way out. Father Donald McDonnell, who was ministering to the farm workers, told Chavez about the Catholic social tradition. As Chavez recalled, "He told me about social justice and the Church's stand on farm labor and reading from the encyclicals of Pope Leo XIII, in which he upheld labor unions." These teachings fascinated the young Chavez. "I would do anything to get the Father to tell me more about labor history. I began going to the Bracero camps with him to help with the Mass, to the city jail with him to talk to the prisoners, anything to be with him."[60]

Chavez learned about the world of Catholic social teaching, which proclaimed the dignity of his work and the rights of workers. Three years later Father McDonnell recommended Chavez as a potential leader to the community organizer Fred Ross, who had come into the community to organize a local chapter of the Community Service Organization (CSO). Chavez eventually worked with Ross for ten years as they organized Mexican Americans in California. This community organization addressed police brutality, school and job discrimination, and inadequate housing. They also worked on citizenship classes and voter registration campaigns. Chavez hoped that the CSO would become a base from which to organize farm workers, but this did not happen. So in 1962, Chavez broke away from CSO because it "got pretty middle class, [and] didn't want to go into the fields. So I left."[61]

Chavez could have had a secure life as an organizer with CSO, enjoying a middle-class existence, but he remembered his people in the fields and made an option for the least of these. As a family man with eight children, leaving CSO was a risk for him and his whole family. With his organizing skills and with a deep spirituality Chavez and Dolores Huerta founded the United Farm Workers Union (UFW). Chavez would often be babysitting his youngest children in the car as he drove through dozens of farm worker towns trying to build up the membership of the new union.

Chavez brought together his charismatic leadership, keen organizing skills, and a solid Catholic spirituality rooted in his Mexican American culture, always with a nonviolent strategy. For the next thirty-one years Chavez worked to organize farm workers so that they might be able to participate more effectively as economic actors with better wages and health benefits and as a community whose collective voice and power would be taken seriously by growers and politicians. By the 1970s the UFW had about eighty thousand members; after a number of setbacks the number in 2003 was about twenty thousand. While not completely successful, Chavez brought the eyes of the church, the media, and politicians to focus on the plight of farm workers, who have a long struggle to achieve justice, with many powerful forces blocking their efforts.

Cesar Chavez stands as an example of a Christian laborer and family man who chose to work for the good of his community even at a great cost to himself and his family. After a long fast in 1968 he summarized his spirituality and his vision of manly courage:

> When we are really honest with ourselves we must admit that our lives are all that really belong to us. So it is how we use our lives that determines what kind of men we are. It is my deepest belief that only by giving our lives do we find life. I am convinced that the truest act of courage, the strongest act of manliness is to sacrifice ourselves for others in [the] totally nonviolent struggle for justice. To be a man is to suffer for others. God help us to be men![62]

He found a way to participate in the economy as a farm worker and an organizer. By bringing his faith to his work, he was truly a minister of the gospel in the marketplace and in the fields.

United Farm Workers' Prayer

(Written by Cesar Chavez [1927–1993], founder of United Farm Workers)

Show me the suffering of the most miserable, so I may
know my people's plight.
Free me to pray for others, for you are present in every person.
Help me to take responsibility for my own life, so that
I can be free at last.
Grant me courage to serve others, for in service there is true life.
Give me honesty and patience, so that I can work with other workers.
Bring forth song and celebration, so that the Spirit will be
alive among us.
Let the Spirit flourish and grow, so that we will never tire
of the struggle.
Let us remember those who have died for justice, for they
have given us life.
Help us love even those who hate us, so we can change the world.
Amen.

Discussion Questions

1. What are the hidden costs of inexpensive chicken that Bishop McRaith "revealed" in the pastoral letter, *Voices and Choices*? Why is the church concerned about these hidden costs?
2. Pope John Paul II said: "The needs of the poor take priority over the desires of the rich; the rights of workers over the maximization of profits; the preservation of the environment over uncontrolled industrial expansion; and production to meet social needs over production for military purposes." Do you see any signs that these principles are "in play" in our society?
3. Pick one of the "ten commandments" of economic justice and explain why you think it is important.
4. In 1891 Pope Leo XIII taught that in justice the worker should "receive what will enable him, housed, clothed, and secure, to live his life without hardship." Is this teaching still valid for today? Explain.

8

Solidarity: War and Peace

Recognizing the solidarity of the human family is a matter of perspective. Astronauts in space are rewarded with a unique perspective of our planet. From outer space Earth is a fragile, blue marble of life in the expansive universe, with the divisions of war, race, religion, and wealth invisible. Indian-born astronaut Kalpana Chawla, who flew on two space shuttle trips, including one that ended in tragedy, noted that she did not feel Indian in space. "When you look at the stars and the galaxy, you feel that you are not just from any particular piece of land, but from the solar system."[1] All of human life and nature are connected, linked in the solidarity of the one planetary home.

This chapter explores the meaning of human solidarity as well as the failure of solidarity in the face of the persistent reality of war. Forgiveness is also discussed as a dimension of solidarity and a requirement for building peace. Finally, the chapter reviews four approaches to war: the just war tradition, pacifism, active nonviolence, and preventive war, as well as the challenge of peace-building.

Solidarity: Ancient Concept, Recent Term

A young German woman has just finished her master's of divinity degree and has a few months open before she will look for a job teaching theology in a German high school. So what should Julie do with her free time? Take a long vacation in Spain, Italy, or the Greek islands? Possibly, but Julie has decided she wants an experience with more depth and meaning. After checking out the internet, she settles on a shelter for homeless women in a tough neighborhood in Rochester, New York. Sight unseen, she arrives in the middle of winter at the doorstep of Bethany House, a Catholic Worker house in one of the snow-belt cities of upstate New York. She has traveled five thousand miles to volunteer at a home for women and children who are homeless, often because of domestic violence or drug abuse.

About the same time, in Washington State Jessica is about to make a similar decision. She has decided to join another Catholic Worker house, St. Joseph House of Hospitality, also in Rochester, which feeds the needy and houses homeless men. Jessica travels three thousand miles to live a life of voluntary poverty and to serve the people most Americans try to avoid.

Katie and Matt are a retired couple living in small town in Wisconsin. While doing all the things grandparents do to help out their grandkids, children, and great-grandchildren, they also make time to be involved in civic organizations and they volunteer one day a week at the clothing and food cupboard in a nearby town.

Why do people do such things? Why do so many people make time to serve the needs of others, in their vocation, in their families, and as citizens? In our world today there are people who respond to the needs of others out of their sense of human solidarity. In some visceral way, although our languages and skin color may be different, we are all connected as human beings. Julie, Jessica, and Katie and Matt are all aware of their connectedness to those in need; they are also mindful of the invitation of Jesus to serve their neighbor. This is the face of solidarity in everyday life.

While the concept of solidarity is as ancient as the Hebrew covenants that God made with Abraham and Moses, the actual word "solidarity" appeared in English only in the middle of the nineteenth century when Catholic thinkers lifted the term from the labor movements in France and Germany.[2] They were looking for a word to express the Catholic vision of human beings as essentially *social* in contrast to the *individualistic* tendencies of capitalism. The term was also intended to counter the subordination of individuals to "the collective will" of communism. The word "solidarity" communicated their vision of society as cooperative and harmonious.

Pope Pius XI used the word solidarity in his 1931 encyclical *Quadragesimo Anno* (*After Forty Years*) as a counterpoint to socialism. His use of solidarity conveyed the God-given dignity of the human person that government and economic policy should recognize; the importance of subsidiarity to establish a role for family and local communal initiatives; and the recognition that solidarity includes all of humanity created and redeemed by God, and not just one group.[3]

Pope Paul VI stressed that "the spirit of solidarity" was essential for full human development of every person. Later Pope John Paul II articulated the Catholic virtue of solidarity by standing with his Polish brothers and sisters in their struggle for freedom. The work of "solidarity" in Poland was not without risk, as the story of Father Jerzy Popieluszko demonstrates.

Jerzy was born to a peasant family in Poland in 1947. His generation had grown up under communism. Like most Poles he shared a disdain for the communist system, but as a priest working as a chaplain to medical students at the university in Warsaw he had never been active in political resistance. Poland was on the verge of change in 1978 when the Polish cardinal, Karol Woytila, was elected pope. In June 1979 Pope John Paul II made the first of four visits to Poland. He stirred up national pride and confidence in millions of Poles as he urged them, "Do not be afraid to insist on your rights. Refuse a life based on lies and double thinking. Do not be afraid to suffer with Christ." Within a year of his visit the militant trade union movement Solidarity was born.

Father Popieluszko became involved in the Solidarity movement almost by chance. In August 1980 when the shipworkers in Gdansk went on strike, the steelworkers in Warsaw expressed their solidarity by going on strike as well. The steelworkers in Warsaw asked the chancery to send a priest who could celebrate mass at the factory. Father Jerzy heard of the request and volunteered to go.

The mass was celebrated in front of the factory where the workers had erected an enormous cross. For the thirty-three year-old priest, this was a turning point in his life. He saw with great clarity that the workers' struggle for justice and freedom was truly a spiritual struggle. With the bishop's support, Jerzy became the chaplain to the striking steelworkers.

The Polish government struck back by declaring martial law in December 1981, resulting in the arrest of thousands of Solidarity members and their supporters. As their chaplain, Jerzy visited the prisoners and organized support for their families. He also drew enormous crowds with his patriotic sermons that highlighted the moral and spiritual aspects of the Solidarity movement. The movement affirmed the spiritual side of humanity and struggled against a foreign-imposed totalitarianism, rejecting a culture built on hatred, lies, and fear: "At this time, when we need so much strength to regain and uphold our freedom, let us pray to God to fill us with the power of His Spirit, to reawaken the spirit of true solidarity in our hearts."[4]

As Father Jerzy's ministry with the workers expanded, so did the government's efforts to silence him. He was followed wherever he went, his masses were often interrupted by provocateurs, and a bomb was hurled at his apartment. However, Jerzy would not be silent or become paralyzed by fear: "The only thing we should fear is the betrayal of Christ for a few silver pieces of meaningless peace."[5]

By 1984 the pressure from the government had increased. Father Jerzy was brought in for interrogation thirteen times and in July he was charged with "abusing freedom of conscience and religion to the detriment of the Polish People's Republic." The indictment brought on a storm of protests, so the government offered him amnesty. The workers who were concerned for his safety asked the cardinal of Warsaw to send him abroad for study. But Father Popieluszko would not abandon the workers in their time of need:

> If we must die it is better to meet death while defending a worthwhile cause than sitting back and letting an injustice take place. . . . The priest is called to bear witness to the truth, to suffer for the truth, and if need be to give up his life for it. We have many such examples in Christianity. From them we should draw conclusions for ourselves.[6]

His death came on October 20, 1984, after being abducted by three men who stuffed him into the trunk of their car. It was Father Jerzy's driver who managed to escape and reported the abduction. Masses were said throughout the country for the priest's safe release and eventually the government buckled under the pressure and launched an immediate investigation, arresting four members of the security police who led them to the priest's body. The abductors confessed that in the early morning hours of October 20, after savagely and repeatedly beating Father Jerzy, they tied him up, weighted his body with stones, and tossed him, still alive, into a reservoir.

Although the security forces had tried to silence his voice, in death the echo of his voice only became louder. Father Jerzy helped to usher in a new day for Polish workers and the Polish people, and within five years of his death, the first free elections were held in postwar Poland. The people peacefully threw out the communist regime and elected a democratic government based on the principles of the Solidarity movement.

A Theology of Solidarity

Pope John Paul II knew from the struggle of solidarity of Poland that solidarity was both a gift and a challenge. In 1981 he maintained in *Laborem Exercens* that humanity is gifted by God in solidarity with each other by the very fact of our shared creation and shared redemption. Solidarity is also a challenge that invites workers and all people to focus their activity on the common good. In his subsequent encyclical, *Sollicitudo Rei Socialis* (1983), he speaks of the "virtue of solidarity," which is not just a vague feeling of compassion, but "*a firm and preserving determination* to commit oneself to the *common good*" (38).

Although the term has a special meaning in Poland's labor history, solidarity is not meant only for workers. All groups of people are invited to practice solidarity—between individuals, professions, classes, communities, and nations. The work of solidarity is to overcome the alienation and injustice that so many people experience.

Theologian Matthew Lamb asks, "Given the massive injustices that sin causes in history, a human justice is inadequate. How can we render justice to the murdered and dead? Human solidarity breaks down in the cycles of violence and counter violence, as one grievance evokes another, as one war is followed by another."[7] It is not difficult to see the lack of solidarity within our country as well as the centuries-old divisions between ethnic groups and nations around the globe.

On the positive side, a theology of solidarity puts us on God's landscape, with a divine perspective. Similar to astronaut Kalpana Chawla, as she looked out of the window of the space shuttle, we locate humanity and creation in a larger context. A God-centered solidarity insists that "the depths of human suffering can only be redeemed by God's loving solidarity with us in Christ. . . . We humans are enabled to forgive as God has forgiven, loving not only our friends but also our enemies, that is, being as universal in our solidarity as God." Such a divine solidarity can "end the cycles of violence, not by muting the cries of the victims, but by transforming, as only God can, those sufferings into new life."[8]

In a Catholic understanding of solidarity, the church is the sacramental presence of human and divine solidarity. This, no doubt, is what Father Popieluszko recognized as he celebrated the Eucharist with the workers. As Jesus was the incarnation of divine solidarity, now the church and individual Christians proclaim the solidarity of all of God's people. "As incarnating the presence of agapic love, the church proclaims the coming fullness of human solidarity with all the just, who are enfolded in the eternal life of the triune God."[9]

Unrestrained Conflict

Pope John Paul II knew that living the virtue of solidarity involves conflict and struggle. He noted that *conflict has a positive role* "when it takes the form of a 'struggle for justice.'"[10] What he did condemn as immoral was unrestrained conflict, whether in class warfare or in military conflict. In the encyclical *Centesimus Annus* he described such conflict as "a conflict which set man against man, almost as if they were 'wolves' . . . a conflict all the more harsh and inhumane because it knew no rule or regulation" (5). The Catholic tradition rejects such conflict because it is unrestrained, not mitigated by the rights of others or the rule of law or reason.

Moral theologian Patrick McCormick explains the immorality of unrestrained violence: "Such unrestrained violence, which intends the complete destruction of the adversary without any attention to moral limits, denies the very dignity of the self, the neighbor, and the covenantal relationship with God."[11] Unrestrained violence leads to the evil of total warfare, as well as the arrogance of militarism, imperialism, and all forms of terrorism.

Pope John Paul II has consistently taught that conflict is part of life, such as in adversarial relationships or groups organizing to defend their common interests vis-à-vis other groups. He admitted that struggle against unjust economic and political systems is justified. For John Paul II the response to injustice cannot be unrestrained conflict. Instead, there must be a twofold approach of: first, addressing the "real and serious grievances" that lead to violence, and secondly, relying on negotiation, arbitration, and compromise to achieve a just and peaceful resolution of the crisis. The goal is to address the root causes of conflict in nonviolent methods of diplomacy and compromise, rather than resorting to violence. Such an approach is called for in the various hot spots around the world, including the Mideast and a number of countries in Africa.

The Catholic tradition, as articulated by Pope John Paul II in *Centesimus Annus*, urges that humanity use "the weapons of truth and justice" rather than smart bombs or suicide attacks. John Paul II pointed to the nonviolent transformation in the Soviet Union and in Eastern Europe, noting that the common "wisdom" of both the East and the West assumed that such drastic political and economic changes could only happen through another major war. The common wisdom about war as the only means of change was proven wrong. Instead, what was successful were nonviolent means of "protest [which] tenaciously insisted on trying every avenue of negotiation, dialogue, and witness to the truth, appealing to the conscience of the adversary and seeking to reawaken in him a sense of shared human dignity."[12]

Pat McCormick notes that "just struggle does not gloss over wrongs but confronts sinful structures in a spirit of solidarity with the marginalized and with respect for the truth and the adversary."[13] John Paul II believed that the moral stance of solidarity and nonviolence is the best hope for humanity but that this moral vision must be translated into structural and institutional responses. Oppressive economic and political structures must be replaced with effective systems that protect the personal and national rights. Nations must also develop international structures of negotiation and arbitration. For instance, why don't countries have Departments of Peace and Peace Colleges to counterbalance the War Colleges and Departments of War such as the Pentagon in the United States? Such structures of peace-building would serve as an alternative and counterweight to the almost automatic use of force, violence, and war.[14]

For John Paul II the continued reliance upon war as a means for resolving international conflicts became increasingly senseless in light of the growing interdependence and militarization of the globe. He made this very clear in the build-up to the Persian Gulf War in 1991, and he made it clear in the build-up to the second U.S. war with Iraq. Regarding the first Iraqi war he wrote:

> I myself, on the occasion of the recent tragic war in the Persian Gulf, repeated the cry "Never again war!" No, never again war, which destroys the lives of innocent people, teaches how to kill, throws into upheaval even the lives of those who do the killing and leaves behind a trail of resentment and hatred, thus making it all the more difficult to find a just solution of the very problems which provoked the war.[15]

Forgiveness as a Building Block of Peace

Pope John Paul II offered the world another strategy for restoring relationships and building peace that is connected to solidarity—forgiveness. His 2002 World Day of Peace message was entitled *No Peace without Forgiveness, No Justice without Forgiveness.* In that document he asked,

> *[H]ow do we restore the moral and social order subjected to such horrific violence?* My reasoned conviction, confirmed in turn by biblical revelation, is that the shattered order cannot be fully restored except by a response that combines justice with forgiveness. *The pillars of true peace are justice and that form of love which is forgiveness* (2).

The pope admitted that talking about justice and forgiveness as a source of peace is not easy: there is a misconception that justice and forgiveness are irreconcilable. He believed that "forgiveness is the opposite of resentment and revenge, not justice," explaining the relationship of peace, justice, and forgiveness in these terms:

> True peace therefore is the fruit of justice, that moral virtue and legal guarantee which ensures full respect for rights and responsibilities, and the just distribution of benefits and burdens. But because human justice is always fragile and imperfect, subject as it is to the limitations and egoism of individuals and groups, it must include and, as it were, be completed by the *forgiveness which heals and rebuilds troubled human relations from their foundations.* This is true in circumstances great and small, at the personal level or on a wider, even international scale. Forgiveness is in no way opposed to justice, as if to forgive meant to overlook the need to right the wrong done. It is rather the fullness of justice, leading to that tranquility of order which is much more than a fragile and temporary cessation of hostilities, involving as it does the deepest healing of the wounds which fester in human hearts. Justice and forgiveness are both essential to such healing (3).

While forgiveness begins with individual people, a "politics of forgiveness" must eventually develop. John Paul reaffirmed that "forgiveness inhabits people's hearts before it becomes a social reality. Only to the degree that an ethics and a culture of forgiveness prevail can we hope for a 'politics' of forgiveness, expressed in society's attitudes and laws. . . ." He explained that forgiveness starts with "a personal choice, a decision of the heart to go against the natural instinct to pay back evil with evil." He noted that all people want to be forgiven, so why not treat others as we would like to be treated? "All human beings cherish the hope of being able to start all over again, and not remain forever shut up in their own mistakes and guilt" (8).

As each individual hopes to be forgiven, so "*society too is absolutely in need of forgiveness.* Families, groups, societies, States and the international community itself need forgiveness in order to renew ties that have been sundered, [to] go beyond sterile situations of mutual condemnation. . . ." In short, "*The ability to forgive lies at the very basis of the idea of a future society marked by justice and solidarity*" (9).

John Paul II's thinking is very much in line with what the Protestant theologian Paul Tillich describes as transforming or creative justice.[16] Creative justice is the ability to forgive in order to reunite. The example of the parable of the Prodigal Son comes to mind. The father forgives his wasteful and repentant son so that he can be reunited with his family, even though this kind of justice seems offensive to the other son, who has remained faithful.

The pope may also have been thinking of the international witness to the power of forgiveness given by Nelson Mandela, who, after twenty-seven years as a political prisoner, led people to reconciliation and forgiveness in South Africa. As newly elected President Mandela invited his white jailer to be an honored guest at his 1994 presidential inauguration. Anglican Archbishop Desmond Tutu, led South Africa's Truth and Reconciliation Commission, which gave notorious violators of human rights a choice: tell the whole truth or face prosecution. Truth about the many atrocities of apartheid was revealed, and many violators were forgiven. These forms of national forgiveness averted a racial bloodbath in South Africa. It is telling that Archbishop Tutu entitled his 1999 book *No Future without Forgiveness*.[17] William Bole calls such examples of merciful acts by national leaders the "politics of forgiveness," a perspective that is not easy to swallow because it is unconventional. "The concept is foreign to most secular political philosophies and peripheral at best to Christian theories of just war and the common good."[18]

Pope John Paul II, who brought a new dimension to the Catholic approach to war, was not alone in his thinking. Among twentieth-century philosophers, the German-Jewish refugee Hannah Arendt is remembered for her writing on forgiveness. After the Holocaust, she described forgiveness as one of two human capacities, along with the ability to enter into covenants, that make it possible to alter the political future to save it from determinism.

Forgiveness does not mean forgetting; instead, it is about remembering in a certain way. Christian ethicist Donald Shriver Jr. defined forgiveness as "an act that joins moral truth, forbearance, empathy, and commitment to repair a fractured human relation."[19] This is not just an academic definition, as Bole points out, it has been tried in the real world:

Moral truth, in particular the social catharsis of truth-telling and public confession, is what South Africa pursued in setting up the Tutu commission. Forbearance is what President Mandela and Kim [of South Korea] signaled at their respective inaugurations. Empathy is what the late King Hussein of Jordan had for eight Israeli families whose children were gunned down by a rogue Jordanian soldier six years ago. Hussein went to their homes and knelt before the parents, begging forgiveness.[20]

While forgiveness is a new reality on the international scene, it has been tried in limited settings. To gain in acceptance it will first have to become part of the lived experience of people in many lands and in many homes, from Palestine to New York City. But what choice do we have? According to Archbishop Tutu and Pope John Paul II there is no future without forgiveness.

The world was shocked by another senseless tragedy in October 2006 as ten young Amish girls were shot in the Old Order Amish one-room school in Nickel Mines in Lancaster County, Pennsylvania. Five of the girls died and five survived. Shocked turned to awe as the Amish community reached out to the family of the killer, Charles Carl Roberts, to forgive him. Terri Roberts, the mother of the shooter, told of the visit to her house:

> On the day that it happened, Henry, our Amish neighbor up on the hill, whom I call an "angel in black," came to our house. My husband provided transportation for the Amish when they needed to travel by car, and he was just devastated. All day long, my husband couldn't lift his head. He kept taking a towel and wiping it over his head—he just kept wiping the tears away and couldn't lift his head up at all. And then Henry came, and he was the first sign of healing for my husband. He put his hand on my husband's shoulder, just stood there and comforted and consoled him for an hour. Henry said, "Roberts, we love you," and just kept affirming and assuring him. The acceptance we have received from the Amish community is beyond any words. To be able to have a community of people that have been hurt so much by what our son did and yet to have them respond to us the way that they have has been an incredible journey.[21]

The Amish midwife who had helped birth several of the girls murdered by the killer said that they were planning to take food over to his family's house, and at the funeral of Charles Roberts half of the seventy-five people in attendance were Amish, including parents of the victims.

We sit back in awe and ponder, "how is this kind of forgiveness possible?" The Amish midwife, as if anticipating our awe, told the reporter "This is possible if you have Christ in your heart."[22] Kenneth Briggs, the author of *The Power of Forgiveness*, noted that Donald Kraybill, a scholar and friend of the Amish, explained "that forgiveness is for these pious people so inculcated that it has become a spiritual reflex. Children learn it by watching their parents and neighbors forgive . . . by looking to the example of Jesus. . . ." Briggs continues:

> The Amish go to the home of the killer to offer the comfort of forgiveness with the faith that they have already been showered with divine comfort. Their errand of mercy is predictable, perhaps, but not automatic. Like all other aspects of faith, they say, forgiveness requires daily practice, a repeated renewal of trust and struggle with doubt. . . . What most sets the Amish apart is their willingness to cultivate those sources [of their convictions] in spiritual solidarity with one another.
>
> Forgiveness . . . is simple to them because they accept it as the will of God as revealed in the Scriptures, and they rehearse their way into it day after day. That doesn't make it easy.[23]

Their acts of forgiveness have touched the world. Professor Kraybill observed on the fourth anniversary of the shooting "I am astonished at the many thousands and millions of lives this event has touched in a profound way. This story has had a major impact on many people who have struggled with bitterness and injustice in their lives."[24]

The Way to Peace: Defend Life

In 1977 Pope Paul VI's statement on peace was very precise: "If you wish peace, defend life."[25] The U.S. bishops reaffirmed that message in their pastoral letter on peace:

> No society can live in peace with itself, or with the world, without a full awareness of the worth and dignity of every human person, and of the sacredness of all human life (Jas 4:1–2). When we accept violence in any form as commonplace, our sensitivities become dulled. When we accept violence, war itself can be taken for granted (285).

Pope John Paul II added his voice about how to avoid "sinking into the abyss" of war. He urged: "[F]irst, a yes to life! Respect life itself and individual lives. . . . Next, respect for law . . . finally, the duty of solidarity."

John Paul, who made solidarity one of the central values and themes of his papacy, went on to explain in very concrete terms why a commitment to human solidarity is so important.

In a world with a superabundance of information but which paradoxically finds it so difficult to communicate, and where living conditions are scandalously unequal, *it is important to spare no effort to ensure that everyone feels responsible for the growth and happiness of all.* Our future is at stake. An unemployed young person, a handicapped person who is marginalized, elderly people who are uncared for, countries which are captives of hunger and poverty: These situations all too often make people despair and fall prey to the temptation either of closing in on themselves or of resorting to violence.[26]

He spoke out against war, urging leaders to have the courage to say: "No to death! . . . no to all that attacks the incomparable dignity of every human being, beginning with that of unborn children. . . . No to war! War is not always inevitable. It is always a defeat for humanity. . . . War itself is an attack on human life, since it brings in its wake suffering and death. The battle for peace is always a battle for life!"[27]

Dorothy Day's (1897–1980) voice was also raised against the violence of war and the violence of poverty. In 1925, when she was twenty-eight years old, Dorothy Day moved into a beach house on Staten Island with her common-law husband Forster Batterham, an anarchist and biologist. Until this time, she had not been a religious person, but Forster's "ardent love of creation brought me to the Creator of all things."[28] Her appreciation of creation led her to prayer, not as the "opiate of the people," but as a way of thanking God for creation. At this point in her life, she started to attend mass, to the consternation of Forster. Dorothy and Forster had a child in March 1927, even though Forster did not think it was right to bring a child into a world that he perceived was evil. The birth of their daughter, Tamar Theresa, was a turning point for Dorothy. Dorothy did not want her daughter to flounder through many years as Dorothy had done—doubting, undisciplined, and amoral. She wanted more structure for her daughter, so she had Tamar baptized. Later that same year Dorothy herself was baptized. The immediate impact of this decision was the painful end of her common-law marriage.

Between 1927 and 1933 Day traveled and worked at a variety of jobs, including as a nurse, and writing for the Catholic periodicals *Commonweal* and *America*. In 1932 she met and was captivated by the vision of Peter Maurin. Maurin, a French peasant, espoused a "gentle personalism," a radical Catholic understanding based on a literal interpretation of the Beatitudes. He rejected the liberal institutions of capitalism and the modern state and their faith in material progress and technology and replaced them with a personal commitment to love in a radical imitation of the gospel, living in voluntary poverty in solidarity with the weak, the poor, the sick, and the alienated.

Day and Maurin complemented each other perfectly: "To the pacifism and abstract social concerns of the intellectual and bohemian Day, Maurin added the fundamental realities of human community and commitment, the radical social gospel, and the French peasant's disdain for institutions."[29] From these roots they shaped a new movement: "Both drew strength and inspiration from the Sermon on the Mount; they combined the commitment to nonviolence with the struggle for social justice that has always characterized true Catholic peacemaking. The result of this combination of talents and spirits was the Catholic Worker movement."[30]

Together, they founded the *Catholic Worker*, a monthly newspaper that was launched on Workers' Day, May 1, 1933. Maurin and Day did not simply denounce injustice; instead, they announced a new social order based on the recognition of Christ in one's neighbor. Maurin's plan of action included houses of hospitality, roundtable discussions, and rural communes. They turned the office of the *Catholic Worker* into a "house of hospitality" to offer food for the hungry and shelter for those uprooted by the Depression. By 1941, only eight years later, thirty-two Worker houses had sprung up around the country. While allowing the supervision of the hierarchy through a chaplain, this grassroots movement was not controlled by the clergy.

In 1935 the *Catholic Worker* spoke out against Mussolini's invasion of Ethiopia, alienating many of its Italian readers. Day was also outspoken in her opposition to the Spanish Civil War. This commitment to pacifism was not accepted by all in the Catholic Worker movement, and it certainly was divisive in the Catholic community.

In August 1940 Dorothy Day published an open letter to all members of the Catholic Worker movement insisting on the pacifist position of the movement. Those who believed in the primacy of the social mission of the Worker or who supported the church's just war tradition abandoned the movement. By 1945, twenty of the thirty-two Catholic Worker Houses had closed and the *Catholic Worker* newspaper lost over one hundred thousand subscribers.[31]

Because of Day's insistence on pacifism, the peace issue became the predominant characteristic of the Catholic Worker movement after 1940. The Catholic Worker helped to establish the groundwork for Catholic resistance during the war and became the seed for Catholic peacemaking after World War II. By her unrelenting stand against war, Dorothy Day "assured a tradition of conscientious objection within the American Catholic Church that would survive the barren winter of World War II and blossom into a new spring of protest in the 1960s."[32]

During the Second Vatican Council, Dorothy lobbied the bishops to include nonviolence as an essential element of living the gospel. The *Catholic Worker*, under her guidance, prepared a special edition on peace and the moral problem of modern warfare. In that issue she wrote:

> One of our Catholic pacifists asked me to write a clear, theoretical, logical pacifist manifesto, and he added [that] so far in these thirty-two years of the Catholic Worker, none had appeared from my pen.
>
> I can write no other than this: unless we use the weapons of the spirit, denying ourselves and taking up our cross and following Jesus, dying with Him and rising with Him, men will go on fighting, and often from the highest motives, believing that they are fighting defensive wars for justice and in self-defense against present or future aggression.[33]

Day airmailed the *Catholic Worker* to the bishops gathered in Rome. Then she went to Rome with copies of this special edition entitled "The Council and the Bomb." She joined a group of women on a ten-day fast in the hope that the Council would speak out clearly against war. Their efforts were not in vain as *Gaudium et Spes* (*Pastoral Constitution on the Church in the Modern World*) condemned total war and destruction of civilians as a "crime against God" (80).

The U.S. bishops acknowledged the legacy of Dorothy Day by naming her in their 1983 pastoral letter on peace. "The nonviolent witness of such figures as Dorothy Day and Martin Luther King has had a profound impact upon the life of the Church in the United States."[34]

Dorothy Day died as she had lived, in Maryhouse, a residence for the destitute on New York City's lower East Side, in a room next to a bag lady. This was on November 29, 1980, when she was 83 years old. Outside the Church of the Nativity where she had worshipped daily for years, Cardinal Cooke was blessing the plain pine coffin and a drifter who gave his name as Lazarus said, with tears oozing down his seamed cheeks: "That fine lady gave me love."[35]

The Bible on Solidarity and Peace

As mentioned earlier, while the *word* "solidarity" entered the English language in the nineteenth century, the *concept* of solidarity as "a unity that produces community" has been present in the Judeo-Christian tradition since its beginning. The origin of solidarity is God's unity with us, which includes all of humanity and all of the created order. The one-word synopsis of God's revelation is "Emmanuel," God with us. As Thomas Merton among others discovered, this divine-human solidarity includes everyone: "Finding God in his solitude, he found God's people, who are inseparable from God and who . . . are at one with one another in God the Hidden Ground of Love of all that is."[36]

One of the most poetic expressions of human solidarity is found in Isaiah 25:6–8.

On this mountain the LORD of hosts will make for all peoples a feast of rich food, a feast of well-aged wines. . . . And he will destroy on this mountain the shroud that is cast over all peoples, the sheet that is spread over all nations; he will swallow up death forever. Then the LORD God will wipe away the tears from all faces, and the disgrace of his people he will take away from all the earth, for the LORD has spoken.

The unity and solidarity of all God's people will be achieved "on God's holy mountain" at the end time, but this vision compels us to make it as real as possible, here and now. War and violence clearly erode the unity and solidarity of the human family and of creation itself. War sets one part of humanity against another.

In the Christian Scriptures Jesus "renounces violence as a strategy for promoting God's kingdom." Scripture scholar Richard Hays concludes that "The evangelists are unanimous in portraying Jesus as a Messiah who subverts all prior expectations by assuming the vocation of suffering rather than conquering Israel's enemies. Despite his stinging criticism of those in positions of authority, he never attempts to exert force as a way of gaining social or political power. . . ."[37] Hays argues that "there is not a syllable in the Pauline letters that can be cited in support of Christians employing violence." In other words, "from Matthew to Revelation *we find a consistent witness against violence* and a calling to the community to follow the example of Jesus in accepting suffering rather than inflicting it."[38] Roman Catholic moralist Lisa Cahill concurs that "nothing is more clear in the moral message of Jesus than his exhortation to and example of forgiveness, mercy, and meekness in the face of abuse or assault."[39]

How can we draw on the insights of the New Testament in shaping our attitude toward war? Is it possible to follow the teachings of first-century Christianity in the twenty-first century? Weren't conditions drastically different during the time of Jesus and the early church in comparison with today? Those are important questions to reflect on as we try to use the Bible as a guide today.

Victor Paul Furnish, a noted scripture scholar, has pointed out three factors that influenced the way the early church approached the question of war. First, the early Christians saw themselves as inhabiting a new way of life that was "in" but not "of" the surrounding culture. They saw themselves apart from the secular culture. Second, prior to the time of Emperor Constantine in the early fourth century, Christianity itself had never been the religion of a nation-state, and thus had little interest in the problem of religion and political power. Finally, the historical and political setting of the Roman Empire at the time of Jesus and the early Christian movement was relatively secure from international aggression. The *Pax Romana* was seen by Christians as a blessing that allowed the travel and communication that facilitated spreading the gospel.[40] Although Jesus and the early leaders of the church articulated their attitude toward war and peace in the political setting of the *Pax Romana*, the political setting had changed drastically by the time of Constantine.

The Early Church and Its Legacy

After the reign of Emperor Constantine in the mid-fourth century and after the Roman Empire fell apart, Christianity became the official religion of the decaying empire and the church became more responsible for public order and security. These changes meant that the church's attitude toward war changed as well. Christian leaders of the first three centuries were generally adamant that discipleship requires close adherence to the nonviolent and countercultural example of Jesus' own life. This was not true after the reign of Constantine (305–327).

As the early Christians set about converting individuals and the entire Roman Empire, they attempted to explain the Christian doctrine and morality to their Greek and Roman counterparts. They backed up their preaching and teaching with their example of nonviolent living, even to the point of martyrdom.

These early Christian teachers were known as apologists, that is, one who speaks or writes in defense of Jesus and the Christian way of life. A typical example was Clement of Alexandria (c. 150–210), who tried to win over the Hellenic world through a synthesis of philosophy and scripture. He pointed out that Christians are educated not for war, but for peace. As soldiers of peace Christians handle the arms of peace, justice, faith, and salvation. Justice and peace need no arms except the word of God and "nowhere will they inflict wounds."[41] Around 210, another apologist, Tertullian, is remembered for saying that "Christ in disarming Peter ungirt every soldier." This became a motto for nonviolence. The document known as the "Apostolic Tradition" offered guidance for the early church, maintaining that "a soldier of the civil authority must be taught not to kill men and to refuse to do so if he is commanded."[42]

While the apologists defended the Christian ethic of pacifism, the martyrs put that vision into action by their living and their dying. The martyrdom of Peter and Paul gave the Christian community in Rome a special recognition among the early churches. The total number of martyrs is uncertain—perhaps a few thousand. The message in their suffering and dying is that many Christians were willing to suffer death rather than inflict it. Their witness was not lost on those who observed their struggle, and their witness became the catalyst that converted many fellow citizens. The power of martyrdom today can be recalled by the death of Father Jerzy Popieluszko in Poland, or that of Oscar Romero, the martyred archbishop of El Salvador, or Sister Dorothy Stang.

Based on the New Testament and the witness of the pre-Constantinian Christians, justification of the use of force by Christians is difficult, if not impossible. Some today argue that we must recover the vision of the early church. Others argue that, as the world has changed drastically from that of the first century, so too must its ethic change. Advocates of nonviolence reply that discipleship permits no compromise with the violence that a sinful world employs to achieve its goals. What is called for is fidelity to our call, not effectiveness in the world.[43] These are the voices of the early church, Reformation thinkers like Anabaptist Menno Simon, the historic peace churches, Dorothy Day, and Martin Luther King, Jr.

Others theologians such as Augustine, Aquinas, Luther, Calvin, and twentieth-century American theologians Reinhold Niebuhr and John Courtney Murray see the kingdom as more distant and stress the *obligation to intervene* to correct injustice. These Christians, sometimes called "realists," do not abandon attempts to live the radical message of love in the real world, but they do see the *demands of love* as entailing measures that seem to contradict the *requirements of love*.

For such realists, the demands of love can include political coercion, violence, and even killing. The example of Lutheran pastor Dietrich Bonhoeffer, who felt he had to resist the evil of Hitler by participating in an attempt to assassinate him, typifies this line of reasoning. Realists would state that sometimes Christians must confront evil and injustice, even to the extent of taking life. In this line of thinking, the ability to love is limited by the injustice and sin in the world. As a result Christians may have to act with coercion and force to bring about justice, which is a primitive form of love.

The debate focuses on how faithful our discipleship can be in these sinful times. If true peace is possible only in the reign of God and if that reign is to be fulfilled only at the end of time by God's action, then we may not always be able to live the Christian ideal of nonviolence. On the other hand, we know that Jesus calls his disciples to a converted life, transformed by the Spirit. As such, how can Christians justify any use of violence, even against enemies in self-defense? The Christian just war theory is an acknowledgment that because God's reign is not yet fully present, Christian behavior cannot be expected to conform fully to its demands in the present age.

Those who are most insistent on the presence of the reign of God breaking into the present reality tend to be pacifists. By contrast, those who support a just war ethic do not deny the New Testament mandate to live a transformed life, but they give that mandate less practical force. Just war proponents give more weight to the social context and use more freedom in interpreting the message of the New Testament.[44] Another way of phrasing this ongoing debate is to ask: Is the teaching of Jesus an *absolute principle* for every situation where we may face violence, or is the teaching of Jesus *an ideal* that encourages us onward, but which we will never completely achieve in this life?[45]

Just War Arguments

St. Augustine was the first Christian theologian to articulate a framework for a just war, that is, a war in which Christians could participate. He argued on the basis of biblical love—just as pacifists use love as their argument for not going to war. Augustine used the example of a group of people walking through a dangerous area. If attacked by thieves and murderers, Augustine argued that a Christian could repel the attackers, especially to defend the women and children. Christian love could justify one's taking up arms and doing violence to the attackers. Augustine also argued that, in imitation of Jesus, he would not use violence to defend his own life, but only to defend the lives of others.

Those who follow Augustine's line of thinking argue that following the biblical command of love is possible even when killing another person. This tradition tends to see the relationship between love and killing, or love and justice, as a paradox, and would argue that "killing someone in the name of love," while a paradox, may be necessary. The example of Dietrich Bonhoeffer is illustrative of this position. Bonhoeffer and his fellow conspirators were willing to kill Hitler in the name of love.

Reinhold Niebuhr, a famous American Protestant ethicist, believed that Christians are sometimes forced by the ambiguities of human historical experience to employ violence to secure the contingent peace of the temporal order. He argued that inaction could be an abdication of moral responsibility for the world in which God has placed us.

Niebuhr and Augustine would contend that historical realities have changed drastically from New Testament times, and the social and political context for Christian moral decision-making is radically different from that of Jesus. This approach would argue that the Sermon on the Mount was addressed to a marginal community outside the circle of power. Therefore, the pacifist teaching of the New Testament cannot be directly applied in a context where Christians hold positions of power and influence or where Christians constitute the majority in a democratic political order.[46]

Another strand of the just war ethic is connected with the thinking of Thomas Aquinas. This version removes killing from the framework of Christian love and thereby does not see killing as a paradox. Rather, war and killing are evaluated in terms of the natural order, natural justice, and the common good. This approach would argue that it may be necessary to use violence to protect the common good from internal or external threats. In other words, for the sake of the good of the many, it may be necessary to take the life of a marauding killer or to declare war on a nation that attacks without provocation. In the approach of Aquinas, the criteria for discriminating among types of killing and their moral evaluations are carefully elaborated. But again, the ideal of nonviolent discipleship of the kingdom becomes more distant.[47]

Just War Criteria

The just war tradition consists of a body of ethical reflection on the justifiable use of force that comprises a combination of theological and ethical traditions. The Catholic bishops note in their 1993 document, *The Harvest of Justice Is Sown in Peace*, that the goals of the just war ethic are to overcome injustice, reduce violence, and prevent the spread of violence. To achieve these goals the just war tradition aims at clarifying when force can be used, limiting the resort to force, and restraining damage done by military forces during war. The bishops summarize the just war tradition in this fashion:

> The *just war tradition begins with a strong presumption against the use of force* and then it establishes the conditions when this presumption may be overridden for the sake of preserving the kind of peace that protects human dignity and human rights.
>
> In a disordered world, where peaceful resolution of conflict sometimes fails, the just war tradition provides an important moral framework for restraining and regulating the limited use of force by governments and international organizations. Since the just war tradition is often misunderstood or selectively applied, we summarize its major components, which are drawn from traditional Catholic teaching.
>
> First, whether lethal force may be used is governed by the following criteria:
>
> * *Just cause*: Force may be used only to correct a grave, public evil, that is, aggression or massive violation of the basic rights of whole populations.
> * *Comparative justice*: While there may be rights and wrongs on all sides of a conflict, to override the presumption against the use of force the injustice suffered by one party must significantly outweigh that suffered by the other.
> * *Legitimate authority*: Only duly constituted public authorities may use deadly force or wage war.
> * *Right intention*: Force may be used only in a truly just cause and solely for that purpose.
> * *Probability of success*: Arms may not be used in a futile cause or in a case where disproportionate measures are required to achieve success.
> * *Proportionality*: The overall destruction expected from the use of force must be outweighed by the good to be achieved.
> * *Last resort*: Force may be used only after all peaceful alternatives have been seriously tried and exhausted.[48]

These criteria must be satisfied in order to override the strong presumption against the use of force. These criteria must be satisfied before *going to war (jus ad bellum)*. Once a war has started, a second set of principles comes into play *(jus in bello)*:

- *Noncombatant immunity*: Civilians may not be the object of direct attack, and military personnel must take due care to avoid and minimize indirect harm to civilians.
- *Proportionality*: In the conduct of hostilities, efforts must be made to attain military objectives with no more force than is militarily necessary and to avoid disproportionate collateral damage to civilian life and property.
- *Right intention*: Even in the midst of conflict, the aim of political and military leaders must be peace with justice, so that acts of vengeance and indiscriminate violence, whether by individuals, military units, or governments, are forbidden.[49]

This set of principles must be rigorously applied when evaluating the decision both to go to war and to evaluate the motivations and strategies during the war.

Bishop Robert McElroy, auxiliary bishop of San Francisco, applied the principles of the just war tradition to the ongoing war in Afghanistan. In 2011, after thirteen years of war in Afghanistan—the longest war in American history—Bishop Robert McElroy wondered if Americans have become comfortable with war. Bishop McElroy believes that it is morally dangerous for the country to accept this prolonged war "without breaking a sweat." He wonders if the United States has become a "society in which major warfare is a permanent part of its national life." He believes that "the church's teaching directly challenges the embrace of warfare as a regular element of state action." The current state of affairs is a serious disregard of church teaching at the level of doctrinal level. He explains:

- *Catholic doctrine does not permit war (or force of arms) to democratize other countries. . . . It is morally illegitimate to use the weapons of war . . . to remake foreign societies in our own image.*
- *Catholic doctrine does not permit the continuation of warfare in order to avoid the damage that will come to one's reputation from defeat.* The church's teaching on right intention in war absolutely precludes starting or continuing a war out of this of any other political motivation.

- *Catholic doctrine does not permit the use of weapons and tactics that eviscerate the distinction between combatants and civilians*—[For example,] the use of drone aircraft for strikes that have generated increasing civilian casualties in Afghanistan and Pakistan. . . .
- *Catholic doctrine does not permit continuation of war based on a mere wisp of hope.* The principle of proportionality . . . require[s] that, in the absence of any clear probability of success after 10 years of major fighting, war must end.[50]

Instead, he urges that "the people of the United States need to engage in a deep and piercing national dialogue on the role of war in their national identity. U.S. citizens need to understand that this nation cannot transform the world by force of arms."[51] Bishop McElroy's work shows the value of the principles of the just war to evaluate the morality of a seemingly endless war, and he concludes that the war in Afghanistan violates the principles of the just war tradition.

The just war tradition is not a finished product. It continues to evolve in light of present realities. A number of theologians have suggested that the tradition needs not only principles for *going to* war (*jus ad bellum*) and moral guidelines *during* war (*jus in bello*), but also ethical guidelines for conduct *after* war (*jus post bellum*).

Such rules of conduct after war ends include: (1) the principle of repentance to express remorse for the death and suffering inflicted by war; (2) a principle of honorable surrender to ensure that the peace does not turn into retribution or revenge; and (3) the principle of restoration to ensure that the damage done by the war be repaired.[52]

The sense of repentance and remorse is particularly important. While there may be relief that the fighting is over, Christians should find it hard to celebrate such a terrible loss of life and suffering. Moral theologian Thomas Shannon notes that "Such principles should not only make us hesitant to enter a war but also encourage our government to plan carefully for the aftermath of the war so that the last state is not worse than the first."[53]

The just war tradition is clearly not a fast track to endorsing the use of violence and war. Rather, it is a rigorous layering of principles that make it very difficult to declare a specific war "just." It shares with pacifism the same underlying assumption against the use of force. In simplified terms, the only difference is that pacifism does not allow any exceptions to the assumption against the use of force, whereas, the just war ethic allows exceptions to the rule. But, of course, the pacifist argument is more complex than that.

Pacifism

Pacifists believe that Christians who accept the use of force are betraying the Christian message and have been co-opted by an ethic that thinks war is the way to peace. John Howard Yoder, a Mennonite ethicist, pointed out that the "irony of history" ought to lead us to recognize the inadequacy of our hope to shape a world that tends toward justice through violence. The pacifist wonders how violence can possibly lead to justice and peace. The pacifist approach means that, practically speaking, Christians would have to relinquish positions of power and influence insofar as the exercise of such positions becomes incompatible with the teaching and example of Jesus. This might well mean that the church would assume a peripheral status in our culture, because our culture seems to be deeply committed to the necessity and glory of violence. The task of the church, then, is to tell an alternative story, to train disciples in the disciplines necessary to resist the seduction of violence, and to offer an alternative home for those who will not succumb to the violence of the world.

Richard Hays concludes that

> [I]t is increasingly the case in Western culture that Christians can participate in public governance only insofar as they suppress their explicitly Christian motivations. Paradoxically, the Christian community might have more impact upon the world if it were less concerned about appearing reasonable in the eyes of the world and more concerned about faithfully embodying the New Testament's teaching against violence.[54]

The Christian church has not resolved this historic debate about the morality of war. There continue to be disagreements about how much responsibility the church should have for protecting the common good and the social order. On the one hand, just war advocates who maintain that Christians have a responsibility for protecting the common good argue that, because of our sinful world, we may have to take up arms. On the other hand, pacifists argue that we can serve the common good more effectively if we witness to the truth of Jesus' pacifism and not compromise the gospel ideals. A certain tension between these two approaches, I believe, is healthy for both. The Catholic tradition is becoming less convinced about its long commitment to the just war ethic and is paying more attention to nonviolent resistance and peace-building.

Nonviolence

It is important to distinguish between pacifism and nonviolence. While today the terms are used interchangeably, nonviolence is a twentieth-century term. The concept of nonviolence came into modern moral reflection through the life and witness of Mahatma Gandhi. Gandhi was a pacifist in that he rejected war and violence as a way to address social injustice. But he developed active nonviolence, which is different from pacifism. He taught a nonviolence that was more active than violence because it presupposes the courage both to die and to absorb the violence of the other. Gandhi's nonviolence was *not passive*; rather it struggled to be victorious. Gandhi called this new form of nonviolence *satyagraha*, the nonviolent struggle. "The victory to be won is not against the enemy but against the enemy's evil. The struggle seeks not to humiliate the aggressors but to elevate and free them."[55]

Gandhian nonviolence was picked up by various Catholic activists in Europe and the United States. In the United States Robert Ludlow, a member of the Catholic Worker movement, was among the first Catholic intellectuals to absorb and interpret Gandhi's theory of nonviolence. Through the 1940s and the 1950s he developed a Catholic theology of nonviolence in the belief that Gandhi's notion of nonviolence could be "a new *Christian* way of social change."[56] This thinking transformed pacifism from an individual opposition to violence into a social effort, a social movement. Ludlow urged Catholic pacifists to move the Catholic Church toward a commitment to peace and then to transform American society.

Martin Luther King Jr. also absorbed and utilized the power of Gandhian nonviolence as a means of social change in the Civil Rights struggle. The tradition of nonviolent struggle against injustice as a means of social change is a recent development in the history of pacifism. While nonviolent resistance has religious underpinnings, it is a means of social change that is no longer necessarily linked to religion. People with diverse religious backgrounds or no religious backgrounds are able to work together in the common cause of social justice, using nonviolence as a force to create social justice.

"Preventive War" after September 11, 2001

A new school of thought regarding the justification for war emerged in the United States after the terrorist attacks on the World Trade Towers, the Pentagon, and the failed attack that ended in Pennsylvania on September 11, 2001, now commonly known as 9/11. This approach asserts that it is justifiable to launch a "preventive war" to confront the threats of terrorism, weapons of mass destruction, and rogue states. The case has been made not only by George W. Bush's administration but also by political philosopher Jean Bethke Elshtain, a professor of social and political ethics at the University of Chicago, and Michael Novak, contributing editor of the *National Review Online*.

Michael Novak created a controversy when he was invited by U.S. ambassador to the Holy See Jim Nicholson to deliver remarks in support of preventive war at a public audience in the Vatican City on February 10, 2003, three weeks before the second war with Iraq was started. Although Novak is a Catholic, he was not considered an official representative of the U.S. government, nor of American Catholics. Novak argued that war against Iraq was justified even though Iraq had not first attacked the United States. He argued that war had been "preemptively declared upon the United States on 09/11/01," and that "no major moral authority had any difficulty in recognizing that a war to prevent this new type of terrorism is not only just but morally obligatory."[57] His reasoning was based on the argument that preemptive or the anticipatory use of force is sometimes morally permissible, but only in the exceptional case where there is a clear and present danger, or a grave and imminent threat. Elshtain and Novak argued that Iraq posed such a threat.

Just war scholar Michael Walzer points out: "No one expects an Iraqi attack tomorrow or next Tuesday, so there is nothing to preempt. The war that is being discussed is preventive, not preemptive—it is designed to respond to a more distant threat." Such an approach is not consistent with Catholic social teaching. Cardinal Joseph Ratzinger, head of the Vatican Congregation for the Doctrine of the Faith at the time, bluntly noted that the concept of preventive war "does not appear in the Catechism of the Catholic Church."[58]

In their November 2002 statement the U.S. bishops expressed grave concern over the expansion of just cause to include preventive wars. Three months later, in February 2003, the bishops, with the strong support of Pope John Paul II, were again highly critical of "preemptive, unilateral use of military [force] . . . [because this] would create deeply troubling moral and legal precedents." The bishops conclude that "Based on the facts that are known, it is difficult to justify resort to war against Iraq, lacking clear and adequate evidence of an imminent attack of a grave nature or Iraq's involvement in the terrorist attacks of September 11."[59]

Bishop Wilton Gregory, president of the United States Conference of Catholic Bishops, reiterated the U.S. bishops' rejection of preventive war on the anniversary of the atomic bombings of Hiroshima and Nagasaki: "The United States Conference of Catholic Bishops will continue . . . and intensify our work on other pressing issues of war and peace, including opposing notions of preventive war, supporting the long-term task of building a just peace in Afghanistan and Iraq. . . ."[60]

Finally, Pope John Paul II sent his delegate Cardinal Pio Laghi, who had previously served as papal nuncio in the United States, to visit President Bush in March 2003 to ask the president not to engage in a preventive war. A year later on June 4, 2004, the pope met personally with President Bush to argue as he had in his message for the 2004 World Day of Peace that "the struggle against terrorism cannot only be 'repressive,' but must start with the 'elimination of the causes' of injustice."[61] Clearly, the Catholic Church has not accepted the arguments of the morality of "preventive war."

Just Peace-making and Just Policing

As is noted in the application of the just war theory to the war in Afghanistan by Bishop McElroy, this tradition still has some value in condemning unjust warfare. But in the age of terrorism, nuclear weapons, and the massive civilian deaths in recent and current wars, the just war theory is "showing its age." It was developed for different times and circumstances. At the same time, many moralists argue some use of force is necessary to protect the innocent and repel the aggressor or the terrorist. One group of scholars and activists working through the Society of Christian Ethics has articulated a new model known as "*just peacemaking.*" They developed "ten empirical practices that have been proven to produce justice and to prevent the resort to war."[62] These practices spell out steps that should be taken before resorting to war. They claim there is empirical and historical evidence that the ten practices are effective in preventing the use of war. This approach is meant to supplement, not replace, the just war and nonviolence frameworks. Proponents of this approach contend that both pacifists and just war advocates should support just peace-making.

Another alternative to the just war theory is emerging that emphasizes the need to respond to terrorism, not with war, but with law enforcement. This approach is called *just policing.* This approach envisions an international police force, working with the International Criminal Court, employing a community policing model to enforce international law and prevent crimes such as terrorism, ethnic cleansing, and genocide. "While just policing is subject to criteria and principles similar to the just war tradition, it is more restrained in the use of violence and force."[63]

The Peace-making Church

Since the time of St. Augustine in the fifth century, leaders in the Catholic Church have accepted some form of the just war ethic. While many peace movements began within the church, as have declarations to limit warfare and violence, the Roman Catholic Church is not a historic peace church.[64] According to Father Drew Christiansen, S.J., a counselor for international affairs at the U.S. Conference of Catholic Bishops, the identification of the Catholic Church as primarily a defender of the just war ethic is no longer true. He believes it is better to describe the Catholic Church as a "peacemaking church."[65]

The emphasis on peace-making developed gradually after the Second World War. The experience of the Holocaust and two very bloody wars in Europe in less than thirty years led German and French theologians to question the ethics of war. In addition, the threat of nuclear weapons challenged the applicability of the just war ethic. The leadership of Pope John XXIII signaled a new direction in the teaching of the church on war and peace. As Father Ken Himes notes, "John never explicitly denied the just-war theory in *Pacem in Terris*, but his silence about the right of national self-defense coupled with his opposition to nuclear war created a mood of questioning on the topic of warfare."[66]

In 1965 the Second Vatican Council gave expression to those concerns by calling for "an evaluation of war with an entirely new attitude" in paragraph 80 of *Gaudium et Spes*. In that same paragraph the bishops uttered a strong condemnation, and the only one that appears in the Vatican II documents: "Every act of war directed to the indiscriminate destruction of whole cities or vast areas with their inhabitants is a crime against God and humanity, which merits firm and unequivocal condemnation."

The primary reason for this shift away from just war theory was the fact that the nature of war itself had changed drastically in the twentieth century. War had become more devastating and deadly, especially for civilians: In World War I (1914–18) over half of the estimated 18.5 million deaths were soldiers; in World War II (1939–45) 60 percent of the estimated 40 million deaths were civilians; and in recent conflicts in Bosnia, Rwanda, Sudan, Afghanistan, and Iraq, 75 to 90 percent of the victims have been civilians.[67]

These statistics show that the principle of "noncombatant immunity" has been violated in the extreme. Is it any wonder that Pope John Paul II proclaimed: "No, never again war, which destroys the lives of innocent people, teaches how to kill, throws into upheaval even the lives of those who do the killing and leaves behind a trail of resentment and hatred, thus making it all the more difficult to find a just solution of the very problems which provoked the war."[68]

Pope Benedict also raised concerns about the value of the just war theory when he was the prefect of the Congregation for the Doctrine of the Faith: "[G]iven the new weapons that make possible destruction that goes beyond the combatant groups, today we should be asking ourselves if it is still licit to admit the very existence of a 'just war.'"[69]

The U.S. bishops also helped to create a new ethic and attitude toward war. In their 1983 pastoral letter *The Challenge of Peace*, the bishops lifted up nonviolence and peace-making as a tradition parallel to the just war ethic. This shift resulted in part from the renewed focus on the Bible, especially the New Testament, as the source of the church's moral theology and social ethic. Previously, the church's teaching was rooted in the Hebrew Scriptures and the writing of St. Augustine. On the tenth anniversary of the peace pastoral, the U.S. bishops issued a statement, *The Harvest of Justice Is Sown in Peace*, which continued to promote the peace-making tradition.

In addition to the death of millions of civilians in recent wars, church leaders have noted the successful nonviolent revolutions in the late 1980s in the Philippines, in Poland, and in other Communist-controlled countries in Eastern Europe. These two factors have led the Catholic hierarchy to strengthen the presumption against war. As a result church leaders are using the just war tradition as a resource that is more likely to *condemn* particular wars than to justify them. An example of this was the Vatican's condemnation of the U.S. war in Iraq in 2003.

Motivated by the evidence of effective nonviolent change, Pope John Paul II and the U.S. bishops have stressed the importance of nonviolent strategies for addressing situations of conflict. Nonviolence is not only the preferred strategy for nations, but also for individual Christians who are urged to live the virtue of solidarity and the vocation of peace-making in their daily lives. The Polish workers set a solid example when they initiated a movement that undermined and eventually destroyed Soviet control of their country.

Because it is no longer confident that the just war ethic is an effective, long-term response to the question of war, the Catholic tradition is moving toward being a "peace-making church." This trajectory of moral reflection suggests that peace-making strategies, pacifism, and effective nonviolence are the better roads for Catholics to pursue. There may be times when war is regrettably necessary, but all of our human creativity and energy should be used to make sure that option is never forced upon us.

Reconciliation, Forgiveness, Peace-building, and Spirituality

The story of the Amish community offering forgiveness to the parents of the man who killed their children reveals the path of reconciliation, forgiveness, and peace. The Amish are part of a Christ-centered culture in which they follow the teaching of the Lord's Prayer: "Forgive us our trespasses as we forgive those who trespass against us." They knew that God has forgiven them first and they are to be people of forgiveness. They lived those words in their daily interactions, developing the habit of forgiveness and the virtue of forgiveness. So, it was part of who they were to forgive; it was part of their DNA. As Kenneth Briggs noted, they did not have to consult Augustine or Aquinas, they accept forgiveness "as the will of God as revealed in the Scriptures, and they rehearse their way into it day after day."[70] They offer an overview of what Catholic peace-building will entail: creating a "culture of life" and a culture of forgiveness and reconciliation.

Reconciliation, forgiveness, and peace-building are part of the Amish way of life. It is how they respond to the daily challenges and problems of life. They are living a spirituality of forgiveness and nonviolence; it is part of their spiritual tradition.

As Catholics we may be influenced by the spirituality of Mother Teresa, Henri Nouwen, Mother Angelica, Dorothy Day, Pope John Paul II, John Dear, and many others, including our own parents and grandparents. All of these diverse Catholic spiritualities share some common elements: personal prayer and contemplation, the sacraments, and the works of charity and justice. The liturgy of the Eucharist is a central ritual of reconciliation for Catholics when we center ourselves in God's act of reconciliation through the life and death of Jesus. As we remember and immerse ourselves in that mystery and gift, we are nourished with the word and the body and blood of Christ to carry that reconciliation into our own lives and into our war-torn world. In addition to the Eucharist, the sacrament of reconciliation in its individual and communal expressions celebrates God's forgiveness of our sins and the message to forgive "seventy times seven."[71] The church's moral and social teachings are given full expression in our preaching, teaching, and celebrating the sacraments.

Peace-building in Rwanda

The Catholic Church of Rwanda knows something about violence, forgiveness, and peace-building. For three months in 1994 an extremist Hutu government unleashed massive killing of the Tutsis tribe in Rwanda. When it was over between 800,000 and 1,000,000 Tutsis and moderate Hutus had been killed out of a total population of 8.1 million Rwandans. Even Catholic Hutu priests and sisters participated in the genocide.

In the face of this horror, the Catholic Church and Catholic Relief Services (CRS) facilitated a grassroots process of truth-telling and forgiveness, with the goal of training twenty thousand leaders across the country to work with twenty thousand base communities that make up the church in Rwanda. Over a five-year period each base community of twenty-five families would discuss the role of ethnicity in the genocide and encourage truth-telling by all who were involved in the bloodshed and forgiveness by the survivors.

CRS brought in outside experts in community trauma healing, conflict management, Catholic social teaching, and human rights. These experts worked with local educators to train parish clergy, staff, and base community "animators" in a month-long program. After this peace-building training the leaders would seek out newly released prisoners to encourage them to confess their crimes and ask forgiveness of the survivors. They also led examinations of conscience within the base communities and encouraged neighbors and friends to come clean about their conduct during the genocide. These leaders also offered to support those willing to confess by accompanying them to the survivors' homes.[72]

As Jeffry Korgen concludes: "Convincing killers to confess and survivors to forgive is difficult work. But it is a ministry that has yielded the improbable: stories of hope and healing over tales of genocide." Church leaders and CRS hope that the successful peace-building efforts will lead to tackling other national disasters, such as the HIV/AIDS epidemic and pervasive poverty. As the CRS leader said: "You can't move forward on any of those things unless people are at peace with their neighbors and themselves."[73]

It is a long road from genocide to reconciliation, but the church is helping Rwandans to build a future of peace.

Ongoing Conversion

It is fitting to conclude this chapter on solidarity, war, and peace with the sober words of Thomas Merton. He reminds us that "Christ our Lord did not come to bring peace as a kind of spiritual tranquilizer. He brought to his disciples a vocation and task: to struggle in the world of violence to establish His peace not only in their own hearts but in society itself."[74]

William Shannon, a Merton scholar, directs us to the core of Merton's nonviolent vision: "We shall only learn to deal effectively with violence when we discover (or recover, for it is really always there) in ourselves that contemplative awareness that enables us—as it had enabled Merton—to see the oneness we share with all God's people—indeed with the whole of God's creation."

The conclusion of this book on Catholic social teachings returns to its beginning: our connectedness and solidarity with all of creation. Wars destroy not only human lives, but also vegetation, trees, rivers and fields, animals, and insects. All of creation pays a price when humans turn to war to solve complex problems.

Shannon continues:

Once a person has achieved this contemplative insight, nonviolence ceases to be a mere option and becomes a choice that brooks no rejection. But let no one think that becoming nonviolent is an easy task. It calls for painful, ongoing conversion, as slowly and almost imperceptibly we begin to realize what it asks of us and to experience the wisdom it imparts to us.[75]

May that ongoing conversion continue in our lives and in our faith communities.

A Muslim, Jewish, and Christian Prayer for Peace

O God, you are the source of life and peace.
Praised be your name forever.
We know it is you who turns
our minds to thoughts of peace.
Hear our prayer in this time of war.
Your power changes hearts.
Muslims, Christians, and Jews remember,
and profoundly affirm,
That they are followers of the one God,
Children of Abraham, brothers and sisters;
Enemies begin to speak to one another;
Those who were estranged

Join hands in friendship;
Nations seek the way of peace together.
Strengthen our resolve to give witness
to these truths by the way we live.
Give to us: Understanding that puts an end to strife;
Mercy that quenches hatred, and
Forgiveness that overcomes vengeance.
Empower all people to live in your law of love.
Amen.[76]

Discussion Questions

1. The just war tradition is a complex set of criteria. In your opinion, do the wars in Iraq and Afghanistan constitute just wars?
2. What is the difference between pacifism and nonviolence?
3. Discuss how forgiveness breaks the cycle of violence and conflict both in personal situations and between groups or nations.
4. Thomas Merton reminds Christians that "Christ our Lord did not come to bring peace as a kind of spiritual tranquilizer. He brought to his disciples a vocation and task: to struggle in the world of violence to establish His peace not only in their own hearts but in society itself." How effectively are we, as American Christians, doing in living out this "vocation"?

Notes

Introduction

[1] *Gaudium et Spes* (Pastoral Constitution on the Church in the Modern World), in *Vatican Council II: Constitutions, Decrees, Declarations*, ed. Austin Flannery, rev. trans. using inclusive language (Northport, NY: Costello, 1996), 1. In this text I will normally quote official church documents by noting the paragraph number when that is available. This is the standard method of noting social documents. It allows the reader to find the quoted text in any of the variety of anthologies of Catholic social teaching as well as the online versions of the texts. This method of notation is preferable to quoting the page number of a specific edition.

[2] "Rochester Child Poverty Rate Increases," September 29, 2010, http://www.13wham.com/news/local/story/Rochester-Child-Poverty-Rate.

[3] http://www.census.gov/hhes/www/poverty/about/overview/index.html.

[4] http://www.worldhunger.org/articles/.

[5] "An Overview of Abortion in the United States," Guttmacher Institute, http://www.guttmacher.org/media/presskits/2008/01/12/abortionoverview.html, accessed March 20, 2011.

[6] J. Milburn Thompson, *Introducing Catholic Social Thought* (Maryknoll, NY: Orbis Books, 2010), 154.

[7] Ibid., 103. Thompson cites Walter C. Clemens and J. David Singer, "The Human Cost of War: Modern Warfare Kills More Civilians than Soldiers," *Scientific American* 282 (June 2000): 56–57; and Ronald Waldman, "Public Health in War: Pursuing the Impossible," *Harvard International Review* 27 (Spring 2005): 60.

[8] Task Force on Catholic Social Teaching and Catholic Education, "Report of the Content Subgroup," *Sharing Catholic Social Teaching* (Washington, DC: United States Catholic Conference, 1998), 23.

[9] *Justice in the World*, in *Catholic Social Thought: The Documentary Heritage*, ed. David O'Brien and Thomas Shannon (Maryknoll, NY: Orbis Books, 1992), 289.

[10] *Caritas in Veritate*, 28 (emphasis added).

[11] Pontifical Council for Justice and Peace, *Compendium of the Social Doctrine of the Church* (Vatican City: Libreria Editrice Vaticana, 2004), 552.

[12] *Communities of Salt and Light: Reflections on the Social Mission of the Parish,* http://www.usccb.org/sdwp/saltandlight.shtml#integration.

[13] Ibid.

[14] For a concise overview of the content of official teachings of Catholic social teaching consult Peter Henriot, Edward DeBerri, and Michael Schulteis, *Catholic So-*

cial Teaching: Our Best Kept Secret (Maryknoll, NY: Orbis, 1992). A careful analysis of the methodology and content of Catholic social teaching is found in Charles Curran, *Catholic Social Teaching 1891–Present: A Historical, Theological, and Ethical Analysis* (Washington, DC: Georgetown University Press, 2002). For an in-depth analysis of the main documents of Catholic social tradition, see the anthology edited by Kenneth Himes, *Modern Catholic Social Teaching: Commentaries and Interpretations* (Washington, DC: Georgetown University Press, 2005).

[15] *Sharing Catholic Social Teaching.* The three committees that worked on this project were the Committee on Education, the Committee on Domestic Policy, and the Committee on International Policy. The statement was approved by the bishops on June 19, 1998.

[16] Ibid., 3. The thirteen principles identified by the "Content Subgroup" are (1) the life and dignity of the human person, (2) human equality, (3) the rights and responsibilities of the human person, (4) the call to family, (5) the call to community and participation, (6) the dignity of work and the right of workers, (7) the option for the poor and vulnerable, (8) solidarity, (9) subsidiarity, (10) the common good, (11) the universal destination of good, the right to private property, and the integrity of creation, (12) economic initiative, and (13) charity and justice (23–26).

[17] Ibid., 6.

[18] *Living the Gospel of Life: A Challenge to American Catholics, A Statement by the Catholic Bishops of the United States,* 1998, 5, http://www.usccb.org/prolife/gospel.shtml.

[19] Benedict XVI, "Conclusion of the Meeting of the Holy Father with the Bishops of Switzerland," November 9, 2006, http://www.vatican.va/holy_father/benedict_xvi/speeches.

[20] Francis Schüssler Fiorenza, "Church, Social Mission of," in *The New Dictionary of Catholic Social Teaching,* ed. Judith Dwyer (Collegeville, MN: The Liturgical Press, 1994), 153.

[21] Joe Holland and Peter Henriot, *Social Analysis: Linking Faith and Social Justice* (Maryknoll, NY: Orbis Books, rev. ed., 1983).

[22] Gustavo Gutiérrez, *Teología de la liberacion: Perspectivas* (Salamanca: Ediciones Sigueme, 1972), 35. This is my translation of "Lo primero es el compromiso de caridad, de servicio. La teologia viene despues, es acto segundo." In the English version these two crucial sentences are translated simply as "Theology follows; it is the second step." The first sentence, "First is the commitment of charity, of service," is missing (*A Theology of Liberation: History, Politics and Salvation,* trans. and ed. Caridad Inda and John Eagleson (Maryknoll, NY: Orbis, 1973), 11).

[23] A version of this section on the pastoral circle was first published in a booklet by the author. See Marvin L. Mich, *I Like Being in Parish Ministry: Social Justice* (Mystic, CT: Twenty-Third Publications, 2002), 34–38.

[24] *Gaudium et Spes,* 43.

[25] Richard Sklba, "Theological Diversity and Dissent within the Church," in *Shepherds Speak: American Bishops Confront the Social and Moral Issues that Challenge Christians Today,* ed. Dennis Corrado and James Hinchey (New York: Crossroad, 1986), 26.

[26] *Gaudium et Spes*, 44.

[27] Ibid., 43.

[28] *Octogesima Adveniens*, 4.

[29] For a directory of Catholic Worker sites see http://www.catholicworker.org/communities/index.cfm.

[30] John Coleman, "Development of Church Social Teaching," *Origins* 11 (June 4, 1981), 41.

1. The Challenge of Being Prophetic: Gospel and Culture

[1] David O'Brien and Thomas Shannon, eds., *Catholic Social Thought: The Documentary Heritage* (Maryknoll, NY: Orbis Books, 1992), 5.

[2] John Coleman, "North American Culture's Receptivity to Catholic Social Teaching," in *Catholic Social Teaching in Global Perspective*, ed. Daniel McDonald (Maryknoll, NY: Orbis Books, 2010), 199.

[3] Charles E. Curran, *The Social Mission of the U. S. Catholic Church: A Theological Perspective* (Washington, DC: Georgetown University Press, 2010), 75.

[4] Committee for Domestic Social Policy, NCCB, *Confronting a Culture of Violence: A Catholic Framework for Action, A Pastoral Message of the U.S. Catholic Bishops* (Washington, DC: USCC, 1994), http://www.usccb.org/sdwp/national/criminal/ccv94.shtml.

[5] *Facts on Induced Abortion in the United States*, Guttmacher Institute, January 2011. The Guttmacher Institute reports that between 1973 and 2008 nearly 50 million abortions took place in the United States (http://www.guttmacher.org/pubs/fb_induced_abortion.html).

[6] Richard Rohr and Joseph Martos, *Why Be Catholic? Understanding Our Experience and Tradition* (Cincinnati, OH: St. Anthony Messenger Press, 1989), 11.

[7] John Kavanaugh, *Following Christ in a Consumer Society*, rev. ed. (Maryknoll, NY: Orbis Books, 1991), xxviii.

[8] Juliet Schor, *The Overworked American: The Unexpected Decline in Leisure* (New York: Basic Books, 1992), as quoted by Charles Murphy, in "The Good Life from a Catholic Perspective: The Problem of Consumption," Environmental Justice Program, National Conference of Catholic Bishops (www.nccbuscc.org.sdwp/ejp/articles/goodlife.htm).

[9] Robert Ellsberg, *All Saints: Daily Reflections on Saints, Prophets, and Witnesses for Our Time* (New York: Crossroad Publishing, 1997), 388.

[10] E. F. Schumacher, "Small Is Beautiful: Toward a Theology of 'Enough,'" *The Christian Century* (July 28, 1971), 902.

[11] Charles Fager, "Small Is Beautiful, and So Is Rome: The Surprising Faith of E. F. Schumacher," *The Christian Century* (April 6, 1977), 326.

[12] Ibid.

[13] Barbara Wood, *E. F. Schumacher: His Life and Thought* (New York: Harper and Row, 1984), 252. This biography written by Schumacher's daughter is available online through the E. F. Schumacher Society at http://www.smallisbeautiful.org/Wood.

[14] Charles Murphy, "The Good Life from a Catholic Perspective: The Problem of Consumption," Environmental Justice Program, United States Conference of Catholic Bishops, http://www.usccb.org/sdwp/ejp/background/articles/consumption.shtml.

[15] Fager, "Small Is Beautiful and So Is Rome," 327.

[16] Ibid.

[17] E. F. Schumacher, *Small Is Beautiful: Economics as if People Mattered* (New York: Harper and Row, 1973), 55.

[18] "Biography of E. F. Schumacher," from World Wisdom, http://www.worldwisdom.com/public/authors/EF-Schumacher.aspx.

[19] Schumacher, "Toward a Theology of 'Enough,'" 901.

[20] Ibid.

[21] Fager, "Small Is Beautiful and So Is Rome," 325.

[22] Ellsberg, *All Saints*, 389.

[23] Murphy, "The Good Life."

[24] Wood, *E. F. Schumacher*, 361.

[25] *Centesimus Annus*, 36.

[26] Ibid., 37.

[27] John Paul II, "Homily at Yankee Stadium," New York, October 2, 1979, 6, http://www.vatican.va/holy_father/john_paul_ii/homilies/1979/.

[28] United States Conference of Catholic Bishops, "Global Climate Change: A Plea for Dialogue, Prudence, and the Common Good," www.nccbuscc.org/sdwp/international/globalclimate.htm, 6.

[29] "And God Saw That It Was Good: A Pastoral Letter of the Bishops of the Boston Province," www.environment.harvard.edu/religion/publications/statements/boston_bishops.html.

[30] Luke T. Johnson, *Sharing Possessions: Mandate and Symbol of Faith* (Philadelphia: Fortress Press, 1981), 79.

[31] Ibid.

[32] Ibid., 49.

[33] Ibid.

[34] Ibid., 62–63.

[35] Ibid., 108.

[36] Ibid., 108–10.

[37] Ibid., 128–29.

[38] Ibid., 102.

[39] William Walsh and John Langan, "Patristic Social Consciousness—The Church and the Poor," in *The Faith That Does Justice*, ed. John Haughey (New York: Paulist Press, 1977), 114.

[40] Ibid., 115.

[41] Martin Hengel, *Property and Riches in the Early Church*, trans. John Bowden (London: SCM Press, 1974), 58.

[42] Walsh and Langan, "Patristic Social Consciousness," 117.

[43] Ibid., 126.

[44] Ibid., 118.

[45] Ibid., 129.

[46] Ibid., 127.

[47] Ibid., 128

[48] Ellsberg, *All Saints*, 432.

[49] Michael Blastic, "Francis of Assisi, St.," in *The Modern Catholic Encyclopedia*, ed. Michael Glazier and Monika Hellwig (Collegeville, MN: Liturgical Press, 1994), 326.

[50] Ellsberg, *All Saints*, 432.

[51] Ibid.

[52] Ibid.

[53] Leonardo Boff, *St. Francis: A Model for Human Liberation* (New York: Crossroad Publishing, 1982), 39.

[54] Ibid., 35.

[55] Ellsberg, *All Saints*, 433.

[56] Rohr and Martos, *Why Be Catholic?* 66.

[57] Kavanaugh, *Following Christ in a Consumer Society*, 170–71.

[58] Walsh and Langan, "Patristic Social Consciousness," 116–17.

[59] Ibid., 116, 117.

[60] Campaign for Human Development, *A Justice Prayer Book* (Washington, DC: United States Catholic Conference, 1982), 20.

2. God's Gift of Creation

[1] Pope Benedict XVI, *2010 World Day of Peace Message: If You Want to Cultivate Peace, Protect Creation*, par. 4, available at www.vatican.va/holy_father/benedict_xvi/messages/.

[2] Task Force on Catholic Social Teaching and Catholic Education, "Report of the Content Subgroup," *Sharing Catholic Social Teaching* (Washington, DC: United States Catholic Conference, 1998), 23.

[3] J. Milburn Thompson, *Introducing Catholic Social Thought* (Maryknoll, NY: Orbis Books, 2010), 155. This section relies on Thompson's summary of Sister Stang's ministry, 153–56.

[4] Thompson, *Introducing Catholic Social Thought*, 156.

[5] *New York Times*, www. topics.nytimes.com, updated: May 3, 2010. Rayfran das Neves Sales and Clodoaldo Carlos Batista were convicted for the murder on December 10, 2005.

[6] "Dorothy Committee" Belim, Brazil, see http://comitedorothy.blogspot.com/, accessed February 8, 2011.

[7] "Nun's Dream Lives on," *The Denver Post*, http://origin.denverpost.com, July 20, 2008.

[8] *NY Times*, May 3, 2010.

[9] "Nun's Dream Lives on."

[10] Maureen Abood, "Chef's Special," *U. S. Catholic* 68 (September 2003), 17.

[11] Lynn White, Jr., "The Historical Roots of Our Ecological Crisis," *Science* 155 (March 1967): 1207.

[12]   Dianne Bergant, "The Earth Is the Lord's," in *Renewing the Face of the Earth: A Resource for Parishes* (Washington, DC: United States Catholic Conference, 1994), 11.

[13]   "The Religious Community Looks Toward the 1992 Earth Summit," *Woodstock Report* (Washington, DC: Woodstock Theological Center, Georgetown University, December 1991): 7–8.

[14]   Ibid., 43.

[15]   Michael Himes and Kenneth Himes, "The Sacrament of Creation: Toward an Environmental Theology," *Commonweal* 117 (January 26, 1990), 44.

[16]   Ibid., 46.

[17]   National Conference of Catholic Bishops, *Renewing the Earth: An Invitation to Reflection and Action on Environment in Light of Catholic Social Teaching*, November 14, 1991 (Washington, DC: United States Catholic Conference), 5.

[18]   Robert Ellsberg, *All Saints: Daily Reflections on Saints, Prophets, and Witnesses for Our Time* (New York: Crossroad Publishing, 1997), 247.

[19]   Leonardo Boff, *St. Francis: A Model for Human Liberation* (New York: Crossroad Publishing, 1982), 39.

[20]   Ibid., 35.

[21]   Ellsberg, *All Saints*, 433.

[22]   Bishop Anthony Pilla, "Christian Faith and the Environment," *Origins* 20 (November 1, 1990): 338.

[23]   Himes and Himes, "The Sacrament of Creation," 45.

[24]   National Catholic Rural Life Conference, www.ncrlc.com.

[25]   Thomas Merton, *New Seeds of Contemplation* (New York: New Directions Publishing Corp., 1961), 30–31.

[26]   John Paul II, "Peace with All Creation," *Origins* 19 (December 14, 1989): 465, also found at www.vatican.va/holy_father/john_paul_ii/messages.

[27]   Sean McDonagh, *The Greening of the Church* (Maryknoll, NY: Orbis Books, 1990), 191.

[28]   National Conference of Catholic Bishops, *Renewing the Earth*, 5–6.

[29]   www.usccb.org/sdwp, 9.

[30]   See http://catholicclimatecovenant.org/the-st-francis-pledge/.

[31]   Available at www.vatican.va/holy_father/benedict_xvi/messages/.

[32]   Elizabeth Johnson, "The Cosmos: Astonishing Image of God," *Catholic International* 12 (February 2001): 43.

[33]   Ibid., 43.

[34]   Thomas Berry, *The Christian Future and the Fate of Earth*, ed. Mary Evelyn Tucker and John Grim (Maryknoll, NY: Orbis Books, 2009), 11.

[35]   Ibid., 117 and 34.

[36]   Thomas Aquinas, *Summa Theologica* Part I, 47, Art. 1.

[37]   Thompson, *Introducing Catholic Social Thought*, 159.

[38]   Aaron Gallegos, "A Partnership for the Earth: Churches and the Environmental Movement," *Sojourners* 26 (March-April 1997), 14.

[39]   Johnson, "The Cosmos," 43.

[40]   Drew Christiansen and Walter Grazier noted that by 1996 there were 48 known statements on ecology issued by bishops' conferences or individual dioceses. See Chris-

tiansen and Grazier, "*And God Saw That It Was Good*": *Catholic Theology and the Environment* (Washington, DC: United States Catholic Conference, 1996), 16, note 4.

[41] *The Columbia River Watershed: Caring for Creation and the Common Good*, An International Pastoral Letter by the Catholic Bishops of the Watershed Region (Seattle: Washington State Catholic Conference, 2000), 5–6, 14.

[42] Ibid., 18.

[43] Ibid., 20.

[44] *Basic Call to Consciousness*, rev. ed. (Roosevelttown, NY: Akwesasne Notes, Mohawk Nation, rev. ed. 1986), 49 (no author given).

[45] Roland Lesseps and Peter Henriot, "Genetically Modified Organisms and Catholic Social Thought," *Blueprint for Social Justice* 57 (January 2004): 2.

3. Human Dignity: Respect for Every Life

[1] Edward Guinan, ed., *Peace and Nonviolence: Basic Writings* (New York: Paulist Press, 1993), 50.

[2] Tom Roberts, "Project H.O.M.E.," *National Catholic Reporter* 35 (December 10, 1999), 3–4; emphasis added.

[3] National Conference Catholic Bishops, *Economic Justice for All* (Washington, DC: United States Catholic Conference, 1986), 32

[4] Pope John Paul II, "The International Situation Today," *Origins* 32 (January 30, 2003): 544.

[5] Ibid., no. 28, emphasis added.

[6] Joseph Cardinal Bernardin, *The Consistent Ethic of Life: Joseph Cardinal Bernardin*, ed. Thomas G. Fuechtmann (Kansas City: Sheed and Ward, 1988), 2.

[7] Ibid., 5.

[8] Ibid., 14.

[9] At least three people articulated the connection between war and abortion in 1971, twelve years before Bernardin's first speech on the topic: Archbishop Humberto Medeiros of Boston, Catholic journalist Margaret O'Brien Steinfels, and Eileen Egan of the Catholic Worker movement. See my discussion of this in *Catholic Social Teaching and Movements* (Mystic, CT: Twenty-Third Publications, 1998), 210–14.

[10] Bernardin, *The Consistent Ethic of Life*, 17.

[11] Bishop Thomas Olmstead, "Catholics and Politics," *Origins* 36, no. 22 (November 9, 2006): 343–44.

[12] Pope John Paul II, *Christifideles Laici* (On the Vocation and the Mission of the Lay Faithful in the Church and in the World) (Washington, DC: USCCB, 1989) 38, emphasis added.

[13] Benedict XVI, Address to the Members of the European People's Party on the Occasion of the Study Days on Europe," March 30, 2006, http://www.vatican.va/holy_father/benedict_xvi/speeches.

[14] http://www.usccb.org/prolife/gospel.shtml.

[15] Ibid.

[16] USCCB, *Forming Consciences for Faithful Citizenship: A Call to Political Responsibility*, 2008, 22–23.

[17]   Benedict XVI, "Conclusion of the Meeting of the Holy Father with the Bishops of Switzerland," November 9, 2006, http://www.vatican.va/holy_father/benedict_xvi/speeches.

[18]   Joint Statement Chairman, Committee on Pro-Life Activities and Chairman, Committee on Domestic Justice and Human Development, USCCB, October 21, 2008. No longer available on website.

[19]   Jim Wallis, *The Great Awakening* (New York: HarperCollins, 2008), 189.

[20]   *Forming Consciences for Faithful Citizenship*, 27–30; Doctrinal Note on Some Questions Regarding the Participation of Catholics in Political Life, 4.

[21]   John Kavanaugh, *Following Christ in a Consumer Society*, rev. ed. (Maryknoll, NY: Orbis Books, 1991), 32.

[22]   New York State Catholic Conference, *Pursuing Justice: Catholic Social Teaching and Issues in Contemporary Society* (Albany: New York State Catholic Conference, 2002), 2–3.

[23]   Ibid.

[24]   United States Catholic Conference of Catholic Bishops, *A Matter of the Heart: A Statement of the United States Conference of Catholic Bishops on the Thirtieth Anniversary of Roe v. Wade*, November 12, 2002 (Washington, DC: United States Conference of Catholic Bishops, 2002), 2.

[25]   Rob Cullivan, "A Birthday for Abortion," *Catholic Courier* (Diocese of Rochester), (January 30, 2003), 6.

[26]   Rob Cullivan, "Teens Speak for Those Never Born," *Catholic Courier* (Diocese of Rochester), (January 30, 2003), 8.

[27]   Bernardin, *Consistent Ethic of Life*, 8–9, 83.

[28]   The 2010 Pew survey results can be found at http://pewforum.org/Politics-and-Elections/.

[29]   Department of Justice, Peace and Human Development, Office of Domestic Social Development, "Death Penalty," February 2011, http://www.usccb.org/death-penalty/index.shtml.

[30]   James Megivern, *The Death Penalty: An Historical and Theological Survey* (New York: Paulist Press, 1997), 444.

[31]   "Statements by the Holy Father on the Death Penalty" found on the website of the United States Conference of Catholic Bishops, www.usccb.org/sdwp/national/criminal.

[32]   Wilton Gregory, Oct 7, 2008, Emory University at http://www.georgiabulletin.org/.

[33]   Archbishop Charles J. Chaput, "Supreme Court Ruling on Death Penalty Encouraging; Now Let's Do More," *Denver Catholic Register* (March 9, 2005), available at http://www.archden.org/dcr/.

[34]   The website for the Catholic Campaign to End the Use of the Death Penalty is http://www.usccb.org/deathpenalty/.

[35]   Helen Prejean, *The Death of Innocents: An Eyewitness Account of Wrongful Executions* (New York: Random House, 2005), xvi.

[36]   Debbie Shelley, "Sister Helen Prejean talks about finding Christ on death row," *The Catholic Commentator* (Baton Rouge, LA), October 8, 2008, at http://www.prejean.org/PressClippings/StJosephsAcademy.html.

[37]   Helen Prejean, *Dead Man Walking: An Eyewitness Account of the Death Penalty in the United States* (New York: Vintage Books, 1994), 6.

[38]   *Gaudium et Spes*, no. 1.

[39]   *Justice in the World*, "Introduction." (No paragraph numbers are used in this document.)

[40]   Prejean, *Dead Man Walking*, 5.

[41]   Ibid., 10.

[42]   Ibid., 10–11.

[43]   Ibid., 22.

[44]   Summary of the cases from *The Death of Innocents* book jacket.

[45]   Prejean, *The Death of Innocents*, xvi.

[46]   Prejean, "*The Abolition of the Death Penalty: A Target for the XXI Century*," September 9, 2003, Aachen, Germany at http://www.prejean.org/.

[47]   "No More Death Penalty," *America* (March 28, 2011), 4.

[48]   "Abolition of the Death Penalty Becomes Law In Illinois: Catholic Conference of Illinois Commends Governor's Approval of Senate Bill 3539," March 9, 2011, at http://www.catholicconferenceofillinois.org/content/StatementSB-3539SignedbyGov(3-9-11).pdf.

[49]   Lark Turner, "Writer of Book Cited by Quinn 'Overwhelmed,'" *Chicago Sun Times* (March 13, 2011).

[50]   Ibid.

[51]   Ibid.

[52]   CNN Opinion, November 25, 2009.

[53]   CBS Evening News, July 22, 2009.

[54]   The Respect Life pamphlet on sex trafficking is available at http://www.usccb.org/prolife. My overview of sex trafficking is taken from this excellent resource written by Diane Bayly, the educational and outreach coordinator for the USCCB Office of Migration and Refugee Services.

[55]   Ibid.

[56]   "Super Bowl a Magnet for Under-age Sex Trade," January 31, 2011, http://www.msnbc.msn.com/id/41360579.

[57]   From the Migrations and Refugee Services human trafficking website: http://www.usccb.org/mrs/trafficking/.

[58]   The programs are described on the website noted above.

[59]   Between 2006 and 2009 the Migration and Refugee Services of the USCCB assisted 1,500 foreign national survivors of human trafficking in the United States.

[60]   Bill Appleby Purcell, *Being Neighbor: The Catechism and Social Justice* (Washington, DC: United States Conference of Catholic Bishops, 1998), 4.

[61]   Prayer written by Sister Prejean, found at http://helenprejean.net/.

4. Community, Family, Participation

[1] Thomas Merton, *Dialogues with Silence: Prayers and Drawings*, ed. Jonathan Montaldo (New York: Harper Collins, 2001), ix–x.

[2] William H. Shannon, ed., *Thomas Merton: Passion for Peace: The Social Essays* (New York: Crossroad, 1995), 2–3.

[3] Thomas Merton, *Conjectures of a Guilty Bystander* (Garden City, NY: Doubleday, 1965), 140–41.

[4] Ibid., 141.

[5] Ibid., 142.

[6] Shannon, *Thomas Merton*, 4.

[7] United States Catholic Conference, *Sharing Catholic Social Teaching* (Washington, DC: United States Catholic Conference, 1998), 22.

[8] John Coleman, *An American Strategic Theology* (New York: Paulist Press, 1982), 10.

[9] John G. Gager, *Kingdom and Community: The Social World of Early Christianity* (Englewood Cliffs, NJ: Prentice Hall, 1976), 96; quoted in William Walsh and John Langan, "Patristic Social Consciousness—The Church and the Poor," in *The Faith That Does Justice*, ed. John Haughey (New York: Paulist Press, 1977), 113.

[10] Walter Brueggemann, *Prophetic Imagination*, 2nd ed., (Philadelphia: Fortress Press, 2001), 21 and 24.

[11] Ibid., 33.

[12] D. N. Premnath, *Eighth Century Prophets: A Social Analysis* (St. Louis: Chalice Press, 2003), 188.

[13] Brueggemann, *Prophetic Imagination*, 40.

[14] Ibid., 66.

[15] Ibid., 68.

[16] "From earliest times, Christians sharply distinguished themselves from surrounding pagan cultures by rejecting abortion and infanticide. The earliest widely used documents of Christian teaching and practice after the New Testament in the 1st and 2nd centuries, the *Didache* (Teaching of the Twelve Apostles) and *Letter of Barnabas*, condemned both practices, as did early regional and particular Church councils" (see "Respect for Unborn Human Life: The Church's Constant Teaching," www.usccb.org/prolifeconstantteaching.shtml).

[17] Robert Ellsberg, *All Saints: Daily Reflections on Saints, Prophets, and Witnesses for Our Time* (New York: Crossroad Publishing, 1997), 259.

[18] Ibid., 260.

[19] Ibid., 258.

[20] John Coleman, "North American Culture's Receptivity to Catholic Social Teaching," in *Catholic Social Teaching in Global Perspective,* ed. Daniel McDonald (Maryknoll, NY: Orbis Books, 2010), 199.

[21] Pope John Paul II, *Sollicitudo Rei Socialis*, 38, emphasis in the original.

[22] Thomas Massaro, *Living Justice: Catholic Social Teaching in Action* (Lanham, MD: Rowman & Littlefield, 2008), 89.

[23] Ibid.

²⁴ *Blessings after the Storms: Catholic Charities 2005 Hurricane Ministry,* Catholic Charities USA, 2006, 16.

²⁵ *Ministering Together Directory,* 5, at www.ministeringtogether.org.

²⁶ *Octogesima Adveniens,* 22, 47.

²⁷ Robert Sirico and Maciej Zieba, *The Social Agenda: A Collection of Magisterial Texts* (Vatican City: Libreria Editrice Vaticana, 2000), 72.

²⁸ United States Conference of Catholic Bishops, *Forming Consciences for Faithful Citizenship: A Call to Political Responsibility from the Catholic Bishops of the United States* (Washington DC: USCCB, 2007), www.faithfulcitizenship.org/.

²⁹ "Events Mark *Roe v. Wade* Anniversary," *Catholic Courier* (Rochester, NY), February, 2011, A4.

³⁰ This is the Jerusalem Bible translation. The New Revised Standard Version (1989) reads: "Then he [Jesus] went home; and the crowd came together again, so that they could not even eat. When his family heard it, they went out to restrain him, for people were saying, 'He has gone out of his mind'" (3:19–21).

³¹ Margaret Farley, "Family," in *The New Dictionary of Catholic Social Thought,* ed. Judith Dwyer (Collegeville, MN: Michael Glazier/The Liturgical Press, 1994), 372.

³² Ibid., 372.

³³ William Lazareth, *Luther on the Christian Home* (Philadelphia: Muhlenberg, 1960), 133, quoted by Farley, in "Family," 373.

³⁴ Farley, "Family," 374.

³⁵ *The Catechism of the Catholic Church,* 2ⁿᵈ ed. (Vatican City: Liberia Editice Vaticana, 1997), 2204 ff.

³⁶ Pope John Paul II, *Familiaris Consortio,* 16.

³⁷ USCCB, *Forming Consciences for Faithful Citizenship,* 70.

³⁸ Benedict XVI, "Address to the Members of The European People's Party on the Occasion of the Study Days on Europe," March 30, 2006, at www.vatican. va/holy_father/benedict_xvi/speeches.

³⁹ Farley, "Family," 379.

⁴⁰ "The family is, so to speak, the domestic Church. In it parents should, by their word and example, be the first preachers of faith to their children" (*Lumen Gentium,* 11). Earlier references to the family as the "church in miniature," the "small church," or the "church of the home" can be found in patristic theologians, including John Chrysostom and Augustine as well as Protestant theologians. See Lisa Sowle Cahill, *Family: A Christian Social Perspective* (Minneapolis: Augsburg Fortress, 2000), 27–82. Also see her article "Familiaris Consortio," in *Modern Catholic Social Teaching,* ed. Kenneth Himes (Washington, DC: Georgetown University Press, 2005), 371.

⁴¹ Michael Fahey, "The Christian Family as Domestic Church at Vatican II," in *The Family,* ed. Lisa Sowle Cahill and Dietmar Mieth (London and Maryknoll, NY: Orbis Books and SCM Press, 1995), 91.

⁴² *Familiaris Consortio,* 42, earlier, 49, 50, and 63.

⁴³ Ibid., 43.

⁴⁴ Ibid., 64, 41, 47, and 48.

⁴⁵ National Conference of Catholic Bishops, *Communities of Salt and Light: Reflections on the Social Mission of the Parish* (Washington, DC: United States Catholic Conference, 1993), 9.

⁴⁶ Ibid., 8.

⁴⁷ Ibid.

⁴⁸ At the supper table we had an hour-long conversation about the event and the meaning of stealing. My daughter stood her ground and felt it was not necessary to return to the store because it had been in our favor. She might have been standing firm for the sake of the argument. Either way, it showed us as parents how our children's morality is shaped by the cultural norms of "looking out for number one" and "it's not wrong unless you get caught."

⁴⁹ National Conference of Catholic Bishops, *Communities of Salt and Light*, 6–7.

⁵⁰ Ibid., 7.

⁵¹ Bill Appleby Purcell, *Being Neighbor: The Catechism and Social Justice* (Washington, DC: United States Catholic Conference, 1998), 5; rewritten by author.

5. Option for the Poor

¹ Rob Cullivan, "Woman Lives Life to Help Homeless," *Catholic Courier* (Rochester, New York, January 9, 2003), 12.

² Jorge Pixley, *Biblical Israel: A People's History* (Minneapolis: Fortress Press, 1992), 12.

³ Ibid., 12.

⁴ David Blanchard, "Session One: Background Piece, Journey to Justice" (Washington, DC: Catholic Campaign for Human Development, n.d.).

⁵ Jim Dinn, *Catholic Wisdom on Welfare Reform* (Chicago: Claretian Publications, no date), 8.

⁶ "Session Two: Background Piece, Journey to Justice," CCHD.

⁷ Robert Ellsberg, *All Saints: Daily Reflections on Saints, Prophets, and Witnesses for Our Time* (New York: Crossroad Publishing, 1997), 479.

⁸ Joseph Gremillion, *The Gospel of Peace and Justice: Catholic Social Teaching since Pope John* (Maryknoll, NY: Orbis Books, 1976), 453.

⁹ Alfred Hennelly, ed., *Liberation Theology: A Documentary History* (Maryknoll, NY: Orbis Books, 1990), 89.

¹⁰ Curt Cadorette, "Medellín," in *New Dictionary of Catholic Social Teaching*, ed. Judith Dwyer (Collegeville, MN: Glazier/Liturgical Press, 1994), 593.

¹¹ Cadorette, "Puebla," in *New Dictionary of Catholic Social Teaching*, 801. Regarding the meeting in Aparecida see Virgilio Elizondo, "Collaborative Theology: Latin American Bishops, the Pope and the Poor," *Commonweal* (January 31, 2008), 8–9.

¹² Daniel Hartnett, "Remembering the Poor: An Interview with Gustavo Gutiérrez," *America* 188 (February 3, 2003), 14.

¹³ Ellsberg, *All Saints*, 527.

¹⁴ Ibid.

15   Ibid.

16   Ibid.

17   Ibid., 526.

18   Ibid.

19   "Martyrs of El Salvador," a card from the Religious Task Force on Central America.

20   National Conference of Catholic Bishops, *Economic Justice for All* (Washington, DC: United States Catholic Conference, 1986), 52, author's formatting.

21   USCCB, *Communities of Salt and Light*, 1994, 1 and 2.

22   Blanchard, "Session One: Background Piece, Journey to Justice."

23   Donal Dorr, "Option for the Poor," in *New Dictionary of Catholic Social Teaching*, ed. Judith Dwyer (Collegeville, MN: Glazier/Liturgical Press, 1994), 755.

24   Ibid., 757.

25   Ibid., 758.

26   Denis Murphy, "Is 'Church of the Poor' Just Rhetoric?" *America* 188 (January 6–13, 2003), 12–14.

27   Ibid., 12–13.

28   Ibid., 13.

29   Ibid., 14.

30   From the 2011 CCHD national brochure available at http://www.usccb.org/cchd/.

31   For more examples of the projects that CCHD funds, see John Hogan, *Credible Signs of Christ Alive: Case Studies from the Catholic Campaign for Human Development* (Lanham, MD: Sheed & Ward, 2003).

32   http://pewhispanic.org/.

33   USCCB, *Strangers No Longer: Together on the Journey of Hope: A Pastoral Letter Concerning Migration from the Catholic Bishops of Mexico and the United States*, January 22, 2003, http://www.usccb.org/mrs.

34   The bishops established the Justice for Immigrants (JFI) campaign to educate and advocate. This postcard petition is part of that campaign, available at http://www.justiceforimmigrants.org.

35   Michael Glazier and Monika Hellwig, eds., *The Modern Catholic Encyclopedia* (Collegeville, MN: The Liturgical Press, 1994), 798. The Sisters of Charity aligned with the Daughters of Charity and continue a vibrant ministry in health care, education, parish, and social services.

36   These suggestions, with my reworking, are offered by Jack Jezreel, *Catholic Wisdom on Option for the Poor* (Chicago: Claretian Publications, no date), 4–7.

37   Department of Social Development and World Peace, *Communities of Salt and Light: Parish Resource Manual* (Washington, DC: United States Catholic Conference, 1994), 21–22.

38   National Conference of Catholic Bishops, *Sharing Catholic Social Teaching* (Washington, DC: United States Catholic Conference, 1998), 5.

39   Bill Appleby Purcell, *Being Neighbor: The Catechism and Social Justice* (Washington, DC: United States Catholic Conference, 1998), 7, adapted by author.

6. Rights and Responsibilities

[1]   Rob Cullivan, "Woman Lives Life to Help Homeless," *Catholic Courier* (Rochester, New York), January 9, 2003, 12.

[2]   *Sharing Catholic Social Teaching* (Washington, DC: United States Catholic Conference, 1998), 5.

[3]   John Donahue, "Biblical Perspectives on Justice," in *Faith That Does Justice*, ed. John Haughey (New York: Paulist Press, 1977), 69.

[4]   Gerhard von Rad, *Old Testament Theology*, trans. D. M. G. Stalker, vol. 1 (New York: Harper and Bros., 1962), 370; quoted by Donahue, "Biblical Perspectives on Justice," 68.

[5]   Ibid., 50.

[6]   Ibid., 50.

[7]   Ibid., 51.

[8]   D. N. Premnath, *Eighth Century Prophets: A Social Analysis* (St. Louis: Chalice Press, 2003), 182.

[9]   Walter Brueggemann, "Voices of the Night—Against Justice," in *To Act Justly, Love Tenderly, Walk Humbly*, ed. Walter Brueggemann (New York: Paulist Press, 1986), 16.

[10]   Vincent Taylor, *The Gospel According to St. Mark*, 2nd ed. (New York: Macmillan and Co., 1966), 462.

[11]   William Herzog, II, *Jesus, Justice, and the Reign of God: A Ministry of Liberation* (Louisville: Westminster John Knox Press, 2000), 133–42.

[12]   Ibid., 142–43.

[13]   Robert Ellsberg, *All Saints: Daily Reflections on Saints, Prophets, and Witnesses for Our Time* (New York: Crossroad Publishing, 1997), 306.

[14]   Quoted by Ronald Musto, in *The Catholic Peace Tradition* (Maryknoll, NY: Orbis Books, 1986), 143.

[15]   It should be noted, however, that Las Casas has been criticized for suggesting that black slaves be substituted for the indigenous peoples of Latin America. For more, see Gustavo Gutiérrez, *Las Casas: In Search of the Poor of Jesus Christ*, trans. Robert R. Barr (Maryknoll, NY: Orbis Books, 1993), 319–30. Later Las Casas realized that "the capture of the blacks [was] as unjust as that of the Indians" (at 328).

[16]   Matthew Lamb, "Solidarity," in *New Dictionary of Catholic Social Teaching*, ed. Judith Dwyer (Collegeville, MN: Glazier/Liturgical Press, 1994), 911.

[17]   Thomas Hoppe, "Human Rights," in *New Dictionary of Catholic Social Teaching*, ed. Judith Dwyer (Collegeville, MN: Glazier/Liturgical Press, 1994), 460.

[18]   Pope John Paul II, "Address at the United Nations" (Washington, DC: United States Catholic Conference, 1979), 13.

[19]   "As a matter of fact, this insight has long been incorporated into U. S. law, which recognizes the principle of eminent domain as an exception to the legal system's usual stance of according nearly absolute property rights to holders of title deeds. Under this legal principle, land or other property that is judged especially critical to the public interest may be altered of even seized outright (usually with

significant compensation to its previous owner) by public authorities in order to provide for crucial public needs, such as security or infrastructure improvements" (Thomas Massaro, *Living Justice: Catholic Social Teaching in Action* [Lanham, MD: Rowman & Littlefield Publishers, 2008], 94).

[20] John Paul II, *Sollicitudo Rei Socialis*, par. 42.

[21] Massaro, *Living Justice*, 94

[22] Bryan Massingale, *Racial Justice and the Catholic Church* (Maryknoll, NY: Orbis Books, 2010), 6.

[23] Ibid., 15.

[24] Ibid., 28. Here Massingale is quoting Charles Lawrence III, "The Id, the Ego, and Equal Protection: Reckoning with Unconscious Racism," *Stanford Law Review* 39 (January 1987): 323.

[25] Massingale, *Racial Justice and the Catholic Church*, 30.

[26] Ibid., 41.

[27] Jamie T. Phelps, "Communion Ecclesio-ology and Black Liberation Theology," *Theological Studies* 61, 4 (2000): 692, as cited by Jon Nilson, "Confessions of a White Catholic Racist Theologians," *Origins* 33 (July 17, 2003): 131 (on-line edition, 2).

[28] The number of souls lost in the slave trade is highly controversial. A BBC reporter uses these numbers: "The exact numbers of Africans shipped overseas during the slave trade are hotly debated—estimates range between 10 and 28 million," http://news.bbc.co.uk/2/hi/africa/1523100.stm. A website at Potsdam College states: "Between the years 1650 and 1900, historians estimate that at least 28 million Africans were forcibly removed from central and western Africa as slaves (but the numbers involved are controversial). A human catastrophe for Africa, the world African Slave Trade was truly a 'Holocaust.'" But then a few sentences later we find: "No one knows exactly how many Africans died at sea during the Middle Passage experience. *Estimates for the total number of Africans lost to the slave trade range from 25 to 50 million.*" So, 50 million appears to be the high end of the estimates, http://www2.potsdam.edu/mausdc/class/495/2002/slavetrade.html.

[29] Nilson, "Confessions of a White Catholic Racist Theologian," 131.

[30] Cyprian Davis, "Two Sides of a Coin: The Black Presence in the History of the Catholic Church in America," in *Many Rains Ago: A Historical and Theological Reflection on the Role of the Episcopate in the Evangelization of African American Catholics*, ed. Secretariat for Black Catholics (Washington, DC: United States Catholic Conference, 1990), 50.

[31] Ibid., 59.

[32] National Conference of Catholic Bishops, *Brothers and Sisters to Us: U.S. Bishops' Pastoral Letter on Racism in Our Day* (Washington, DC: United States Catholic Conference, 1979), 1. For global perspectives on racism see Dawn Nothwehr, *That They May Be One: Catholic Social Teaching on Racism, Tribalism, and Xenophobia* (Maryknoll, NY: Orbis Books, 2008).

[33] Ibid.

[34] Archbishop Sean O'Malley, "Solidarity: The Antidote to Resurgent Racism," *Origins* 29 (February 3, 2000): 531–32.

[35]   Massingale, *Racial Justice and the Catholic Church*, 76.

[36]   Ibid., 77–78.

[37]   Ibid., 105.

[38]   *L'Osservatore Romano*, Eng. ed. (March 22, 2000), 4; cited in Pontifical Council for Justice and Peace, "Contribution to World Conference against Racism, Racial Discrimination, Xenophobia and Related Intolerance," 7; as cited by Massingale, *Racial Justice and the Catholic Church*, 112.

[39]   Ibid., 112–13.

[40]   *Poverty and Racism: Overlapping Threats to the Common Good*, Catholic Charities USA, 2008, 1. Bryan Massingale was the primary author of this brief.

[41]   Ibid., 1–2.

[42]   Ibid., 3.

[43]   Ibid., 11.

[44]   Ibid., 11–12.

[45]   Ibid., 13.

[46]   United States Conference of Catholic Bishops, *A Place at the Table: A Catholic Recommitment to Overcome Poverty and to Respect the Dignity of All God's Children, A Pastoral Reflection of the U.S. Catholic Bishops* (Washington, DC: United States Conference of Catholic Bishops, 2002), 3, at www.usccb.org/bishops/table.htm.

[47]   In 2009, 43.6 million people were in poverty, up from 39.8 million in 2008—the third consecutive annual increase in the number of people in poverty, http://www.census.gov/hhes/www/poverty/about/overview/index.html.

[48]   *A Place at the Table*, 4.

[49]   Ibid., 2.

[50]   Ibid.

[51]   Ibid., 7–8.

[52]   Ibid., 8.

[53]   Ibid.

[54]   Ibid., 8–9.

[55]   Monika Hellwig, "Principle of Subsidiarity," in *The Modern Catholic Encyclopedia*, ed. Michael Glazier and Monika Hellwig (Collegeville, MN: Liturgical Press, 1994), 836.

[56]   *Sharing Catholic Social Teaching*, 25.

[57]   *A Place at the Table*, 10.

[58]   Frank Turner, S.J., "Exploring the Encyclical," *Thinking Faith: The Online Journal of the British Jesuits* (December 2, 2009): 2, at www.thinkingfaith.org.

[59]   *"The social question has become a radically anthropological question"* (75, emphasis in original).

[60]   Austen Ivereigh, "Building Civil Society," *Thinking Faith: The Online Journal of the British Jesuits* (December 23, 2009): 4, at www.thinkingfaith.org. Also see Ivereigh's *Faithful Citizens: A Practical Guide to Catholic Social Teaching and Community Organising* (London: Darton, Longman and Todd, 2010).

[61]   Bill Appleby Purcell, *Being Neighbor: The Catechism and Social Justice* (Washington, DC: United States Catholic Conference, 1998), 6; adapted by author.

7. *The Dignity of Work and Workers' Rights*

¹ *New York Times*, March 2, 2011, at http://topics.nytimes.com.

² Archbishop Jerome Listecki, "Statement Regarding the Rights of Workers and the Value of Unions," February 23, 2011, at www.wisconsincatholic.org.

³ Bishop Stephen E. Blaire, "USCCB Chairman Supports Wisconsin Bishops on the Rights of Workers," February 24, 2011, at http://www.usccb.org/comm/archives/2011/11-038.shtml.

⁴ *Voices and Choices: A Pastoral Letter from the Catholic Bishops of the South* (November 2000), at www.americancatholic.org/News/PoultryPastoral/english.asp, 2.

⁵ John Rausch, "Cheap Chicken Actually Costs a Lot," National Catholic Rural Life Conference website: www.ncrlc.com/poultrypastoral.html, 2. For a view of the working conditions in a poultry processing plant read Steve Striffler, "Undercover in a Chicken Factory," *Utne* (January-February 2004), 68–74.

⁶ "Our team of reporters and editors spent 22 months interviewing more than 200 poultry workers throughout the Southeast and analyzing industry documents. Their investigation soon led them to focus on one of the largest Carolinas-based poultry producers, House of Raeford. Its eight plants have been cited for more serious safety violations than all but two other poultry companies in recent years—and more than some companies several times their size.

"Our journalists found evidence that House of Raeford has failed to report serious injuries, including broken bones and carpal tunnel syndrome. They discovered that plant officials often dismissed workers' requests for medical care that would cost the company money" (Rick Thames, "Poultry Series Exposes a New, Silent Subclass," *Charlotte Observer,* Friday, June 25, 2010), www.CharlotteObserver.com.

⁷ *Voices and Choices*, 12.

⁸ Ibid.

⁹ Ibid., 4.

¹⁰ J. Milburn Thompson, *Introducing Catholic Social Thought* (Maryknoll, NY: Orbis Books, 2010), 86.

¹¹ Chuck Collins and Mary Wright, *The Moral Measure of the Economy* (Maryknoll, NY: Orbis Books, 2007), 68.

¹² Ibid., 69.

¹³ Ibid., 70. Collins and Wright speak of "two or three Americas." I see "two Rochesters" in my work and family life in Rochester, New York. My wife, Kristine, and I found that Rochester was a great city in which to raise our two children. At the same time, Rochester is a terrible place to raise a child as *42 percent of the children in Rochester live below the federal poverty level*. It all depends on which Rochester you are part of—our middle-class neighborhood or the poor urban neighborhoods.

¹⁴ Helen Prejean, *Dead Man Walking: An Eyewitness Account of the Death Penalty in the United States* (New York: Vintage Books, 1993), 4.

¹⁵ Ibid., 10.

[16] William L. Pickett, *Catholic Social Teaching and the Consequences of Income Inequality: A Message for American Catholics?* M.A. thesis, St. Bernard's School of Theology and Ministry, Rochester, New York, July 2010, http://williampickett. com/writing.shtml. Also see Richard Wilkinson and Kate Pickett, *The Spirit Level: Why More Equal Societies Almost Always Do Better* (London: Allen Lane, 2009).

[17] Jim Wallis, *God's Politics: Why the Right Gets It Wrong and the Left Doesn't Get It* (San Francisco: HarperSanFrancisco, 2005), 212.

[18] William R. Herzog II, *Parables as Subversive Speech* (Louisville: Westminster/ John Knox Press, 1994), 79–97.

[19] Scriptural texts that address worker rights include Exodus 23:9; Leviticus 25:23–38; Deuteronomy 27:19; Psalms 72 and 103:6; Jeremiah 7:1–11; Isaiah 3:11–15; 58; 61; Amos 2:6–7; 6:4–8; 8:4–7; Micah 6:8; Luke 4:18; and Matthew 25:31–46.

[20] John Paul II, "Address on Christian Unity in a Technological Age," in Gerald Darring, *A Cathechism of Catholic Social Teaching* (Kansas City: Sheed and Ward, 1987), 29.

[21] *A Decade after Economic Justice for All: Continuing Principles, Changing Context, New Challenges* (Washington, DC: United States Catholic Conference, 1996).

[22] John Allen, "Indiana Firm Can Claim a Papal Thumbs-Up from New Social Encyclical," *National Catholic Reporter* (July 7, 2009), http://ncronline.org.

[23] Smriti Jacob, "The Power of Disclosure," *Rochester Business Journal* 19 (December 5, 2003), 33.

[24] E-mail correspondence to the author from Bob Fien, December 23, 2003. Two associations that promote employee stock ownership are the National Center for Employee Ownership (NCEO), 1736 Franklin Street, 8th floor, Oakland, CA 94614, (510) 208–1300, and the Employee Stock Ownership Plan (ESOP) Association, 1726 M Street, Suite 501, Washington, D.C., 20036, (202) 293–2971. And a 2011 update from an email from Bob Fien dated March 7, 2011 reported: "A significant portion of our business is in the housing market and that business totally dried up and is still very, very weak. Years ago, we hedged against the housing market by broadening our product lines and establishing a strong international effort. Traditionally, when the U.S. goes into a recession the rest of the world is strong and vice versa. This time for the first time the whole world went down.

For three and a half years, we have been going through hell. We still are. There were a number of times when I thought we would not make it. The most difficult thing was laying off the people. Before the recession we employed 280 people. Today we are down to 40. Surprisingly, or perhaps not surprisingly, most of the people we laid off have taken part time jobs and have told us they are waiting to come back. Prior to the recession we were a $60 million company. Last year we shipped $15 million and this year we will do about $22 million. *In spite of the hardships, we are still maintaining our culture. I think that is one of the reasons that, in spite of our distressed condition, we seem to be doing better than most of our competitors.* I am confident that we will pull out of this and get back to the way we were" [emphasis added].

[25] Vincent Gallagher, *The True Costs of Low Prices: The Violence of Globalization* (Maryknoll, NY: Orbis Books, 2006), 102.

[26] Human Rights Watch, "Easy Targets: Violence against Children Worldwide," September 1, 2001, www.hrw.org.

[27] Human Rights Watch, "Fields of Peril: Child Labor in US Agriculture," May 5, 2010, www.hrw.org.

[28] Craig Kielburger, *Free the Children* (Toronto: McClelland & Stewart, 1998), 5.

[29] Ibid., 7.

[30] Ibid., 308.

[31] Ibid., 311.

[32] Ibid., 314.

[33] Data from Free the Children website, http://www.freethechildren.com.

[34] Tom Schindler, "Work," in *The Modern Catholic Encyclopedia*, ed. Michael Glazier and Monika Hellwig (Collegeville, MN: Michael Glazier/Liturgical Press, 1994), 917.

[35] Christine Firer Hinze, "Dirt and Economic Inequality: A Christian-Ethical Peek under the Rug," *Annual of the Society of Christian Ethics* 21 (2001): 47–48.

[36] Barbara Ehrenreich, "Maid to Order: The Politics of Other Women's Housework," *Harper's Magazine* 300 (1799), April 17, 2000, 59–70, as cited by Firer Hinze, "Dirt and Economic Inequality," 58.

[37] Firer Hinze, "Dirt and Economic Inequality," 59.

[38] USCCB, "Themes of Catholic Social Teaching," from http://www.usccb.org/sdwp/projects/socialteaching/excerpt.shtml.

[39] USCCB, *Economic Justice for All: Pastoral Letter on Catholic Social Teaching and the U.S. Economy* (Washington, DC: United States Catholic Conference, 1986), 103.

[40] Ibid.

[41] Tom Schindler, "Unions," in *The Modern Catholic Encyclopedia*, eds., Michael Glazier and Monika Hellwig (Collegeville, MN: Michael Glazier/Liturgical Press, 1994), 881–82.

[42] *Economic Justice for All*, 104

[43] Maryanne Stevens, "Strike, Right to," in *The New Dictionary of Catholic Social Thought*, ed. Judith Dwyer (Collegeville, MN: Glazier/Liturgical Press, 1994), 926.

[44] Frank Almade, "Just Wage," in *The New Dictionary of Catholic Social Thought*, ed. Judith Dwyer (Collegeville, MN: Michael Glazier/Liturgical Press, 1994), 493.

[45] Ibid., 493–94. "Indirect employers" is found in *Laborem Exercens*, 17.

[46] Jon Gertner, "What Is a Living Wage?" *The New York Times Magazine*, January 15, 2006, www.nytimes.com.

[47] William Bole, *Our Sunday Visitor*, September 3, 1995; www.ewtn.com on October 25, 2005.

[48] Stephen Hart. "Getting Organized," *The Christian Century* (November 7, 2001), 20–25; found at www.religion-online.org.

[49] Living-wage rate in Baltimore found at www.baltimorecity.gov.

[50] See www.livingwagesonoma.org and www.livingwagenyc.org.

[51] The living-wage rate in Rochester for 2011 is $11.83 without any health insurance benefit and $10.59 with health insurance. For a fuller discussion of the living wage see my essay, "The Living Wage Movement and Catholic Social Teach-

ing," *Journal of Catholic Social Thought* 6, no. 1 (2009): 231–52. Other helpful resources are Robert Pollin and Stephanie Luce, *The Living Wage: Building a Fair Economy*, rev. ed. (New York: The New Press, 2000); Deborah Figart, "Ethical Foundations of the Contemporary Living Wage Movement," *International Journal of Social Economics* 28 (2001); Robert Pollin, Mark Brenner, Jeannette Wicks-Lim, and Stephanie Luce, *A Measure of Fairness: The Economics of Living Wages and Minimum Wages in the United States* (Ithaca, NY: Cornell University Press, 2008); and Jerold Waltman, *The Case for the Living Wage* (New York: Algora Publishing, 2004).

[52]   *Economic Justice for All*, 353.

[53]   Jeff Guntzel, "A Century of Catholic Church Defense of Workers," *National Catholic Reporter* (August 1, 2003), 1.

[54]   Gerald Costello, *Without Fear or Favor: George Higgins on the Record* (Mystic, CT: Twenty-Third Publications, 1984), 105.

[55]   Ibid., 134–37.

[56]   "Monsignor George Higgins: An Appreciation," May 1, 2002, at www.aflcio.org.

[57]   National Conference of Catholic Bishops, *A Fair and Just Workplace: Principles and Practices for Catholic Health Care* (Washington, DC: United States Catholic Conference, 1999), www.usccb.org/sdwp, 5–6.

[58]   USCCB Committee on Domestic Justice and Human Development, *Respecting the Just Rights of Workers: Guidance and Options for Catholic Health Care and Unions*, June 22, 2009, at www.usccb.org/sdwp.

[59]   Jerry Filteau, "Bishops' Labor Document Seen as Breakthrough," *National Catholic Reporter*, June 24, 2009, at www.ncronline.org.

[60]   Ronald Taylor, *Chavez and the Farm Workers* (Boston: Beacon Press, 1975), 81.

[61]   Jean Maddern Pitrone, *Chavez: Man of the Migrants: A Plea for Social Justice* (New York: Alba House, 1971), 53.

[62]   Robert Ellsberg, *All Saints: Daily Reflections on Saints, Prophets, and Witnesses for Our Time* (New York: Crossroad Publishing, 1997), 180–81.

8. Solidarity: War and Peace

[1]   "India Mourns Loss of Native-born Hero on 2nd Spaceflight," *Democrat and Chronicle*, February 2, 2003, A13.

[2]   The *Langenscheidt's New College Merriam-Webster English Dictionary* (Maspeth, NY: Langenscheidt Pub., 1998) cites 1841 as the first time "solidarity" was used in English.

[3]   Matthew Lamb, "Solidarity," in *The New Dictionary of Catholic Social Thought*, ed. Judith Dwyer (Collegeville, MN: Glazier/Liturgical Press, 1994), 909.

[4]   Robert Ellsberg, *All Saints: Daily Reflections on Saints, Prophets, and Witnesses for Our Time* (New York: Crossroad Publishing, 1997), 456.

[5]   Ibid., 457.

[6]   Ibid., 457–58.

⁷ Lamb, "Solidarity," 912.

⁸ Ibid.

⁹ Ibid., 912.

¹⁰ *Centesimus Annus*, 14. Patrick McCormick, "Centesimus Annus," in *The New Dictionary of Catholic Social Thought*, ed. Judith Dwyer (Collegeville, MN: Glazier/Liturgical Press, 1994), 141.

¹¹ Ibid.

¹² *Centesimus Annus*, 23.

¹³ McCormick, "Centesimus Annus," 142.

¹⁴ Ibid.

¹⁵ *Centesimus Annus*, 52.

¹⁶ Paul Tillich, *Love, Power and Justice* (London: Oxford University Press, 1954), 63ff.

¹⁷ Desmond Tutu, *No Future without Forgiveness* (Garden City, NY: Doubleday/Image, 2000).

¹⁸ William Bole, "Forgiveness: A Radical New Factor," *America* (April 21, 2003), 18.

¹⁹ Donald Shriver Jr., *An Ethic for Enemies* (London: Oxford University Press, 1995), as quoted by Bole, "Forgiveness," 18.

²⁰ Bole, "Forgiveness," 18.

²¹ "Healing on Both Sides of the Nickel Mines Tragedy, Four Years on," posted on October 2, 2010 at http://amishamerica.com/healing-on-both-sides-of-the-nickel-mines-tragedy-four-years-on/.

²² "The Amish: The Massacre of Six Innocents," Oct, 3, 2006, http://www.religioustolerance.org/amish7.htm.

²³ Kenneth Briggs, *The Power of Forgiveness* (Minneapolis: Fortress Press: 2008): 12–13.

²⁴ "Amish Tragedy Marked Quietly," October 2, 2010, http://articles.lancasteronline.com/local/4/296630.

²⁵ Paul VI, *World Day of Peace Message*, 1977.

²⁶ Pope John Paul II, "The International Situation Today," *Origins* 32 (January 30, 2003): 544, emphasis added.

²⁷ Ibid.

²⁸ Dorothy Day, *The Long Loneliness* (New York: Harper, 1952; reprint Harper Collins, 1980), 134. Dorothy was born in Brooklyn in 1897; her family subsequently relocated to Chicago. At age sixteen, she headed to the University of Illinois at Urbana where she joined the Socialist Party. After two years she left college and moved to New York City, where she found a job with the Socialist daily, *The Call*. She wrote about poverty from a radical perspective, covering speeches by people like Leon Trotsky, and writing about poverty, labor strikes, and the women's suffrage movement. In 1917, at the age of twenty, Dorothy was arrested in Washington, D.C., while protesting with the suffragettes. Several of the women including Dorothy were given thirty-day jail sentences, which they protested with a hunger strike. After ten days of fasting, they were released on the eighteenth day by order of President Woodrow Wilson.

[29] Ronald Musto, *The Catholic Peace Tradition* (Maryknoll, NY: Orbis Books, 1986), 242

[30] Ibid. Other resources on Dorothy Day include her autobiography, Dorothy Day, *The Long Loneliness* (New York: Harper, 1952) and three works by Robert Ellsberg, *The Duty of Delight: The Diaries of Dorothy Day* (Milwaukee, WI: Marquette University Press, 2008); *All the Way to Heaven: The Selected Letters of Dorothy Day* (Milwaukee, WI: Marquette University Press, 2010); and *Dorothy Day: Selected Writings* (Maryknoll, NY: Orbis Books, 2005).

[31] Ibid., 243.

[32] Ibid.

[33] *The Catholic Worker* (July–August 1965), 7.

[34] *The Challenge of Peace*, 117.

[35] "Street Saint," *Time* Magazine (December 15, 1980), 74.

[36] William H. Shannon, ed., *Thomas Merton: Passion for Peace: The Social Essays* (New York: Crossroad, 1995), 2–3.

[37] Richard Hays, *The Moral Vision of the New Testament* (New York: Harper Collins, 1996), 329–30.

[38] Ibid., 331, 332; emphasis added.

[39] Lisa Cahill, *Love Your Enemies: Discipleship, Pacifism, and Just War Theory* (Minneapolis: Fortress Press, 1944), 3.

[40] Ibid., 39.

[41] Musto, *The Catholic Peace Tradition*, 35.

[42] Ibid., 36.

[43] Cahill, *Love Your Enemies*, 7.

[44] Ibid., 12.

[45] Ibid., 13.

[46] Hays, *The Moral Vision of the New Testament*, 342.

[47] Cahill, *Love Your Enemies*, 14

[48] USCCB, *The Harvest of Justice Is Sown in Peace: A Reflection of the National Conference of Catholic Bishops on the Tenth Anniversary of "The Challenge of Peace"* (Washington, DC: United States Catholic Conference, 1993), http://www.usccb.org/sdwp/harvest.shtml, 10–11.

[49] Ibid.

[50] Robert McElroy, "War without End," *America* (February 21, 2011), 13.

[51] Ibid.

[52] Michael Schuck, "When the Shooting Stops: Missing Elements in Just War Theory," *Christian Century* 111, no. 30 (October 26, 1994), 982–83; Mark Allman and Tobias Winright, *After the Smoke Clears: The Just War Tradition and Post War Justice* (Maryknoll, NY: Orbis Books, 2010).

[53] Thomas Shannon, "What Is 'Just War' Today?" *Catholic Update* (May 2004), 4.

[54] Hays, *The Moral Vision of the New Testament*, 342–43. The official Catholic position would argue that pacifism and nonviolence can be seen as "reasonable" and participating in public governance can actually be a Christian vocation.

[55] Musto, *The Catholic Peace Tradition*, 200.

[56] Ibid., 247.

[57] Michael Novak, "'Asymmetrical Warfare' and Just War: A Moral Obligation," *National Review Online,* www.nationalreview.com (February 10, 2003), 4, 3.

[58] Gerard Powers, "An Ethical Analysis of War Against Iraq," *Blueprint for Social Justice* 56 (March 2003), 3.

[59] Quoted by Thomas Shannon, "What Is 'Just War' Today?" 4.

[60] Wilton Gregory, "Blessed Are the Peacemakers: Reflections on Two Anniversaries," August 4, 2003, 4, www.uscsb.org/sdwp.

[61] Zenit News Agency, "Pope to Ask Bush for Radical Shift in Policy, Says Cardinal Laghi, Changes Sought in Approach to Iraq and Holy Land," www.Zenit. org/English, May 13, 2004, 1.

[62] J. Milburn Thompson, *Introducing Catholic Social Thought* (Maryknoll, NY: Orbis Books, 2010), 136. Milburn lists the ten practices as: (1) support nonviolent direct action, (2) take independent initiatives to reduce threat, (3) use cooperative conflict resolution, (4) acknowledge responsibility for conflict and injustice and seek repentance and forgiveness, (5) advance democracy, human rights, religious liberty, and interdependence, (6) foster just and sustainable economic development, (7) work with emerging cooperative forces in the international system, (8) strengthen the United Nations and international efforts for cooperation and human rights, (9) reduce offensive weapons and weapons trade, and (10) encourage grassroots peacemaking groups and other voluntary associations. Also see Glen Stassen, ed., *Just Peacemaking: Ten Practices for Abolishing War,* rev. ed. (Cleveland: Pilgrim Press, 2008).

[63] Thompson, *Introducing Catholic Social Thought,* 138. Also see Gerald Schlabach, ed., *Just Policing, Not War: An Alternative Response to World Violence* (Collegeville, MN: A Michael Glazier Book/Liturgical Press, 2007).

[64] For a treatment of peace history within Catholicism, see Musto, *The Catholic Peace Tradition.*

[65] Drew Christiansen, "Catholic Theology of Peace—and War," Lecture delivered at Nazareth College, Rochester, New York, October 30, 2003.

[66] Kenneth Himes, "War," in *The New Dictionary of Catholic Social Thought,* ed. Judith Dwyer (Collegeville, MN: Glazier/Liturgical Press, 1994), 979.

[67] Thompson, *Introducing Catholic Social Thought,* 103. Thompson cites Walter C. Clemens and J. David Singer, "The Human Cost of War: Modern Warfare Kills More Civilians than Soldiers," *Scientific American* 282 (June 2000), 56–57; and Ronald Waldman, "Public Health in War: Pursuing the Impossible," *Harvard International Review* 27 (Spring 2005): 60.

[68] Pope John Paul II, *Centesimus Annus,* 52.

[69] Cited by Bishop Robert McElroy, "War without End," *America* (February 21, 2011), 12–13.

[70] Briggs, *The Power of Forgiveness,* 13.

[71] Robert Schreiter, "The Catholic Social Imaginary and Peacebuilding: Ritual, Sacrament, and Spirituality," *Peacebuilding: Catholic Theology, Ethics, and Praxis* (Maryknoll, NY: Orbis Books, 2010), 221–39.

[72] Jeffry Odell Korgen, *Solidarity Will Transform the World: Stories of Hope from Catholic Relief Services* (Maryknoll, NY: Orbis Books, 2007), 101–04. Korgen reported that "Rwanda released confessing prisoners due to illness, age, or half sentence served in groups of forty thousand at a time" (159, n. 4).

[73] Ibid., 121.

[74] Shannon, *Thomas Merton*, 3–4.

[75] Ibid., 4.

[76] Distributed by Pax Christi USA and the Fellowship of Reconciliation, www.paxchristiusa.org.

Catholic Social Teaching:
Selected Bibliography

Charles E. Curran. *The Social Mission of the U.S. Catholic Church: a Theological Perspective*. Washington, DC: Georgetown University Press, 2011. An historical and theological overview and critique of the social mission of the U.S. Catholic Church by a preeminent moral theologian.

Edward DeBerri and James Hug, eds. *Catholic Social Teaching: Our Best Kept Secret*, 4th edition. Maryknoll, NY: Orbis Books, 2003. Outline of the documents from Latin America, Africa, Asia, Australia, and Europe along with papal, Vatican, and U.S. bishops' statements.

Bernard Evans. *Lazarus at the Table: Catholics and Social Justice*. Collegeville, MN: Liturgical Press, 2006. A very brief text that articulates the principles at the heart of Catholic social teaching.

Kenneth R. Himes, Lisa Sowle Cahill, Charles E. Curran, and David Hollenbach, eds. *Modern Catholic Social Teaching: Commentaries and Interpretations*. Washington, DC: Georgetown University Press, 2004. An in-depth analysis of the key documents by leading American theologians.

Jeffry Odell Korgen. *My Lord and My God: Engaging Catholics in Social Ministry*. New York: Paulist Press, 2007. Packed with great ideas and passion.

Thomas Massaro. *Living Justice: Catholic Social Teaching in Action*. Lanham, MD: Rowman & Littlefield Publishers, 2008. A popular updated explanation of the Catholic social teaching.

Bryan Massingale. *Racial Justice and the Catholic Church*. Maryknoll, NY: Orbis Books, 2010. A powerful analysis and critique of racism and the Catholic Church.

Marvin L. Krier Mich. *Catholic Social Teaching and Movements*. Mystic, CT: Twenty-Third Publications, 1998. Introduces the reader to both the official documents and grassroots movements that make up the Catholic social tradition.

Pontifical Council on Justice and Peace. *Compendium of the Social Doctrine of the Church*. Washington, DC: USCCB, 2005. The official Vatican summary of Catholic social teaching.

J. Milburn Thompson. *Introducing Catholic Social Thought*. Maryknoll, NY: Orbis Books, 2010. A lively introduction to Catholic social thought.

Tom Ulrich. *Parish Social Ministry: Strategies for Success*. Notre Dame, IN: Ave Maria Press, 2001. The guru of parish social ministry offers his best insights.

Related Websites

Bread for the World
www.bread.org

Catholic Campaign for Human Development
www.usccb.org/cchd

Catholic Charities USA/Parish Social Ministry
www.catholiccharitiesusa.org

Catholic Relief Service
www.catholicrelief.org

Center of Concern
www.coc.org

JustFaith Ministries
www.justfaith.org

Interfaith Committee for Worker Justice
www.iwj.org

National Conference of Catechetical Leadership
www.nccl.org

National Catholic Rural Life Conference
www.ncrlc.com

NETWORK
www.networklobby.org

Office of Social Justice St. Paul and Minneaplis
www.osjspm.org/ (resources on CST)

Pax Christi USA
www.paxchristiusa.org

US Conference of Catholic Bishops
www.usccb.org

Dept. of Justice, Peace and Human Development
www.usccb.org/jphd

Pro-life Activities
www.usccb.org/prolife

Vatican
www.vatican.va

Index